THE ARCTIC PRAIRIES

HARPER NATURE LIBRARY
New Paperback Editions of Outstanding Nature Classics

THE
ARCTIC PRAIRIES

A CANOE-JOURNEY
OF 2,000 MILES IN SEARCH OF THE CARIBOU;
BEING THE ACCOUNT OF A
VOYAGE TO THE REGION NORTH OF
AYLMER LAKE

BY

ERNEST THOMPSON SETON

HARPER COLOPHON BOOKS
Harper & Row, Publishers
New York, Cambridge, Hagerstown, Philadelphia, San Francisco
London, Mexico City, São Paulo, Sydney

A hardcover edition of this book was originally published by Charles Scribner's Sons.

THE ARCTIC PRAIRIES. Copyright 1911 by Ernest Thompson Seton. All rights reserved. Printed in the United States of America. No part of this book may be used or reproduced in any manner whatsoever without written permission except in the case of brief quotations embodied in critical articles and reviews. For information address Harper & Row, Publishers, Inc., 10 East 53rd Street, New York, N.Y. 10022. Published simultaneously in Canada by Fitzhenry & Whiteside Limited, Toronto.

First HARPER COLOPHON edition published 1981.

ISBN: 0-06-090841-6

81 82 83 84 85 10 9 8 7 6 5 4 3 2 1

CONTENTS

PREFACE

WHAT young man of our race would not gladly give a year of his life to roll backward the scroll of time for five decades and live that year in the romantic bygone days of the Wild West; to see the great Missouri while the Buffalo pastured on its banks, while big game teemed in sight and the red man roamed and hunted, unchecked by fence or hint of white man's rule; or, when that rule was represented only by scattered trading-posts, hundreds of miles apart, and at best the traders could exchange the news by horse or canoe and months of lonely travel?

I, for one, would have rejoiced in tenfold payment for the privilege of this backward look in our age, and had reached the middle life before I realised that, at a much less heavy cost, the miracle was possible to-day.

For the uncivilised Indian still roams the far reaches of absolutely unchanged, unbroken forest and prairie leagues, and has knowledge of white men only in bartering furs at the scattered trading-posts, where locomotive and telegraph are unknown; still the wild Buffalo elude the hunters, fight the Wolves, wallow, wander, and breed; and still there is hoofed game by the million to be found where the Saxon is as seldom seen as on the Missouri in the times of Lewis and Clarke. *Only* we must seek it all, not in the West, but in the far North-west; and for "Missouri and Mississippi" read "Peace and Mackenzie Rivers," those noble streams that northward roll their mile-wide turbid floods a thousand leagues to the silent Arctic Sea.

This was the thought which spurred me to a six-months' journey by canoe. And I found what I went in search of, but found, also, abundant and better rewards that were not in mind, even as Saul, the son of Kish, went seeking asses and found for himself a crown and a great kingdom.

My thanks are due here to the Right Honourable Lord Strathcona, G. C. M. G., Governor of the Hudson's Bay Company, for giving me access to the records of the Company whenever I needed them for historical purposes; to the Honourable Frank Oliver, Minister of the Interior, Canada, for the necessary papers and permits to facilitate scientific collection, and also to Clarence C. Chipman, Esq., of Winnipeg, the Hudson's Bay Company's Commissioner, for practical help in preparing my outfit, and for letters of introduction to the many officers of the Company, whose kind help was so often a Godsend.

ERNEST THOMPSON SETON

THE ARCTIC PRAIRIES

CHAPTER I

DEPARTURE FOR THE NORTH

In 1907 I set out to journey by canoe down the Athabaska and adjoining waters to the sole remaining forest wilds—the far north-west of Canada—and the yet more desert Arctic Plains, where still, it was said, were to be seen the Caribou in their primitive condition.

My only companion was Edward A. Preble, of Washington, D. C., a trained naturalist, an expert canoeist and traveller, and a man of three seasons' experience in the Hudson's Bay Territory and the Mackenzie Valley. While my chief object was to see the Caribou, and prove their continued abundance, I was prepared incidentally to gather natural-history material of all kinds, and to complete the shore line of the ambiguous lake called "Aylmer," as well as explore its sister, the better-known Clinton-Colden.

I went for my own pleasure at my own expense, and yet I could not persuade my Hudson's Bay Company friends that I was not sent by some government, museum or society for some secret purpose.

On the night of May 5 we left Winnipeg, and our observations began with the day at Brandon.

From that point westward to Regina we saw abundant evidence that last year had been a "rabbit year," that is, a year in which the ever-fluctuating population of Northern Hares (Snowshoe-rabbits or White-rabbits) had reached its maximum, for nine-tenths of the bushes in sight from the train had been barked at the snow level. But the fact that we saw not one

Map showing the north limit of trees and of the successful culture of potatoes, barley, and wheat

The dotted line from the Saskatchewan northward is my canoe-route

Rabbit shows that "the plague" had appeared, had run its usual drastic course, and nearly exterminated the species in this particular region.

Early next morning at Kininvie (40 miles west of Medicine Hat, Alberta) we saw a band of 4 Antelope south of the track; later we saw others all along as far as Gleichen. All were south of the track. The bands contained as follows: 4, 14, 18, 8, 12, 8, 4, 1, 4, 5, 4, 6, 4, 18, 2, 6, 34, 6, 3, 1, 10, 25, 16, 3, 7, 9 (almost never 2, probably because this species does not pair), or 232 Antelope in 26 bands along 70 miles of track;

but all were on the south side; not one was noted on the north.

The case is simple. During the past winter, while the Antelope were gone southward, the Canadian Pacific Railway Company had fenced its track. In spring the migrants, returning, found themselves cut off from their summer feeding-grounds by those impassable barb-wires, and so were gathered against the barrier. One band of 8, at a stopping place, ran off when they saw passengers alighting, but at half a mile they turned, and again came up against the fence, showing how strong is the northward impulse.

Unless they learn some way of mastering the difficulty, it means extermination for the Antelope of the north Saskatchewan.

From Calgary we went by train to Edmonton. This is the point of leaving the railway, the beginning of hard travel, and here we waited a few days to gather together our various shipments of food and equipment, and to await notice that the river was open.

In the north the grand event of the year is the opening of the rivers. The day when the ice goes out is the official first day of spring, the beginning of the season; and is eagerly looked for, as every day's delay means serious loss to the traders, whose men are idle, but drawing pay as though at work.

On May 11, having learned that the Athabaska was open, we left Edmonton in a livery rig, and drove 94 miles northward though a most promising, half-settled country, and late the next day arrived at Athabaska Landing, on the great east tributary of the Mackenzie, whose waters were to bear us onward for so many weeks.

Athabaska Landing is a typical frontier town. These are hard words, but justified. We put up at the principal hotel; the other lodgers told me it was considered the worst hotel in the world. I thought I knew of two worse, but next morning accepted the prevailing view.

Our canoe and provisions arrived, but the great convoy of scows that were to take the annual supplies of trade stuff for the far north was not ready, and we needed the help and guidance of its men, so must needs wait for four days.

This gave us the opportunity to study the local natural history and do a little collecting, the results of which appear later.

The great size of the timber here impressed me. I measured a typical black poplar (*P. balsamifera*), 100 feet to the top, 8 feet 2 inches in circumference, at 18 inches from the ground, and I saw many thicker, but none taller.

At the hotel, also awaiting the scows, was a body of four (dis-)Mounted Police, bound like ourselves for the far north. The officer in charge turned out to be an old friend from Toronto, Major A. M. Jarvis. I also met John Schott, the gigantic half-breed, who went to the Barren Grounds with Caspar Whitney in 1895. He seemed to have great respect for Whitney as a tramper, and talked much of the trip, evidently having forgotten his own shortcomings of the time. While I sketched his portrait, he regaled me with memories of his early days on Red River, where he was born in 1841. I did not fail to make what notes I could of those now historic times. His accounts of the Antelope on White Horse Plain, in 1855, and Buffalo about the site of Carberry, Manitoba, in 1852, were new and valuable light on the ancient ranges of these passing creatures.

All travellers who had preceded me into the Barren Grounds had relied on the abundant game, and in consequence suffered dreadful hardships; in some cases even starved to death. I proposed to rely on no game, but to take plenty of groceries, the best I could buy in Winnipeg, which means the best in the world; and, as will be seen later, the game, because I was not relying on it, walked into camp every day.

But one canoe could not carry all these provisions, so most of it I shipped on the Hudson's Bay Company scows, taking with us, in the canoe, food for not more than a week, which with camp outfit was just enough for ballast.

Of course I was in close touch with the Hudson's Bay people. Although nominally that great trading company parted with its autocratic power and exclusive franchise in 1870, it is still the sovereign of the north. And here let me correct an error that is sometimes found even in respectable print—the Company has at all times been ready to assist scientists to the utmost of its very ample power. Although jealous of its trading rights, every one is free to enter the territory without taking count of the Company, but there has not yet been a *successful* scientific expedition into the region without its active co-operation.

The Hudson's Bay Company has always been the guardian angel of the north.

I suppose that there never yet was another purely commercial concern that so fully realized the moral obligations of its great power, or that has so uniformly done its best for the people it ruled.

At all times it has stood for peace, and one hears over and over again that such and such tribes were deadly enemies, but the Company insisted on their smoking the peace pipe. The Sioux and Ojibway, Black-Foot and Assiniboine, Dog-Rib and Copper-Knife, Beaver and Chipewyan, all offer historic illustrations in point, and many others could be found for the list.

The name Peace River itself is the monument of a successful effort on the part of the Company to bring about a better understanding between the Crees and the Beavers.

Besides human foes, the Company has saved the Indian from famine and plague. Many a hunger-stricken tribe owes its continued existence to the fatherly care of the Company, not simply general and indiscriminate, but minute and personal, carried into the details of their lives. For instance, when bots so pestered the Caribou of one region as to render their hides useless to the natives, the Company brought in hides from a district where they still were good.

The Chipewyans were each spring the victims of snow-blindness until the Company brought and succeeded in popularizing their present ugly but effectual and universal peaked hats. When their train-dogs

were running down in physique, the Company brought
in a strain of pure Huskies or Eskimo. When the
Albany River Indians were starving and unable to
hunt, the Company gave the order for 5,000 lodge
poles. Then, not knowing how else to turn them to
account, commissioned the Indians to work them into
a picket garden-fence. At all times the Indians had
a friend in the Company, and it was the worst thing
that ever happened in the region when the irrespon-
sible free-traders with their demoralizing methods
were allowed to enter and traffic where or how they
pleased.

Indian Pilot.   May 19, 1907

CHAPTER II

DOWN THE NOISY RIVER WITH THE VOYAGEURS

At Athabaska Landing, on May 18, 1907, 10.15 a. m., we boarded the superb Peterborough canoe that I had christened the *Ann Seton*. The Athabaska River was a-flood and clear of ice; 13 scows of freight, with 60 half-breeds and Indians to man them, left at the same time, and in spite of a strong headwind we drifted northward fully 3½ miles an hour.

The leading scow, where I spent some time, was in charge of John MacDonald himself, and his passengers comprised the Hudson's Bay Company officials, going to their posts or on tours of inspection. They were a jolly crowd, like a lot of rollicking schoolboys, full of fun and good-humour, chaffing and joking all day; but when a question of business came up, the serious business man appeared in each, and the Company's interest was cared for with their best powers. The bottle was not entirely absent in these scow fraternities, but I saw no one the worse for liquor on the trip.

The men of mixed blood jabbered in French, Cree, and Chipewyan chiefly, but when they wanted to swear, they felt the inadequacy of these mellifluous or lisping tongues, and fell back on virile Saxon, whose tang, projectivity, and wealth of vile epithet evidently supplied a long-felt want in the Great Lone Land of the Dog and Canoe.

10

In the afternoon Preble and I pushed on in our boat, far in advance of the brigade. As we made early supper I received for the twentieth time a lesson in photography. A cock Partridge or Ruffed Grouse came and drummed on a log in open view, full sunlight, fifty feet away. I went quietly to the place. He walked off, but little alarmed. I set the camera eight feet from the log, with twenty-five feet of tubing, and retired to a good hiding-place. But alas! I put the tube on the left-hand pump, not knowing that that was a dummy. The Grouse came back in three minutes, drumming in a superb pose squarely in front of the camera. I used the pump, but saw that it failed to operate; on going forward the Grouse skimmed away and returned no more. Preble said, "Never mind; there will be another every hundred yards all the way down the river, later on." I could only reply, "The chance never comes but once," and so it proved. We heard Grouse drumming many times afterward, but the sun was low, or the places densely shaded, or the mosquitoes made conditions impossible for silent watching; the *perfect* chance came but once, as it always does, and I lost it.

About twenty miles below the Landing we found the abandoned winter hut of a trapper; on the roof were the dried up bodies of 1 Skunk, 2 Foxes, and 30 Lynxes, besides the bones of 2 Moose, showing the nature of the wild life about.

That night, as the river was brimming and safe, we tied up to the scows and drifted, making 30 more miles, or 60 since embarking.

In the early morning, I was much struck by the life-lessness of the scene. The great river stretched away northward, the hills rose abruptly from the water's edge, everywhere extended the superb spruce forest, here fortunately unburnt; but there seemed no sign of living creature outside of our own numerous, noisy,

The Roll Call

and picturesque party. River, hills, and woods were calm and silent. It was impressive, if disappointing; and, when at last the fir stillness was broken by a succession of trumpet notes from the Great Pileated Woodpecker, the sound went rolling on and on, in reverberating echoes that might. well have alarmed the bird himself.

The white spruce forest along the banks is most inspiring; magnificent here. Down the terraced slopes and right to the water's edge on the alluvial soil it stands in ranks. Each year, of course, the floods undercut the banks, and more trees fall, to become at last the flotsam of the shore a thousand miles away.

There is something sad about these stately trees, densely packed, all a-row, unflinching, hopelessly awaiting the onset of the inexorable, invincible river. One group, somewhat isolated and formal, was a forest life parallel to Lady Butler's famous "Roll Call of the Grenadiers."

At night we reached the Indian village of Pelican Portage, and landed by climbing over huge blocks of ice that were piled along the shore. The adult male inhabitants came down to our camp, so that the village was deserted, except for the children and a few women.

As I walked down the crooked trail along which straggle the cabins, I saw something white in a tree at the far end. Supposing it to be a White-rabbit in a snare, I went near and found, to my surprise, first that it was a dead house-cat, a rare species here; second, under it, eyeing it and me alternately, was a hungry-looking Lynx. I had a camera, for it was near sun-down, and in the woods, so I went back to the boat and returned with a gun. There was the Lynx still prowling, but now farther from the village. I do not believe he would have harmed the children, but a Lynx is game. I fired, and he fell without a quiver or a sound. This was the first time I had used a gun in many years, and was the only time on the trip. I felt rather guilty, but the carcass was a godsend to two old Indians who were sickening on a long diet of salt pork, and that Lynx furnished them tender meat for three days afterward; while its skin and skull went to the American Museum.

On the night of May 20, we camped just above
Grand Rapids—Preble and I alone, for the first time,
under canvas, and glad indeed to get away from the
noisy rabble of the boatmen, though now they were
but a quarter mile off. At first I had found them
amusing and picturesque, but their many unpleasant
habits, their distinct aversion to strangers, their greedi-
ness to get all they could out of one, and do nothing in
return, combined finally with their habit of gambling
all night to the loud beating of a tin pan, made me
thankful to quit their company for a time.

At Grand Rapids the scows were unloaded, the
goods shipped over a quarter-mile hand tramway, on
an island, the scows taken down a side channel, one
by one, and reloaded. This meant a delay of three
or four days, during which we camped on the island
and gathered specimens.

Being the organizer, equipper, geographer, artist,
head, and tail of the expedition, I was, perforce, also
its doctor. Equipped with a "pill-kit," an abundance
of blisters and bandages and some "potent purgatives,"
I had prepared myself to render first and last aid to the
hurt in my own party. In taking instructions from our
family physician, I had learned the value of a profound
air of great gravity, a noble reticence, and a total absence of doubt, when I did speak. I compressed his
creed into a single phrase: "In case of doubt, look wise
and work on his 'bowels.'" This simple equipment soon
gave me a surprisingly high standing among the men.
I was a medicine man of repute, and soon had a larger
practice than I desired, as it was entirely gratuitous.

The various boatmen, Indians and half-breeds, came with their troubles, and, thanks chiefly to their faith, were cured. But one day John MacDonald, the chief pilot and a mighty man on the river, came to my tent on Grand Island. John complained that he couldn't hold anything on his stomach; he was a total peristaltic wreck indeed (my words; his were more simple and more vivid, but less sonorous and professional). He said he had been going down hill for two weeks, and was so bad now that he was "no better than a couple of ordinary men."

"Exactly so," I said. "Now you take these pills and you'll be all right in the morning." Next morning John was back, and complained that my pills had no effect; he wanted to feel something take hold of him. Hadn't I any pepper-juice or brandy?

I do not take liquor on an expedition, but at the last moment a Winnipeg friend had given me a pint flask of pure brandy—"for emergencies." An emergency had come.

"John! you shall have some extra fine brandy, nicely thinned with pepper-juice." I poured half an inch of brandy into a tin cup, then added half an inch of "pain-killer."

"Here, take this, and if you don't feel it, it means your insides are dead, and you may as well order your coffin."

John took it at a gulp. His insides were not dead; but I might have been, had I been one of his boatmen.

He doubled up, rolled around, and danced for five minutes. He did not squeal—John never squeals—but he suffered some, and an hour later announced that he was about cured.

Next day he came to say he was all right, and would soon again be as good as half a dozen men.

At this same camp in Grand Rapids another cure on a much larger scale was added to my list. An Indian had "the bones of his foot broken," crushed by a heavy weight, and was badly crippled. He came leaning on a friend's shoulder. His foot was blackened and much swollen, but I soon satisfied myself that no bones were broken, because he could wriggle all the toes and move the foot in any direction.

"You'll be better in three days and all right in a week," I said, with calm assurance. Then I began with massage. It seemed necessary in the Indian environment to hum some tune, and I found that the "Koochy-Koochy" lent itself best to the motion, so it became my medicine song.

With many "Koochy-Koochy"-ings and much ice-cold water he was nearly cured in three days, and sound again in a week. But in the north folk have a habit (not known elsewhere) of improving the incident. Very soon it was known all along the river that the Indian's *leg was broken*, and I had set and healed it in three days. In a year or two, I doubt not, it will be his neck that was broken, not once, but in several places.

Grand Island yielded a great many Deermice of the *arcticus* form, a few Red-backed Voles, and any number of small birds migrant.

As we floated down the river the eye was continu-

ally held by tall and prominent spruce trees that had
been cut into peculiar forms as below. These were
known as "lob-sticks," or "lop-sticks," and are usually the monuments of some distinguished visitor in
the country or records of some heroic achievement.
Thus, one would be pointed out as Commissioner
Wrigley's lob-stick, another as John MacDonald's the
time he saved the scow.

The inauguration of a lob-stick is quite a ceremony.
Some person in camp has impressed all with his importance or other claim to
notice. The men, having
talked it over, announce
that they have decided on
giving him a lob-stick.
"Will he make choice of
some prominent tree in

Lob-sticks, or trees trimmed as
monuments, along the river

view?" The visitor usually selects one back from the
water's edge, often on some far hilltop, the more
prominent the better; then an active young fellow is
sent up with an axe to trim the tree. The more
embellishment the higher the honor. On the trunk
they then inscribe the name of the stranger, and he is
supposed to give each of the men a plug of tobacco
and a drink of whiskey. Thus they celebrate the man
and his monument, and ever afterwards it is pointed
out as "So-and-so's lob-stick."

It was two months before my men judged that I was
entitled to a lob-stick. We were then on Great Slave
Lake where the timber was small, but the best they
could get on a small island was chosen and trimmed

into a monument. They were disappointed however, to find that I would by no means give whiskey to natives, and my treat had to take a wholly different form.

Grand Rapids, with its multiplicity of perfectly round pot-hole boulders, was passed in four days, and then, again in company with the boats, we entered the real canyon of the river.

> Down Athabaska's boiling flood
> Of seething, leaping, coiling mud.

CHAPTER III

HUMAN NATURE ON THE RIVER

Sunday morning, 26th of May, there was something like a strike among the sixty half-breeds and Indians that composed the crews. They were strict Sabbatarians (when it suited them); they believed that they should do no work, but give up the day to gambling and drinking. Old John, the chief pilot, wished to take advantage of the fine flood on the changing river, and drift down at least to the head of the Boiler Rapids, twenty miles away. The men maintained, with many white swear words, for lack of strong talk in Indian, that they never yet knew Sunday work to end in anything but disaster, and they sullenly scattered among the trees, produced their cards, and proceeded to gamble away their property, next year's pay, clothes, families, anything, and otherwise show their respect for the Lord's Day and defiance of old John MacDonald. John made no reply to their arguments; he merely boarded the *cook's boat*, and pushed off into the swift stream with the cooks and all the grub. In five minutes the strikers were on the twelve big boats doing their best to live up to orders. John said nothing, and grinned at me only with his eyes.

The crews took their defeat in good part after the first minute, and their commander rose higher in their respect.

19

At noon we camped above the Boiler Rapids. In
the evening I climbed the 400- or 500-foot hill behind
camp and sketched the canyon looking northward.
The spring birds were now beginning to arrive, but

Canyon of the Athabaska River, looking north

were said to be a month late this year. The ground
was everywhere marked with moose sign; prospects
were brightening.

The mania for killing that is seen in many white men
is evidently a relic of savagery, for all of these Indians
and half-breeds are full of it.   Each carries a rifle, and
every living thing that appears on the banks or on the
water is fusilladed with Winchesters until it is dead or
out of sight.   This explains why we see so little from
the scows.   One should be at least a day ahead of
them to meet with wild life on the river.

This morning two Bears appeared on the high bank
—and there was the usual uproar and fusillading; so far
as could be learned without any effect, except the ex-
penditure of thirty or forty cartridges at five cents each

On the 27th we came to the Cascade Rapids. The first or Little Cascade has about two feet fall, the second or Grand Cascade, a mile farther, is about a six foot sheer drop. These are considered very difficult

Natural amphitheatre on Athabaska Canyon

to run, and the manner of doing it changes with every change in season or water level.

We therefore went through an important ceremony, always carried out in the same way. All 13 boats were beached, the 13 pilots went ahead on the bank to study the problem, they decided on the one safe place and manner, then returned, and each of the 13 boats was run over in 13 different places and manners. They always do this. You are supposed to have run the Cascades successfully if you cross them alive, but to have failed if you drown. In this case all were successful.

Below the Cascades I had a sample of Indian gratitude that set me thinking. My success with John

MacDonald and others had added the whole community to my medical practice, for those who were not sick thought they were. I cheerfully did my best for all, and was supposed to be *persona grata*. Just below the Cascade Rapids was a famous sucker pool, and after we had camped three Indians came, saying that the pool was full of suckers—would I lend them my canoe to get some?

Away they went, and from afar I was horrified to see them clubbing the fish with my beautiful thin-bladed maple paddles. They returned with a boat load of 3- and 4-pound Suckers (*Catostomus*) and 2 paddles broken. Each of their friends came and received one or two fine fish, for there were plenty. I, presumably part owner of the catch, since I owned the boat, selected one small one for myself, whereupon the Indian insolently *demanded 25 cents for it;* and these were the men I had been freely doctoring for two weeks! Not to speak of the loaned canoe and broken paddles! Then did I say a few things to all and sundry—stinging, biting things, ungainsayable and forcible things—and took possession of all the fish that were left, so the Indians slunk off in sullen silence.

Gratitude seems an unknown feeling among these folk; you may give presents and help and feed them all you like, the moment you want a slight favour of them they demand the uttermost cent. In attempting to analyse this I was confronted by the fact that among themselves they are kind and hospitable, and at length discovered that their attitude toward us is founded on the ideas that all white men are very rich,

that the Indian has made them so by allowing them
to come into this country, that the Indian is very poor
because he never was properly compensated, and that
therefore all he can get out of said white man is much
less than the white man owes him.

As we rounded a point one day a Lynx appeared
statuesque on a stranded cake of ice, a hundred yards
off, and gazed at the approaching boats. True to their
religion, the half-breeds seized their rifles, the bullets
whistled harmlessly about the "Peeshoo"—whereupon
he turned and walked calmly up the slope, stopping to
look at each fresh volley, but finally waved his stumpy
tail and walked unharmed over the ridge. Distance
fifty yards.

On May 28 we reached Fort MacMurray.

Here I saw several interesting persons: Miss Chris-
tine Gordon, the postmaster; Joe Bird, a half-breed
with all the advanced ideas of a progressive white
man; and an American ex-patriot, G———, a tall,
raw-boned Yank from Illinois. He was a typical
American of the kind that knows little of America
and nothing of Europe; but shrewd and successful in
spite of these limitations. In appearance he was not
unlike Abraham Lincoln. He was a rabid American,
and why he stayed here was a question.

He had had no detailed tidings from home for years,
and I never saw a man more keen for the news. On
the banks of the river we sat for an hour while he plied
me with questions, which I answered so far as I could.
He hung on my lips; he interrupted only when there
seemed a halt in the stream; he revelled in all the de-

tails of wrecks by rail and sea. Roosevelt and the trusts—insurance scandals—the lynchings in the South —the burnings in the West—massacres—murders— horrors—risings—these were his special gloats, and yet he kept me going with "Yes—yes—and then?" or "Yes, by golly—that's the way we're a-doing it. Go on."

Then, after I had robbed New York of $100,000,000 a year, burnt 10 large towns and 45 small ones, wrecked 200 express trains, lynched 96 negroes in the South— and murdered many men every night for 7 years in Chicago—he broke out:

"By golly, we are a-doing it. We *are* the people. We are a-moving things now; and I tell you I give the worst of them there European countries, the very worst of 'em, just 100 years to become Americanised."

Think of that, ye polished Frenchmen; ye refined, courteous Swedes; ye civilised Danes; you have 100 years to become truly Americanised!

All down the river route we came on relics of another class of wanderers—the Klondikers of 1898. Sometimes these were empty winter cabins; sometimes curious tools left at Hudson's Bay Posts, and in some cases expensive provisions; in all cases we heard weird tales of their madness.

There is, I am told, a shanty on the Mackenzie above Simpson, where four of them made a strange record. Cooped up for months in tight winter quarters, they soon quarrelled, and at length their partnership was dissolved. Each took the articles he had contributed, and those of common purchase they divided in four equal parts. The stove, the canoe, the lamp, the spade, were broken relentlessly and savagely into four parts—four piles of useless rubbish. The shanty was divided in four. One man had some candles of his own bringing. These he kept and carefully screened off his corner of the room so no chance rays might reach the others to comfort them; they spent the winter in darkness. None spoke to the other, and they parted, singly and silently, hatefully as ever, as soon as the springtime opened the way.

CHAPTER IV

DOWN THE SILENT RIVER WITH THE MOUNTED POLICE

At Fort MacMurray we learned that there was no telling when the steamer might arrive; Major Jarvis was under orders to proceed without delay to Smith Landing; so to solve all our difficulties I bought a 30-foot boat (sturgeon-head) of Joe Bird, and arranged to join forces with the police for the next part of the journey.

I had made several unsuccessful attempts to get an experienced native boatman to go northward with me. All seemed to fear the intending plunge into the unknown; so was agreeably surprised when a sturdy young fellow of Scottish and Cree parentage came and volunteered for the trip. A few inquiries proved him to bear a good reputation as a river-man and worker, so William C. Loutit was added to my expedition and served me faithfully throughout.

In time I learned that Billy was a famous traveller. Some years ago, when the flood had severed all communication between Athabaska Landing and Edmonton, Billy volunteered to carry some important despatches, and covered the 96 miles on foot in one and a half days, although much of the road was under water. On another occasion he went alone and afoot from House River up the Athabaska to Calling River, and across the Point to the Athabaska again, then up to the Landing—150 rough miles in four days. These exploits I had to find out for myself later on, but much more important to me at the time was the fact that he was a first-class cook, a steady, cheerful worker, and a capable guide as far as Great Slave Lake.

The Athabaska below Fort MacMurray is a noble stream, one-third of a mile wide, deep, steady, un-

Floating down the Slave

marred; the banks are covered with unbroken virginal forests of tall white poplar, balsam poplar, spruce, and birch. The fire has done no damage here as yet, the axe has left no trace, there are no houses, no sign of man except occasional teepee poles. I could fancy myself floating down the Ohio two hundred years ago.

These were bright days to be remembered, as we drifted down its placid tide in our ample and comfortable boat, with abundance of good things. Calm, lovely, spring weather; ducks all along the river; plenty of food, which is the northerner's idea of bliss; plenty of water, which is the river-man's notion of joy; plenty of leisure, which is an element in most men's heaven, for we had merely to float with the stream, three miles an hour, except when we landed to eat or sleep.

The woods were donning their vernal green and re-
sounded with the calls of birds now.   The mosquito
plague of the region had not yet appeared, and there
was little lacking to crown with a halo the memory of
those days on the Missouri of the North.

Native quadrupeds seemed scarce, and we were all
agog when one of the men saw a black fox trotting
along the opposite bank.   However, it turned out to

Fort McKay

be one of the many stray dogs of the country.   He
followed us a mile or more, stopping at times to leap
at fish that showed near the shore.   When we landed
for lunch he swam the broad stream and hung about
at a distance.   As this was twenty miles from any
settlement, he was doubtless hungry, so I left a boun-
tiful lunch for him, and when we moved away, he
claimed his own.

At Fort McKay I saw a little half-breed boy shooting with a bow and displaying extraordinary marks-
manship.   At sixty feet he could hit the bottom of a
tomato tin nearly every time; and even more surprising was the fact that he held the arrow with what is
known as the Mediterranean hold.   When, months
later, I again stopped at this place, I saw another boy

doing the very same.   Some residents assured me that this was the style of all the Chipewyans as well as the Crees.

That night we camped far down the river and on the side opposite the Fort, for experience soon teaches one to give the dogs no chance of entering camp on marauding expeditions while you rest.   About ten, as I was going to sleep, Preble put his head in and said: "Come out here if you want a new sensation."

In a moment I was standing with him under the tall spruce trees, looking over the river to the dark forest, a quarter mile away, and listening intently to a new and wonderful sound.   Like the slow tolling of a soft but high-pitched bell, it came.   *Ting, ting, ting, ting,* and on, rising and falling with the breeze, but still keeping on about two *"tings"* to the second, and on, dulling as with distance, but rising again and again.

It was unlike anything I had ever heard, but Preble knew it of old.   "That," says he, "is the love-song of the Richardson Owl.   *She* is sitting demurely in some spruce top while he sails around, singing on the wing, and when the sound seems distant, he is on the far side of the tree."

Ting, ting, ting, ting, it went on and on, this soft belling of his love, this amorous music of our northern bell-bird.

Ting, TING, *ting, ting, ting,* TING, *ting, ting, ting, ting,* TING, *ting*—oh, how could any lady owl resist such strains?—and on, with its *ting, ting, ting,* TING, *ting, ting, ting,* TING, the whole night air was vibrant.   Then, as though by plan, a different note—the deep boom-

ing *"Oho—oh—who—oh who hoo"* of the Great Horned
Owl—was heard singing a most appropriate bass.

But the little Owl went on and on; 5 minutes, 10
minutes, 20 minutes at last had elapsed before I
turned in again and left him. More than once that
night I awoke to hear his *"tinging"* serenade upon the
consecrated air of the piney woods.

Yet Preble said this one was an indifferent performer.
On the Mackenzie he had heard far better singers of

Athabaska River looking north from Poplar Point

the kind; some that introduce many variations of the
pitch and modulation. I thought it one of the most
charming bird voices I had ever listened to—and felt
that this was one of the things that make the journey
worth while.

On June 1 the weather was so blustering and wet
that we did not break camp. I put in the day exam-
ining the superb timber of this bottom-land. White
spruce is the prevailing conifer and is here seen in perfection. A representative specimen was 118 feet high,
11 feet 2 inches in circumference, or 3 feet 6½ inches
in diameter 1 foot from the ground, *i. e.*, above any
root spread. There was plenty of timber of similar
height. Black spruce, a smaller kind, and tamarack

are found farther up and back in the bog country. jackpine of fair size abounds on the sandy and gravelly parts. Balsam poplar is the largest deciduous tree; its superb legions in upright ranks are crowded along all the river banks and on the islands not occupied by the spruce. The large trees of this kind often have deep holes; these are the nesting sites of the Whistler Duck, which is found in numbers here and as far north as this tree, but not farther. White poplar is plentiful

Male Lynx. June 3, 1907

also; the hillsides are beautifully clad with its purplish masses of twigs, through which its white stems gleam like marble columns. White birch is common and large enough for canoes. Two or three species of willow in impenetrable thickets make up the rest of the forest stretches.

At this camp I had the unique experience of showing all these seasoned Westerners that it was possible to make a fire by the friction of two sticks. This has long been a specialty of mine; I use a thong and a bow as the simplest way. Ordinarily I prefer balsam-fir or tamarack; in this case I used a balsam block and a spruce drill, and, although each kind failed when used with drill and block the same, I got the fire in half a minute.

On June 3 we left this camp of tall timber. As we floated down we sighted a Lynx on the bank looking contemplatively into the flood. One of the police boys seized a gun and with a charge of No. 6 killed the Lynx. Poor thing, it was in a starving condition, as indeed are most meat-eaters this year in the north. Though it was fully grown, it weighed but 15 pounds.

Poplar Point, Athabaska River, from north

In its stomach was part of a sparrow (white-throat?) and a piece of rawhide an inch wide and 4 feet long, evidently a portion of a dog-harness picked up somewhere along the river. I wonder what he did with the bells.

That night we decided to drift, leaving one man on guard. Next day, as we neared Lake Athabaska, the shores got lower, and the spruce disappeared, giving way to dense thickets of low willow. Here the long expected steamer, *Graham*, passed, going upstream. We now began to get occasional glimpses of Lake Athabaska across uncertain marshes and sand bars. It was very necessary to make Fort Chipewyan while there was a calm, so we pushed on. After four hours' groping among blind channels and mud banks, we reached the lake at midnight—though of course there was no night, but a sort of gloaming even at the darkest—and it took us four hours' hard rowing to cover the ten miles that separated us from Chipewyan.

It sounds very easy and commonplace when one says "hard rowing," but it takes on more significance when one is reminded

Mouth of Peace River

that those oars were 18 feet long, 5 inches through, and weighed about 20 pounds each; the boat was 30 feet long, a demasted schooner indeed, and rowing her through shallow muddy water, where the ground suction was excessive, made labour so heavy that 15-minute spells were all any one could do. We formed four relays, and all worked in turn all night through, arriving at Chipewyan 4 A. M., blistered, sore, and completely tired out.

Fort Chipewyan (pronounced Chip-we-yań) was Billy Loutit's home, and here we met his father, mother, and numerous as well as interesting sisters. Mean-

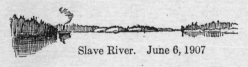

Slave River.   June 6, 1907

while I called at the Roman Catholic Mission, under Bishop Gruard, and the rival establishment, under Reverend Roberts, good men all, and devoted to the cause, but loving not each other. The Hudson's Bay Company, however, was here, as everywhere in the north, the really important thing.

There was a long stretch of dead water before we

could resume our downward drift, and, worse than that, there was such a flood on the Peace River that it was backing the Athabaska, that is, the tide of the latter was

reversed on the Rocher River, which extends twenty-five miles between here and Peace mouth. To meet this, I hired Colin Fraser's steamer. We left Chipewyan at 6.15; at 11.15 camped below the Peace on Great Slave River, and bade farewell to the steamer.

Crow's Nest, Fort Smith Landing

The reader may well be puzzled by these numerous names; the fact is the Mackenzie, the Slave, the Peace, the Rocher, and the Unchaga are all one and the same river, but, unfortunately, the early explorers thought proper to give it a new name each time it did something, such as expand into a lake. By rights it should be the Unchaga or Unjiza,

Female Lynx.   June 6, 1907

from the Rockies to the Arctic, with the Athabaska as its principal southern tributary.

The next day another Lynx was collected. In its stomach were remains of a Redsquirrel, a Chipmunk, and a Bog-lemming. The last was important as it made a new record.

The Athabaska is a great river, the Peace is a greater, and the Slave, formed by their union, is worthy of its parents. Its placid flood is here nearly a mile wide, and its banks are covered with a great continuous forest of spruce trees of the largest size. How far back this extends I do not know, but the natives say the best timber is along the river.

More than once a Lynx was seen trotting by or staring at us from the bank, but no other large animal.

On the night of June 7 we reached Smith Landing.

CHAPTER V

A CONFERENCE WITH THE CHIEFS

A few bands of Buffalo are said to exist in the country east of Great Slave River. Among other matters, Major Jarvis had to report on these, find out how many were left, and exactly where they were. When he invited me to join his expedition, with these questions in view, I needed no pressing.

Our first business was to get guides, and now our troubles began.

Through the traders we found four Indians who knew the Buffalo range—they were Kiya, Sousi, Kirma, and Peter Squirrel. However, they seemed in no way desirous of guiding any one into that country. They dodged and delayed and secured many postponements, but the Royal Mounted Police and the Hudson's Bay Company are the two mighty powers of the land, so, urged by an officer of each, these worthies sullenly assembled to meet us in Sousi's cabin.

Sousi, by the way, is Chipewyan for Joseph, and this man's name was Joseph Beaulieu. Other northern travellers have warned all that came after them to beware of the tribe of Beaulieu, so we were on guard.

Sullen silence greeted us as we entered; we could feel their covert antagonism. Jarvis is one of those affable, good-tempered individuals that most persons take for "easy." In some ways he may be so, but I soon realised that he was a keen judge of men and their ways, and he whispered to me: "*They* mean to block us if possible." Sousi understood French and had some English, but the others professed ignorance of everything but Chipewyan. So it was necessary to call in an interpreter. How admirably he served us may be judged from the following sample secured later.

Q. Are the Buffalo near?

A. Wah-hay-was-ki busquow Kai-ah taw nip-ee-wat-chow-es-kee nee-moy-ah. Kee-as-o-win sug-ee-meesh i-mush-wa mus-tat-e-muck ne-mow-ah pe-muk-te-ok ne-moy-ah dane-tay-tay-ah.

Interpreter. He say "no."

Q. How long would it take to get them?

A. Ne-moy-ah mis-chay-to-ok Way-hay-o ay-ow-ok-i-man-kah-mus-to-ok. Mis-ta-hay cha-gow-os-ki wah-hay-o musk-ee-see-seepi. Mas-kootch e-goot-ah-i-ow mas-kootch ne-moy-ah muk-e-boy sak-te-muk mas-kootch gahk-sin-now ne-moy-ah gehk-kee-win-tay dam-foole-Inglis.

Interpreter. He say "don't know."

Q. Can you go with us as guide?

A. Kee-ya-wah-lee nas-bah a-lash-tay wah-lee-lee lan-day. (Answer literally) "Yes, I could go if I could leave the transport."

Interpreter's answer, "Mebby."

After a couple of hours of this bootless sort of thing we had made no headway toward getting a guide, nor could we get definite information about the Buffaloes or the Wolves. Finally the meeting suffered a sort of natural disintegration.

Next day we tried again, but again there were

technical difficulties, grown up like mushrooms over night.

Kiya could not go or lend his horses, because it was mostly Squirrel's country, and he was afraid Squirrel would not like it. Squirrel could not go because it would be indelicate of him to butt in after negotiations had been opened with Kiya. Kirma was not well. Sousi could not go because his wife was sick, and it preyed on his mind so that he dare not trust himself away from the settlement; at least, not without much medicine to fortify him against rheumatism, home-sickness, and sadness.

Next day Kiya sent word that he had business of great moment, and could not meet us, but would see that early in the morning Squirrel was notified to come and do whatever we wished. In the morning Squirrel also had disappeared, leaving word that he had quite overlooked a most important engagement to "portage some flour across the rapids," not that he loved the tump line, but he had "promised," and to keep his word was very precious to him.

Jarvis and I talked it over and reviewed the information we had. At Ottawa it was reported that the Wolves were killing the calves, so the Buffalo did not increase. At Winnipeg the Wolves were so bad that they killed yearlings; at Edmonton the cows were not safe.

At Chipewyan the Wolves, reinforced by large bands from the Barren Grounds, were killing the young Buffalo, and later the cows and young bulls. At Smith's Landing the Wolves had even tackled an old bull whose head was found with the large bones. Horses and dogs were now being devoured. Terrible battles were taking place between the dark Wolves of Peace River and the White Wolves of the Barrens for possession of the Buffalo grounds. Of course the Buffalo were disappearing; about a hundred were all that were left.

But no one ever sees any of these terrible Wolves, the few men who know that country have plenty of pemmican, that is neither Moose nor Caribou, and the Major briefly summed up the situation: "The Wolves are indeed playing havoc with the Buffalo, and the ravenous leaders of the pack are called Sousi, Kiya, Kirma, and Squirrel."

Now of all the four, Sousi, being a Beaulieu and a half-breed, had the worst reputation, but of all the four he was the only one that had admitted a possibility of guiding us, and was to be found on the fifth morning. So his views were met, a substitute found to watch his fishing nets, groceries to keep his wife from pining during his absence, a present for himself, the regular rate of wages doubled, his horses hired, his rheumatism, home-sickness, and sadness provided against, a present of tobacco, some more presents, a promise of reward for every Buffalo shown, then another present, and we set out.

Rake. Smith Landing, June 12,
1907. Typical of agriculture
on Great Slave River

CHAPTER VI

OUT WITH SOUSI BEAULIEU

IT's a fine thing to get started, however late in the day, and though it was 3.20 P. M. before everything was ready, we gladly set out—Sousi, Major Jarvis, and myself—all mounted, Sousi leading a pack-horse with provisions.

And now we had a chance to study our guide. A man's real history begins, of course, about twenty years before he is born. In the middle of the last century was a notorious old ruffian named Beaulieu. Montreal was too slow for him, so he invaded the north-west with a chosen crew of congenial spirits. His history can be got from any old resident of the north-west. I should not like to write it as it was told to me.

His alleged offspring are everywhere in the country, and most travellers on their return from this region, sound a note of warning: "Look out for every one of the name of Beaulieu. They are a queer lot." And now we had committed ourselves and our fortunes into the hands of Beaulieu's second or twenty-second son—I could not make sure which. He is a typical half-breed, of medium height, thin, swarthy, and very active, although he must be far past 50. Just how far is not

known, whether 59 69 or 79, he himself seemed uncertain, but he knows there is a 9 in it.   The women
of Smith's Landing say 59, the men say 79 or 89.

He is clad in what might be the cast-off garments
of a white tramp, except for his beaded moccasins.
However sordid these people may be in other parts
of their attire, I note that they always have some
redeeming touch of color and beauty about the moc-

Camp on Salt River.   June 13, 1907

casins which cover their truly shapely feet.   Sousi's
rifle, a Winchester, also was clad in a native mode.
An embroidered cover of moose leather protected it
night and day, except when actually in use; of his
weapons he took most scrupulous care.   Unlike the
founder of the family, Sousi has no children of his own.
But he has reared a dozen waifs under prompting of
his own kind heart.   He is quite a character—does not
drink or smoke, and I never heard him swear.   This
is not because he does not know how, for he is con-
versant with the vigor of all the five languages of the
country, and the garment of his thought is like Joseph's
coat.   Ethnologically speaking, its breadth and sub-

stance are French, but it bears patches of English, with
flowers and frills, strophes, and classical allusions of
Cree and Chipewyan—the last being the language of
his present "home circle."

There was one more peculiarity of our guide that
struck me forcibly. He was forever considering his
horse. Whenever the trail was very bad, and half of
it was, Sousi dismounted and walked—the horse usually following freely, for the pair were close friends.

This, then, was the dark villain against whom we
had been warned. How he lived up to his reputation
will be seen later.

After four hours' march through a level, swampy
country, forested with black and white spruce, black
and white poplar, birch, willow, and tamarack, we came
to Salt River, a clear, beautiful stream, but of weak,
salty brine.

Not far away in the woods was a sweet spring, and
here we camped for the night. Close by, on a place recently burnt over, I found the nest of a Green-winged
Teal. All cover was gone and the nest much singed,
but the down had protected the 10 eggs. The old one
fluttered off, played lame, and tried to lead me away.
I covered up the eggs and an hour later found she had
returned and resumed her post.

That night, as I sat by the fire musing, I went over
my life when I was a boy in Manitoba, just too late to
see the Buffalo, recalling how I used to lie in some old
Buffalo wallow and peer out over the prairie through
the fringe of spring anemones and long to see the big
brown forms on the plains. Once in those days I got

a sensation, for I did see them. They turned out to be a herd of common cattle, but still I got the thrill.

Now I was on a real Buffalo hunt, some twenty-five years too late. Will it come? Am I really to see the Wild Buffalo on its native plains? It is too good to be true; too much like tipping back the sands of time.

Anemones.   June 15, 1907

CHAPTER VII

THE BUFFALO HUNT

WE left camp on Salt River at 7.45 in the morning and travelled till 11 o'clock, covering six miles. It was all through the same level country, in which willow swamps alternated with poplar and spruce ridges. At 11 it began to rain, so we camped on a slope under some fine, big white spruces till it cleared, and then continued westward. The country now undulated somewhat and was varied with openings.

Sousi says that when first he saw this region, 30 years ago, it was all open prairie, with timber only in hollows and about water. This is borne out by the facts that all the large trees are in such places, and that all the level open stretches are covered with sapling growths of aspen and fir. This will make a glorious settlement some day. In plants, trees, birds, soil, climate, and apparently all conditions, it is like Manitoba.

We found the skeleton of a *cow Buffalo*, apparently devoured by Wolves years ago, because all the big bones were there and the skull unbroken.

About two in the afternoon we came up a 200-foot rise to a beautiful upland country, in which the forests were diversified with open glades, and which everywhere showed a most singular feature. The ground is

44

pitted all over with funnel-shaped holes, from 6 to 40 feet deep, and of equal width across the rim; none of them contained water. I saw one 100 feet across and about 50 feet deep; some expose limestone; in one place we saw granite.

At first I took these for extinct geysers, but later I learned that the whole plateau called Salt Mountain is pitted over with them. Brine is running out of the mountain in great quantities, which means that the upper strata are being undermined as the salt washes out, and, as these crack, the funnels are formed no doubt by the loose deposits settling.

In the dry woods Bear tracks became extremely numerous; the whole country, indeed, was marked with the various signs. Practically every big tree has bear-claw markings on it, and every few yards there is evidence that the diet of the bears just now is chiefly berries of *Uva ursi*.

As we rode along Sousi prattled cheerfully in his various tongues; but his steady flow of conversation abruptly ended when, about 2 P. M., we came suddenly on some Buffalo tracks, days old, but still Buffalo tracks. All at once and completely he was the hunter. He leaped from his horse and led away like a hound.

Ere long, of course, the trail was crossed by two fresher ones; then we found some dry wallows and several very fresh tracks. We tied up the horses in an old funnel pit and set about an elaborate hunt. Jarvis minded the stock, I set out with Sousi, after he had tried the wind by tossing up some grass. But he stopped, drew a finger-nail sharply across my canvas

coat, so that it gave a little shriek, and said "Va pa,"
which is "Cela ne va pas" reduced to its bony frame-
work. I doffed the offending coat and we went forward as shown on the map. The horses were left at
A; the wind was east. First we circled a little to eastward, tossing grass at intervals, but, finding plenty of
new sign, went northerly and westward till most of the

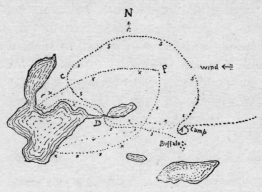

x x x x course taken when I got lost. At F I turned
back to the lake. s s s shows Sousi's course
when stalking the Buffalo

new sign was east of us. Sousi then led for *C*, telling
me to step in his tracks and make no noise. I did so
for long, but at length a stick cracked under my foot;
he turned and looked reproachfully at me. Then a
stick cracked under *his* foot; I gave him a poke in the
ribs. When we got to the land between the lakes
at *D*, Sousi pointed and said, "They are here." We
sneaked with the utmost caution that way—it was impossible to follow any one trail—and in 200 yards Sousi
sank to the ground gasping out, "La! la! maintenon
faites son portrait au tant que vous voudrez." I

crawled forward and saw, not one, *but half a dozen*
Buffalo. "I must be nearer," I said, and, lying flat on
my breast, crawled, toes and elbows, up to a bush
within 75 yards, where I made shot No. 1, and saw
here that there were 8 or 9 Buffalo, one an immense
bull.

Sousi now cocked his rifle—I said emphatically:
"Stop! you must not fire." "No?" he said in aston-

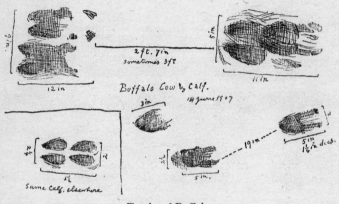

Tracks of Buffalo

ished tones that were full of story and comment.
"What did we come for?" Now I saw that by backing out and crawling to another bunch of herbage I
could get within 50 yards.

"It is not possible," he gasped.

"Watch me and see," I replied. Gathering all the
near vines and twisting them around my neck, I covered my head with leaves and creeping plants, then
proceeded to show that it *was* possible, while Sousi
followed. I reached the cover and found it was a bed

of spring anemones on the far side of an old Buffalo
wallow, and there in that wallow I lay for a moment
revelling in the sight. All at once it came to me:
Now, indeed, was fulfilled the long-deferred dream of
my youth, *for in shelter of those flowers of my youth, I
was gazing on a herd of wild Buffalo.* Then slowly I
rose above the cover and took my second picture.

The Buffalo herd

But the watchful creatures, more shy than Moose here,
saw the rising mass of herbage, or may have caught
the wind, rose lightly and went off. I noticed now, for
the first time, a little red calf; ten Buffalo in all I
counted. Sousi, standing up, counted 13. At the
edge of the woods they stopped and looked around,
but gave no third shot for the camera.

I shook Sousi's hand with all my heart, and he, good
old fellow, said: "Ah! it was for this I prayed last

night; without doubt it was in answer to my prayer that the Good God has sent me this great happiness."

Then back at camp, 200 yards away, the old man's tongue was loosed, and he told me how the chiefs in conference, and every one at the Fort, had ridiculed him and his Englishmen—"who thought they could walk up to Buffalo and take their pictures."

We had not been long in camp when Sousi went off to get some water, but at once came running back, shouting excitedly, "My rifle, my rifle!" Jarvis handed it to him; he rushed off to the woods. I followed in time to see him shoot an old Bear and two cubs out of a tree. She fell, sobbing like a human being, "Oh! Oh! Oh-h-h-h!" It was too late to stop him, and he finished her as she lay helpless. The little ones were too small to live alone, so shared her fate.

It seems, as Sousi went to the water hole, he came on an old Bear and her two cubs. She gave a warning "*koff, koff.*" The only enemies they knew about and feared, were Buffalo, Moose, and Wolves; from these a tree was a safe haven. The cubs scrambled up a tall poplar, then the mother followed. Sousi came shouting in apparent fear; I rushed to the place, thinking he was attacked by something, perhaps a Buffalo bull, but too late to stop the tragedy that followed.

That night he roasted one of the cubs, and as I watched the old cannibal chewing the hands off that little baby Bear it gave me a feeling of disgust for all flesh-eating that lasted for days. Major Jarvis felt much as I did, and old Sousi had exclusive joy in all his bear meat.

Next morning I was left at camp while Jarvis and
Sousi went off to seek for more Buffalo. I had a pre-
sentiment that they would find none, so kept the
camera and went off to the Lake a mile west, and there
made drawings of some tracks, took photos, etc., and
on the lake saw about twenty-five pairs of ducks,
identified Whitewinged Scoter, Pintail, Green-winged
Teal, and Loon. I also watched the manœuvres of a
courting Peetweet. He approached the only lady with

Tracks of the Blackbear

his feathers up and his wings raised; she paid no heed
(apparently), but I noticed that when he flew away
she followed. I saw a large garter snake striped black
and green, and with 2 rows of red spots, one on each
side. It was very fat and sluggish. I took it for a
female about to lay. Later I learned from Sousi and
others that this snake is quite common here, and the
only kind found, but in the mountains that lie not far
away in the west is another kind, much thicker, fatter,
and more sluggish. Its bite is fearfully poisonous,
often fatal; "but the Good God has marked the beast
by putting a cloche (bell) in its tail."

About 10 I turned campward, but after tramping
for nearly an hour I was not only not at home, I was in
a totally strange kind of country, covered with a con-

tinuous poplar woods. I changed my course and tried a different direction, but soon was forced to the conclusion that (for the sixth or seventh time in my life) I was lost.

"Dear me," I said, "this is an interesting opportunity. It comes to me now that I once wrote an essay on 'What To Do and What Not To Do When Lost In the Woods.' Now what in the world did I say in it, and which were the things not to do. Yes, I remember now, these were the pieces of advice:

"1st. 'Don't get frightened.' Well, I'm not; I am simply amused.

"2d. 'Wait for your friends to come.' Can't do that; I'm too busy; they wouldn't appear till night.

"3d. 'If you must travel, go back to a place where you were sure of the way.' That means back to the lake, which I know is due west of the camp and must be west of me now."

So back I went, carefully watching the sun for guidance, and soon realised that whenever I did not, I *swung to the left*. After nearly an hour's diligent travel I did get back to the lake, and followed my own track in the margin to the point of leaving it; then, with a careful corrected bearing, made for camp and arrived in 40 minutes, there to learn that on the first attempt I had swung so far to the left that I had missed camp by half a mile, and was half a mile beyond it before I knew I was wrong. (See map on p. 46.)

At noon Jarvis and Sousi came back jubilant; they had seen countless Buffalo trails, had followed a large bull and cow, but had left them to take the trail of a

considerable Band; these they discovered in a lake.
There were 4 big bulls, 4 little calves, 1 yearling, 3
2-year-olds, 8 cows. These allowed them to come
openly within 60 yards. Then took alarm and gal-
loped off. They also saw a Moose and a Marten—and

Buffalo dry wallows for the relief from flies

2 Buffalo skeletons. How I did curse my presenti-
ment that prevented them having the camera and
securing a really fine photograph!

At 2 P. M. Sousi prepared to break camp. He
thought that by going back on our trail he might
strike the trail of another herd off to the south-east
of the mountain. Jarvis shrewdly suspected that our
guide wanted to go home, having kept his promise,
won the reward, and got a load of Bear meat. How-

ever, Sousi was the guide, so we set out in a shower which continued more or less all day and into the night, so we camped in the rain.

Next day it was obvious, and Sousi no longer concealed the fact, that he was making for home as fast as he could go.

At Salt River I found the little Teal back on her eggs in the burnt ground. At 3.30 we reached Smith Landing, having been absent exactly 3 days, and having seen in that time 33 Buffalo, 4 of them calves of this year, 3 old Buffalo skeletons of ancient date, but not a track or sign of a Wolf, not a howl by night, or any evidence of their recent presence, for the buffalo skeletons found were obviously very old.

And our guide—the wicked one of evil ancestry and fame—he was kind, cheerful, and courteous throughout; he did exactly as he promised, did it on time, and was well pleased with the pay we gave him. Speak as you find. If ever I revisit that country I shall be glad indeed to secure the services of good old Sousi, even if he is a Beaulieu.

CHAPTER VIII

THOMAS ANDERSON

WE were now back at Smith Landing, and fired with
a desire to make another Buffalo expedition on which
we should have ampler time and cover more than a
mere corner of the range. We aimed, indeed, to strike
straight into the heart of the Buffalo country. The
same trouble about guides arose. In this case it was
less acute, because Sousi's account had inspired con-
siderably more respect. Still it meant days of delay
which, however, I aimed to make profitable by inves-
tigations near at hand.

After all, the most interesting of creatures is the
two-legged one with the loose and changeable skin,
and there was a goodly colony of the kind to choose
from. Most prominent of them all was Thomas
Anderson, the genial Hudson's Bay Company officer
in charge of the Mackenzie River District. His head-
quarters are at Fort Smith, 16 miles down the river,
but his present abode was Smith Landing, where all
goods are landed for overland transport to avoid the
long and dangerous navigation on the next 16 miles of
the broad stream. Like most of his official brethren,
he is a Scotchman; he was born in Nairn, Scotland, in
1848. At 19 he came to the north-west in service of

the company, and his long and adventurous life, as he climbed to his present responsible position, may be thus skeletonised:

He spent six months at Fort Temiscamingue,
1 year at Grand Lac,
3 years at Kakabonga,
5 years at Hunter's Lodge, Chippeway,
10 years at Abitibi,
3 years at Dunvegan, Peace River,
1 year at Lesser Slave Lake,
2 months at Savanne, Fort William,
10 years at Nipigon House,
3 years at Isle à la Crosse,
4 years on the Mackenzie River, chiefly at Fort Simpson,
6 months at Fort Smith.

Which tells little to the ears of the big world, but if we say that he spent 5 years in Berlin, then was moved for 3 years to Gibraltar, 2 years to various posts on the Rhine, whence he went for 4 years to St. Petersburg; thence to relieve the officer in charge of Constantinople, and made several flying visits to Bombay and Pekin, we shall have some idea of his travels, for all were afoot, on dogsled, or by canoe.

What wonderful opportunities he had to learn new facts about the wood folk—man and beast—and how little he knew the value of the glimpses that he got! I made it my business to gather all I could of his memories, so far as they dwelt with the things of my world, and offer now a résumé of his more interesting observations on hunter and hunted of the North.[1]

The following are among the interesting animal notes:

Cougar. Ogushen, the Indian trapper at Lac des Quinze, found tracks of a large cat at that place in the fall of 1879 (?). He saw them all winter on South Bay of that Lake. One day he came on the place where it had killed a Caribou. When he came back about March he saw it. It came toward him. It was evidently a cat longer than a Lynx and it had a very long tail, which swayed from side to side as it walked. He shot it dead, but feared to go near it believing it to be a Wendigo. It had a very bad smell. Anderson took it to be a Puma. It was unknown to the Indian. Ogushen was a first-class hunter and Anderson firmly believes he was telling the truth. Lac des Quinze is 15 miles north of Lake Temiscamingue.

Seals. In old days, he says, small seals were found in Lake Ashkeek. This is 50 miles north-east from Temiscamingue. It empties into Kippewa River, which empties into Temiscamingue. He never saw one, but the Indians of the vicinity told of it as a thing which commonly happened 50 or 60 years ago. Ashkeek is Ojibwa for seal. It is supposed that they wintered in the open water about the Rapids.

White Foxes, he says, were often taken at Cree Lake. Indeed one or two were captured each year. Cree Lake is 190 miles south-east of Fort Chipewyan. They

---

[1] Since these notes were made, Thomas Anderson has "crossed the long portage."

are also taken at Fort Chipewyan from time to time. One was taken at Fondulac, east end of Lake Athabaska, and was traded at Smith Landing in 1906. They are found regularly at Fondulac, the east end of Great Slave Lake, each year.

In the winter of 1885–6 he was to be in charge of Nipigon House, but got orders beforehand to visit the posts on Albany River. He set out from Fort William on Lake Superior on his 1,200-mile trip through the snow with an Indian whose name was Joe Eskimo, from Manitoulin Island, 400 miles away. At Nipigon House he got another guide, but this one was in bad shape, spitting blood. After three days' travel the guide said: "I will go to the end if it kills me, because I have promised, unless I can get you a better guide. At Wayabimika (Lake Savanne) is an old man named Omeegi; he knows the road better than I do." When they got there, Omeegi, although very old and half-blind, was willing to go on condition that they should not walk too fast. Then they started for Osnaburgh House on Lake St. Joseph, 150 miles away. The old man led off well, evidently knew the way, but sometimes would stop, cover his eyes with his hands, look at the ground and then at the sky, and turn on a sharp angle. He proved a fine guide and brought the expedition there in good time.

Next winter at Wayabimika (where Charley de la Ronde [1] was in charge, but was leaving on a trip of 10 days) Omeegi came in and asked for a present—"a new shirt and a pair of pants." This is the usual

[1] Count de la Ronde.

outfit for a corpse. He explained that he was to die before Charley came back; that he would die "when the sun rose at that island" (a week ahead). He got the clothes, though every one laughed at him. A week later he put on the new garments and said: "To-day I die when the sun is over that island!" He went out, looking at the sun from time to time, placidly smoking. When the sun got to the right place he came in, lay down by the fire, and in a few minutes was dead.

We buried him in the ground, to his brother's great indignation when he heard of it. He said: "You white men live on things that come out of the ground, and are buried in the ground, and properly, but we Indians live on things that run above ground, and want to take our last sleep in the trees."

Another case of Indian clairvoyance ran thus: About 1879, when Anderson was at Abitibi, the winter packet used to leave Montreal, January 2, each year, and arrive at Abitibi January 19. This year it did not come. The men were much bothered as all plans were upset. After waiting about two weeks, some of the Indians and half-breeds advised Anderson to consult the conjuring woman, Mash-kou-tay Ish-quay (Prairie woman, a Flathead from Stuart Lake, B. C.). He went and paid her some tobacco. She drummed and conjured all night. She came in the morning and told him: "The packet is at the foot of a rapid now, where there is open water; the snow is deep and the travelling heavy, but it will be here to-morrow when the sun is at that point."

Sure enough, it all fell out as she had told. This

woman married a Hudson's Bay man named Mac-
Donald, and he brought her to Lachine, where she
bore him 3 sons; then he died of small-pox, and Sir
George Simpson gave orders that she should be sent
up to Abitibi and there pensioned for as long as she
lived. She was about 75 at the time of the incident.
She many times gave evidence of clairvoyant power.
The priest said he "knew about it, and that she was
helped by the devil."

A gruesome picture of Indian life is given in the
following incident.

One winter, 40 or 50 years ago, a band of Algonquin
Indians at Wayabimika all starved to death except one
squaw and her baby; she fled from the camp, carrying the child, thinking to find friends and help at
Nipigon House. She got as far as a small lake near Deer
Lake, and there discovered a cache, probably in a tree.
This contained one small bone fish-hook. She rigged
up a line, but had no bait. The wailing of the baby
spurred her to action. No bait, but she had a knife;
a strip of flesh was quickly cut from her own leg, a
hole made through the ice, and a fine jack-fish was
the food that was sent to this devoted mother. She
divided it with the child, saving only enough for bait.
She stayed there living on fish until spring, then safely
rejoined her people.

The boy grew up to be a strong man, but was cruel
to his mother, leaving her finally to die of starvation.
Anderson knew the woman; she showed him the scar
where she cut the bait.

A piece of yet more ancient history was supplied
him in Northern Ontario, and related to me thus:

Anderson was going to Kakabonga in June, 1879, and camped one night on the east side of Birch Lake on the Ottawa, about 50 miles north-east of Grand Lake Post.

He and his outfit of two canoes met Pah-pah-tay, chief of the Grand Lake Indians, travelling with his family. He called Anderson's attention to the shape of the point which had one good landing-place, a little sandy bay, and told him the story he heard from his people of a battle that was fought there with the Iroquois long, long ago.

Four or five Iroquois war-canoes, filled with warriors, came to this place on a foray for scalps. Their canoes were drawn up on the beach at night. They lighted fires and had a war-dance. Three Grand Lake Algonquins, forefathers of Pah-pah-tay, saw the dance from hiding. They cached their canoe, one of them took a sharp flint—"we had no knives or axes then"—swam across to the canoes, and cut a great hole in the bottom of each.

The three then posted themselves at three different points in the bushes, and began whooping in as many different ways as possible. The Iroquois, thinking it a great war-party, rushed to their canoes and pushed off quickly. When they were in deep water the canoes sank and, as the warriors swam back ashore, the Algonquins killed them one by one, saving alive only one, whom they maltreated, and then let go with a supply of food, as a messenger to his people, and to carry the warning that this would be the fate of every Iroquois that entered the Algonquin country.

CHAPTER IX

MOSQUITOES

REFERENCE to my Smith Landing Journal for June 17 shows the following:

"The Spring is now on in full flood, the grass is high, the trees are fully leaved, flowers are blooming, birds are nesting, *and the mosquitoes are a terror to man and beast.*"

If I were to repeat all the entries in that last key, it would make dreary and painful reading; I shall rather say the worst right now, and henceforth avoid the subject.

Every traveller in the country agrees that the mosquitoes are a frightful curse. Captain Back, in 1833 (Journal, p. 117), said that the sand-flies and mosquitoes are the worst of the hardships to which the northern traveller is exposed.

T. Hutchins, over a hundred years ago, said that no one enters the Barren Grounds in the summer, because no man can stand the stinging insects. I had read these various statements, but did not grasp the idea until I was among them. At Smith Landing, June 7, mosquitoes began to be troublesome, quite as numerous as in the worst part of the New Jersey marshes. An estimate of those on the mosquito bar over my bed, showed 900 to 1,000 trying to get at me; day and night, without change, the air was ringing with their hum.

This was early in the season. On July 9, on Nyarling River, they were much worse, and my entry was as follows:

"On the back of Billy's coat, as he sat paddling before me, I counted a round 400 mosquitoes boring away; about as many were on the garments of his head and neck, a much less number on his arms and legs. The air about was thick with them; at least as many more, fully 1,000, singing and stinging and filling the air with a droning hum. The rest of us were equally pestered.

"The Major, fresh, ruddy, full-blooded, far over 200 pounds in plumpness, is the best feeding ground for mosquitoes I (or they, probably) ever saw; he must be a great improvement on the smoke-dried Indians. No matter where they land on him they strike it rich, and at all times a dozen or more bloated bloodsuckers may be seen hanging like red currants on his face and neck. He maintains that they do not bother him, and scoffs at me for wearing a net. They certainly do not impair his health, good looks, or his perennial good-humour, and I, for one, am thankful that his superior food-quality gives us a corresponding measure of immunity."

At Salt River one could kill 100 with a stroke of the palm, and at times they obscured the colour of the horses. A little later they were much worse. On 6 square inches of my tent I counted 30 mosquitoes, and the whole surface was similarly supplied; that is, there were 24,000 on the tent and apparently as many more flying about the door. Most of those that bite

us are killed, but that makes not the slightest perceptible difference in their manners or numbers.   They
reminded me of the Klondike gold-seekers.   Thousands
go; great numbers must die a miserable death; not
more than one in 10,000 can get away with a load of
the coveted stuff, and yet each believes that he is to
be that one, and pushes on.

Dr. L. O. Howard tells us that the mosquito rarely
goes far from its birthplace.   That must refer to the
miserable degenerates they have in New Jersey, for
these of the north offer endless evidence of power to
travel, as well as to resist cold and wind.

On July 21, 1907, we camped on a small island on
Great Slave Lake.   It was about one-quarter mile
long, several miles from mainland, at least half a mile
from any other island, apparently all rock, and yet it
was swarming with mosquitoes.   Here, as elsewhere,
they were mad for our blood; those we knocked off
and maimed, would crawl up with sprained wings and
twisted legs to sting as fiercely as ever, as long as the
beak would work.

We thought the stinging pests of the Buffalo country
as bad as possible, but they proved mild and scarce
compared with those we yet had to meet on the Arctic
Barrens of our ultimate goal.

Each day they got worse; soon it became clear that
mere adjectives could not convey any idea of their
terrors.   Therefore I devised a mosquito gauge.   I
held up a bare hand for 5 seconds by the watch, then
counted the number of borers on the back; there were
5 to 10.   Each day added to the number, and when

we got out to the Buffalo country, there were 15 to 25 on the one side of the hand and elsewhere in proportion. On the Nyarling, in early July, the number was increased, being now 20 to 40. On Great Slave Lake, later that month, there were 50 to 60. But when we reached the Barren Grounds, the land of open breezy plains and cold water lakes, the pests were so bad that the hand held up for 5 seconds often showed from 100 to 125 long-billed mosquitoes boring away into the flesh. It was possible to number them only by killing them and counting the corpses. What wonder that all men should avoid the open plains, that are the kingdom of such a scourge.

Yet it must not be thought that the whole country is similarly and evenly filled. There can be no doubt that they flock and fly to the big moving creatures they see or smell. Maybe we had gathered the whole mosquito product of many acres. This is shown by the facts that if one rushes through thick bushes for a distance, into a clear space, the mosquitoes seem absent at first. One must wait a minute or so to gather up another legion. When landing from a boat on the Northern Lakes there are comparatively few, but even in a high wind, a walk to the nearest hilltop results in one again moving in a cloud of tormentors. Does not this readiness to assemble at a bait suggest a possible means of destroying them?

Every one, even the seasoned natives, agree that they are a terror to man and beast; but, thanks to our fly-proof tents, we sleep immune. During the day I wear my net and gloves, uncomfortably hot, but a blessed relief from the torment. It is easy to get used to those coverings; it is impossible to get used to the mosquitoes.

For July 10 I find this note: "The Mosquitoes are worse now than ever before; even Jarvis, Preble, and the Indians are wearing face protectors of some kind. The Major has borrowed Preble's closed net, much to the latter's discomfiture, as he himself would be glad to wear it."

This country has, for 6 months, the finest climate in the world, but $2\frac{1}{2}$ of these are ruined by the malignancy of the fly plague. Yet it is certain that knowledge will confer on man the power to wipe them out.

No doubt the first step in this direction is a thorough understanding of the creature's life-history. This understanding many able men are working for. But there is another line of thought that should not be forgotten, though it is negative—many animals are immune. Which are they? Our first business is to list them if we would learn the why of immunity.

Frogs are among the happy ones. One day early in June I took a wood-frog in my hand. The mosquitoes swarmed about. In a few seconds 30 were on my hand digging away; 10 were on my forefinger, 8 on my thumb; between these was the frog, a creature with many resemblances to man—red blood, a smooth, naked, soft skin, etc.—and yet not a mosquito attacked it. Scores had bled my hand before one alighted on the frog, and it leaped off again as though the creature were red hot. The experiment repeated with another frog gave the same result. Why? It can hardly be because the frog is cold-blooded, for many birds also seem to be immune, and their blood is warmer than man's.

Next, I took a live frog and rubbed it on my hand over an area marked out with lead pencil; at first the place was wet, but in a few seconds dry and rather shiny. I held up my hand till 50 mosquitoes had alighted on it and begun to bore; of these, 4 alighted on the froggy place, 3 at once tumbled off in haste, but one, No. 32, did sting me there. I put my tongue to the frog's back; it was slightly bitter.

I took a black-gilled fungus from a manure pile to-day, rubbed a small area, and held my hand bare till 50 mosquitoes had settled and begun to sting; 7 of these alighted on the fungus juice, but moved off at once, except the last; it stung, but at that time the juice was dry.

Many other creatures, including some birds, enjoy immunity, but I note that mosquitoes did attack a dead crane; also they swarmed onto a widgeon plucked while yet warm, and bored in deep; but I did not see any filling with blood.

There is another kind of immunity that is equally important and obscure. In the summer of 1904, Dr. Clinton L. Bagg, of New York, went to Newfoundland for a fishing trip. The Codroy country was, as usual, plagued with mosquitoes, but as soon as the party crossed into the Garnish River Valley, a land of woods and swamps like the other, the mosquitoes had disappeared. Dr. Bagg spent the month of August there, and found no use for nets, dopes, or other means of fighting winged pests; there were none. What the secret was no one at present knows, but it would be a priceless thing to find.

Now, lest I should do injustice to the Northland that will some day be an empire peopled with white men, let me say that there are three belts of mosquito country— the Barren Grounds, where they are worst and endure for $2\frac{1}{2}$ months; the spruce forest, where they are bad and continue for 2 months, and the great arable region of wheat, that takes in Athabaska and Saskatchewan, where the flies are a nuisance for 6 or 7 weeks, but no more so than they were in Ontario, Michigan, Manitoba, and formerly England; and where the cultivation of the land will soon reduce them to insignificance, as it has invariably done in other similar regions. It is quite remarkable in the north-west that such plagues are most numerous in the more remote regions, and they disappear in proportion as the country is opened up and settled.

Finally, it is a relief to know that these mosquitoes convey no disease—even the far-spread malaria is unknown in the region.

Why did I not take a "dope" or "fly repellent," ask many of my friends.

In answer I can only say I have never before been where mosquitoes were bad enough to need one. I had had no experience with fly-dope. I had heard that they are not very effectual, and so did not add one to the outfit. I can say now it was a mistake to

leave any means untried. Next time I carry "dope."
The following recipe is highly recommended:

> Pennyroyal,   one part,
> Oil of Tar,   "   "
> Spirits of Camphor, "   "
> Sweet Oil, or else vaseline, three parts.

Their natural enemies are numerous; most small
birds prey on them; dragon-flies also, and the latter
alone inspire fear in the pests. When a dragon-fly
comes buzzing about one's head the mosquitoes move
away to the other side, but it makes no considerable
difference.

On Buffalo River I saw a boatman or water-spider
seize and devour a mosquito that fell within reach;
which is encouraging, because, as a rule, the smaller
the foe, the deadlier, and the only creature that really
affects the whole mosquito nation is apparently a
small red parasite that became more and more numerous as the season wore on. It appeared in red lumps
on the bill and various parts of the stinger's body, and
the victim became very sluggish. Specimens sent to
Dr. L. O. Howard, the authority on mosquitoes, elic-
ited the information that it was a fungus, probably
new to science. But evidently it is deadly to the Culex.
More power to it, and the cause it represents; we cannot
pray too much for its increase.

Now to sum up: after considering the vastness of the
region affected—three-quarters of the globe—and the
number of diseases these insects communicate, one is
inclined to say that it might be a greater boon to

mankind to extirpate the mosquito than to stamp out tuberculosis. The latter means death to a considerable proportion of our race, the former means hopeless suffering to all mankind; one takes off each year its toll of the weaklings, the other spares none, and in the far north at least has made a hell on earth of the land that for six months of each year might be a human Paradise.

The pests of the Peace

CHAPTER X

A BAD CASE

MY unsought fame as a medicine man continued to grow. One morning I heard a white voice outside asking, "Is the doctor in?" Billy replied: "Mr. Seton is inside." On going forth I met a young American who thus introduced himself: "My name is Y———, from Michigan. I was a student at Ann Arbor when you lectured there in 1903. I don't suppose you remember me; I was one of the reception committee; but I'm mighty glad to meet you out here."

After cordial greetings he held up his arm to explain the call and said: "I'm in a pretty bad way."

"Let's see."

He unwound the bandage and showed a hand and arm swollen out of all shape, twice the natural size, and of a singular dropsical pallor.

"Have you any pain?"

"I can't sleep from the torture of it."

"Where does it hurt now?"

"In the hand."

"How did you get it?"

"It seemed to come on after a hard crossing of Lake Athabaska. We had to row all night."

I asked one or two more questions, really to hide my puzzlement. "What in the world is it?" I said to

myself; "all so fat and puffy." I cudgelled my brain
for a clue. As I examined the hand in silence to play
for time and conceal my ignorance, he went on:

"What I'm afraid of is blood-poisoning. I couldn't
get out to a doctor before a month, and by that
time I'll be one-armed or dead. I know which I'd
prefer."

Knowing, at all events, that nothing but evil could
come of fear, I said: "Now see here. You can put
that clean out of your mind. You never saw blood-
poisoning that colour, did you?"

"That's so," and he seemed intensely relieved.

While I was thus keeping up an air of omniscience
by saying nothing, Major Jarvis came up.

"Look at this, Jarvis," said I; "isn't it a bad
one?"

"Phew," said the Major, "that's the worst felon I
ever saw."

Like a gleam from heaven came the word *felon*.
That's what it was, a felon or whitlow, and again I
breathed freely. Turning to the patient with my
most cock-sure professional air, I said:

"Now see, Y., you needn't worry; you've hurt your
finger in rowing, and the injury was deep and has set
up a felon. It is not yet headed up enough; as soon
as it is I'll lance it, unless it bursts of itself (and in-
wardly I prayed it might burst). Can you get any
linseed meal or bran?"

"Afraid not."

"Well, then, get some clean rags and keep the place
covered with them dipped in water as hot as you can

stand it, and we'll head it up in twenty-four hours;
then in three days I'll have you in good shape to
travel." The last sentence, delivered with the calm
certainty of a man who knows all about it and never
made a mistake, did so much good to the patient that
I caught a reflex of it myself.

He gave me his good hand and said with emotion:
"You don't know how much good you have done me.
I don't mind being killed, but I don't want to go
through life a cripple."

"You say you haven't slept?" I asked.

"Not for three nights; I've suffered too much."

"Then take these pills. Go to bed at ten o'clock and
take a pill; if this does not put you to sleep, take
another at 10.30. If you are still awake at 11, take
the third; then you will *certainly* sleep."

He went off almost cheerfully.

Next morning he was back, looking brighter. "Well,
I said, "you slept last night, all right."

"No," he replied, "I didn't; there's opium in those
pills, isn't there?"

"Yes."

"I thought so. Here they are. I made up my
mind I'd see this out in my sober senses, without
any drugs."

"Good for you," I exclaimed in admiration. "They
talk about Indian fortitude. If I had given one of
those Indians some sleeping pills, he'd have taken them
all and asked for more. But you are the real American
stuff, the pluck that can't be licked, and I'll soon have
you sound as a dollar."

Then he showed his immense bladder-like hand. "I'll have to make some preparation, and will operate in your shanty at 1 o'clock," I said, thinking how very professional it sounded.

The preparation consisted of whetting my penknife and, much more important, screwing up my nerves. And now I remembered my friend's brandy, put the flask in my pocket, and went to the execution.

He was ready. "Here," I said; "take a good pull at this brandy."

"I will not," was the reply. "I'm man enough to go through on my mettle."

"'Oh! confound your mettle,'" I thought, for I wanted an excuse to take some myself, but could not for shame under the circumstances.

"Are you ready?"

He laid his pudding-y hand on the table.

"You better have your Indian friend hold that hand."

"I'll never budge," he replied, with set teeth, and motioned the Indian away. And I *knew* he would not flinch. He will never know (till he reads this, perhaps) what an effort it cost me. I knew only I must cut deep enough to reach the pus, not so deep as to touch the artery, and not across the tendons, and must do it firmly, at one clean stroke. I did.

It was a *horrid success*. He never quivered, but said: "Is that all? That's a pin-prick to what I've been through every minute for the last week."

I felt faint, went out behind the cabin, and—shall I confess it?—took a long swig of brandy. But I was as good as my promise: in three days he was well enough to travel, and soon as strong as ever.

I wonder if real doctors ever conceal, under an air of professional calm, just such doubts and fears as worried me.

CHAPTER XI

THE SECOND BUFFALO HUNT

THOUGH so trifling, the success of our first Buffalo hunt gave us quite a social lift. The chiefs were equally surprised with the whites, and when we prepared for a second expedition, Kiya sent word that though he could not act as guide, I should ride his own trained hunter, a horse that could run a trail like a hound, and was without guile.

I am always suspicious of a horse (or man) without guile. I wondered what was the particular weakness of this exceptionally trained, noble, and guileless creature. I have only one prejudice in horse-flesh—I do not like a white one. So, of course, when the hunter arrived he was white as marble, from mane to tail and hoofs; his very eyes were of a cheap china colour, suggestive of cataractine blindness. The only relief was a morbid tinge of faded shrimp pink in his nostrils and ears. But he proved better than he looked. He certainly did run tracks by nose like a hound, provided I let him choose the track. He was a lively walker and easy trotter, and would stay where the bridle was dropped. So I came to the conclusion that Kiya was not playing a joke on me, but really had lent me his best hunter, whose sepulchral whiteness I could see would be of great advantage in snow time when chiefly one is supposed to hunt.

Not only Kiya, but Pierre Squirrel, the head chief, seemed to harbour a more kindly spirit. He now suddenly acquired a smattering of English and a fair knowledge of French. He 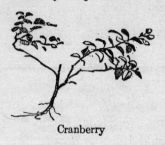 even agreed to lead us through his own hunting-grounds to the big Buffalo-range, stipulating that we be back by July 1, as that was Treaty Day, when all the tribe assembled to receive their treaty money, and his presence as head chief was absolutely necessary.

Cranberry

We were advised to start from Fort Smith, as the trail thence was through a dryer country; so on the morning of June 24, at 6.50, we left the Fort on our second Buffalo hunt.

Major A. M. Jarvis, Mr. E. A. Preble, Corporal Selig, Chief Pierre Squirrel, and myself, all mounted, plus two pack-horses, prepared for a week's campaign.

Riding ahead in his yellow caftan and black burnoose was Pierre Squirrel on his spirited charger, looking most picturesque.

Uva ursi

But remembering that his yellow caftan was a mosquito net, his black burnoose a Hudson's Bay coat, and his charger an ornery Indian Cayuse, robbed the picture of most of its poetry.

We marched westerly 7 miles through fine, dry,

jack-pine wood, then 3 miles through mixed poplar, pine, and spruce, and came to the Slave River opposite Point Gravois. Thence we went a mile or so into similar woods, and after another stretch of muskegs. We camped for lunch at 11.45, having covered 12 miles.

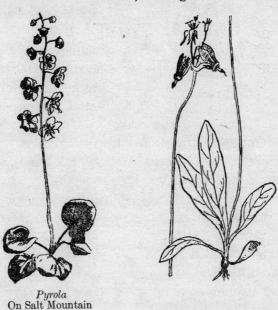

Pyrola
On Salt Mountain

At two we set out, and reached Salt River at three, but did not cross there. It is a magnificent stream, 200 feet wide, with hard banks and fine timber on each side; but its waters are brackish.

We travelled north-westerly, or northerly, along the east banks for an hour, but at length away from it on a wide prairie, a mile or more across here, but evidently extending much farther behind interruptions of willow clumps. Probably these prairies join with those we

saw on the Beaulieu trip. They are wet now, though
a horse can go anywhere, and the grass is good. We
camped about six on a dry place back from the river.
At night I was much interested to hear at intervals the

familiar *Kick-kick-
kick-kick* of the Yel-
low Rail in the ad-
joining swamps. This
must be its northmost
range; we did not
actually see it.

Uva-ursi

Here I caught a garter-snake. Preble says it is the
same form as that at Edmonton. Our guide was as
much surprised to see me take it in my hands, as he
was to see me let it go unharmed.

Next morning, after a short hour's travel, we came
again to Salt River and proceeded to cross. Evidently Squirrel had selected the wrong place, for the
sticky mud seemed bottomless, and we came near los-
ing two of the horses.

After two hours we all got across and went on, but
most of the horses had
shown up poorly, as spirit-
less creatures, not yet recovered from the effects
of a hard winter.

Linnæa

Our road now lay over the high upland of the Salt
Mountain, among its dry and beautiful woods. The
trip would have been glorious but for the awful things
that I am not allowed to mention outside of Chapter IX.

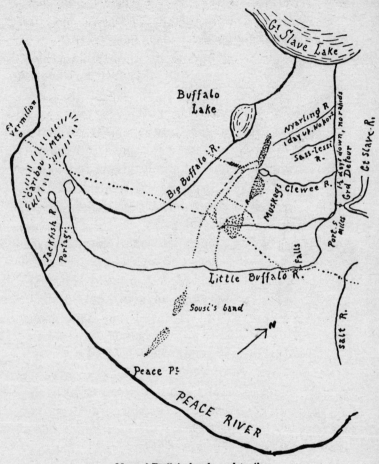

Map of Buffalo herds and trails

Drawn by Chief Pierre Squirrel, June 26, 1907

Pierre proved a pleasant and intelligent companion; he did his best, but more than once shook his head and said: "Chevaux no good."

Unifolium

We covered 15 miles before night, and all day we got glimpses of some animal on our track, 300 yards behind in the woods. It might easily have been a Wolf, but at night he sneaked into camp— a forlorn and starving Indian dog.

Next day we reached the long-looked-for Little Buffalo River. Several times of late Pierre had commented on the slowness of our horses and enlarged on the awful muskegs that covered the country west of the Little Buffalo. Now he spoke out frankly and said we had been 2½ days coming 40 miles when the road was good; we were now coming to very bad roads and had to go as far again. These horses could not do it, and get him back to Fort Smith for July 1 —and back at any price he must be.

He was willing to take the whole outfit half a day farther westward, or, if we preferred it, he would go afoot or on horseback with the pick of the men and horses for a hasty dash forward; but to take the whole outfit on to the Buffalo country and get back on time was not possible.

This was a bad shake. We held a council of war, and the things that were said of that Indian should have riled him if he understood. He preserved his calm demeanour; probably this was one of the convenient times when all his English forsook him. We were simply raging: to be half-way to our goal, with abundance of provisions, fine weather, good health and everything promising well, and then to be balked because our guide wanted to go back.

Juniperus nana

I felt as savage as the others, but on calmer reflection pointed out that Pierre told us before starting that he must be back for Treaty Day, and even now he was ready to do his best.

Then in a calm of the storm (which he continued to ignore) Pierre turned to me and said: "Why don't you go back and try the canoe route? You can go down the Great River to Grand Detour, then portage 8 miles over to the Buffalo, go down this to the Nyarling, then up the Nyarling into the heart of the Buffalo country; $2\frac{1}{2}$ days will do it, and it will be easy, for there is plenty of water and no rapids," and he drew a fairly exact map which showed that he knew the country thoroughly.

There was nothing to be gained by going half a day farther.

To break up our party did not fit in at all with our plans, so, after another brief stormy debate in which the guide took no part, we turned without crossing the Little Buffalo, and silently, savagely, began the homeward journey; as also did the little Indian dog.

Next morning we crossed the Salt River at a lower place where was a fine, hard bottom. That afternoon we travelled for 6 miles through a beautiful and level country, covered with a forest of large poplars, not very thick; it will some day be an ideal cattle-range, for it had rank grass everywhere, and was varied by occasional belts of jack-pine. In one of these Preble found a nest with six eggs that proved to be those of the Bohemian Chatterer. These he secured, with photograph of the nest and old bird. It was the best find of the journey.

The eggs proved of different incubation—at least a week's difference—showing that the cool nights necessitated immediate setting.

We camped at Salt River mouth, and next afternoon were back at Fort Smith, having been out five days and seen nothing, though there were tracks of Moose and Bear in abundance.

Here our guide said good-bye to us, and so did the Indian dog.

CHAPTER XII

BEZKYA AND THE PILLS

DURING this journey I had successfully treated two of
the men for slight ailments, and Squirrel had made
mental note of the fact. A result of it was that in the
morning an old, old, black-looking Indian came hob-
bling on a stick to my tent and, in husky Chipewyan,
roughly translated by Billy, told me that he had pains
in his head and his shoulder and his body, and his
arms and his legs and his feet, and he couldn't hunt,
couldn't fish, couldn't walk, couldn't eat, couldn't lie,
couldn't sleep, and he wanted me to tackle the case. I
hadn't the least idea of what ailed the old chap, but
conveyed no hint of my darkness. I put on my very
medical look and said: "Exactly so. Now you take
these pills and you will find a wonderful difference in
the morning." I had some rather fierce rhubarb pills;
one was a dose but, recognising the necessity for *éclat*,
I gave him two.

He gladly gulped them down in water. The Indian
takes kindly to pills, it's so easy to swallow them, so
obviously productive of results, and otherwise satisfactory. Then the old man hobbled off to his lodge.

A few hours later he was back again, looking older
and shakier than ever, his wet red eyes looking like
plague spots in his ashy brown visage or like volcanic

eruptions in a desert of dead lava, and in husky, clicking accents he told Billy to tell the Okimow that the
pills were no good—not strong enough for him.

"Well," I said, "he shall surely have results this
time." I gave him three big ones in a cup of hot tea.
All the Indians love tea, and it seems to help them.
Under its cheering power the old man's tongue was
loosened. He talked more clearly, and Billy, whose
knowledge of Chipewyan is fragmentary at best, suddenly said:

"I'm afraid I made a mistake. Bezkya says the pills
are *too strong*. Can't you give him something to stop
them?"

"Goodness," I thought; "here's a predicament," but
I didn't know what to do. I remembered a western
adage, "When you don't know a thing to do, don't do
a thing." I only said: "Tell Bezkya to go home, go to
bed, and stay there till to-morrow, then come here
again."

Away went the Indian to his lodge. I felt rather
uneasy that day and night, and the next morning
looked with some eagerness for the return of Bezkya.
But he did not come and I began to grow unhappy. I
wanted some evidence that I had not done him an injury. I wished to see him, but professional etiquette
forbade me betraying myself by calling on him. Noon
came and no Bezkya; late afternoon, and then I sallied
forth, not to seek him, but to pass near his lodge, as
though I were going to the Hudson's Bay store. And
there, to my horror, about the lodge I saw a group of
squaws, with shawls over their heads, whispering to-

gether. As I went by, all turned as one of them
pointed at me, and again they whispered.

"Oh, heavens!" I thought; "I've killed the old
man." But still I would not go in. That night I
did not sleep for worrying about it. Next morning I
was on the point of sending Billy to learn the state of
affairs, when who should come staggering up but old
Bezkya. He was on two crutches now, his com-
plexion was a dirty gray, and his feeble knees were
shaking, but he told Billy—yes, unmistakably this
time—to tell the Okimow that that was great medicine I had given him, and he wanted a dose just like it
for his wife.

CHAPTER XIII

FORT SMITH AND THE SOCIAL QUEEN

SEVERAL times during our river journey I heard reference to an extraordinary woman in the lower country, one who gave herself great airs, put on style, who was so stuck up, indeed, that she had "two pots, one for tea, one for coffee." Such incredible pomposity and arrogance naturally invited sarcastic comment from all the world, and I was told I should doubtless see this remarkable person at Fort Smith.

After the return from Buffalo hunt No. 2, and pending arrangements for hunt No. 3, I saw more of Fort Smith than I wished for, but endeavoured to turn the time to account by copying out interesting chapters from the rough semi-illegible, perishable manuscript accounts of northern life called "old-timers." The results of this library research work appear under the chapter heads to which they belong.

At each of these northern posts there were interesting experiences in store for me, as one who had read all the books of northern travel and dreamed for half a lifetime of the north; and that was—almost daily meeting with famous men. I suppose it would be similar if one of these men were to go to London or Washington and have some one tell him: that gentle old man there is Lord Roberts, or that meek, shy, re-

tiring person is Speaker Cannon; this on the first bench
is Lloyd-George, or that with the piercing eyes is
Aldrich, the uncrowned King of America. So it was
a frequent and delightful experience to meet with
men whose names have figured in books of travel for
a generation. This was Roderick MacFarlane, who
founded Fort Anderson, discovered the MacFarlane
Rabbit, etc.; here was John Schott, who guided Caspar Whitney; that was Hanbury's head man; here
was Murdo McKay, who travelled with Warburton
Pike in the Barrens and starved with him on Peace
River; and so with many more.

Very few of these men had any idea of the interest
attaching to their observations. Their notion of val-
ues centres chiefly on things remote from their daily
life. It was very surprising to see how completely
one may be outside of the country he lives in. Thus
I once met a man who had lived sixteen years in northern Ontario, had had his chickens stolen every year by
Foxes, and never in his life had seen a Fox. I know
many men who live in Wolf country, and hear them at
least every week, but have never seen one in twenty
years' experience. Quite recently I saw a score of folk
who had lived in the porcupiniest part of the Adiron-
dacks for many summers and yet never saw a Porcupine, and did not know what it was when I brought one
into their camp. So it was not surprising to me to find
that although living in a country that swarmed with
Moose, in a village which consumes at least a hundred
Moose per annum, there were at Fort Smith several of
the Hudson's Bay men that had lived on Moose meat

all their lives and yet had never seen a live Moose.   It
sounds like a New Yorker saying he had never seen a
stray cat.   But I was simply dumfounded by a final
development in the same line.

Quite the most abundant carpet in the forest here
is the uva-ursi or bear-berry.   Its beautiful evergreen
leaves and bright red berries cover a quarter of the
ground in dry woods and are found in great acre beds.
It furnishes a staple of food to all wild things, birds
and beasts, including Foxes, Martens, and Coyotes; it
is one of the most abundant of the forest products, and
not one hundred yards from the fort are solid patches
as big as farms, and yet when I brought in a spray to
sketch it one day several of the Hudson's Bay officers
said: "Where in the world did you get that?   It must
be very rare, for I never yet saw it in this country."
A similar remark was made about a phœbe-bird.
"It was never before seen in the country"; and yet
there is a pair nesting every quarter of a mile from
Athabaska Landing to Great Slave Lake.

Fort Smith, being the place of my longest stay, was
the scene of my largest medical practice.

One of my distinguished patients here was Jacob
McKay, a half-breed born on Red River in 1840.   He
left there in 1859 to live 3 years at Rat Portage.
Then he went to Norway House, and after 3 years
moved to Athabaska in 1865.   In 1887 he headed a
special government expedition into the Barren Grounds
to get some baby Musk-ox skins.   He left Fort Rae,
April 25, 1887, and, travelling due north with Dogrib
Indians some 65 miles, found Musk-ox on May 10, and

later saw many hundreds.   They killed 16 calves for their pelts, but no old ones.   McKay had to use all his influence to keep the Indians from slaughtering wholesale; indeed, it was to restrain them that he was sent.

He now lives at Fort Resolution.

One morning the chief came and said he wanted me to doctor a sick woman in his lodge.   I thought sick women a good place for an amateur to draw the line, but Squirrel did not.   "Il faut venir; elle est bien malade."

At length I took my pill-kit and followed him. Around his lodge were a score of the huge sled dogs, valuable animals in winter, but useless, sullen, starving, noisy nuisances all summer.   If you kick them out of your way, they respect you; if you pity them, they bite you.   They respected us.

We entered the lodge, and there sitting by the fire were two squaws making moccasins.   One was old and ugly as sin; the second, young and pretty as a brown fawn.   I looked from one to the other in doubt, and said:

"Laquelle est la malade?"

Then the pretty one replied in perfect English: "You needn't talk French here; I speak English," which she certainly did.   French is mostly used, but the few that speak English are very proud of it and are careful to let you know.

"Are you ill?" I asked.

"The chief thinks I am," was the somewhat impatient reply, and she broke down in a coughing fit.

"How long have you had that?" I said gravely.

"What?"

I tapped my chest for reply.

"Oh! since last spring."

"And you had it the spring before, too, didn't you?"

"Why, yes! (a pause).   But that isn't what bothers me."

"Isn't your husband kind to you?"

"Yes—sometimes."

"Is this your husband?"

"No!   F—— B—— is; I am K——."

Again she was interrupted by coughing.

"Would you like something to ease that cough?" I asked.

"No!   It isn't the body that's sick; it's the heart."

"Do you wish to tell me about it?"

"I lost my babies."

"When?"

"Two years ago.   I had two little ones, and both died in one month.   I am left much alone; my husband is away on the transport; our lodge is nearby. The chief has all these dogs; they bark at every little thing and disturb me, so I lie awake all night and think about my babies.   But that isn't the hardest thing."

"What is it?"

She hesitated, then burst out: "The tongues of the women.   You don't know what a hell of a place this is to live in.   The women here don't mind their work; they sit all day watching for a chance to lie about their neighbours.   If I am seen talking to you now, a story will be made of it.   If I walk to the store for a pound of tea, a story is made of that.   If I turn my head, another story; and everything is carried to my husband to make mischief.   It is nothing but lies, lies, lies, all day, all night, all year.   Women don't do that way in your country, do they?"

"No," I replied emphatically.   "If any woman in my country were to tell a lie to make another woman unhappy, she would be thought very, very wicked."

"I am sure of it," she said.   "I wish I could go to your country and be at rest."   She turned to her work and began talking to the others in Chipewyan.

Now another woman entered.   She was dressed in semi-white style, and looked, not on the ground, as does an Indian woman, on seeing a strange man, but straight at me.

"Bon jour, madame," I said.

"I speak Ingliss," she replied with emphasis.

"Indeed!   And what is your name?"

"I am Madame X——."

And now I knew I was in the presence of the stuck-up social queen.

After some conversation she said: "I have some things at home you like to see."

"Where is your lodge?" I asked.

"Lodge," she replied indignantly; "I have no lodge. I know ze Indian way.   I know ze half-breed way.   I know ze white man's way.   I go ze white man's way. I live in a house—and my door is *painted blue.*"

I went to her house, a 10 by 12 log cabin; but the door certainly was painted blue, a gorgeous sky blue, the only touch of paint in sight.   Inside was all one room, with a mud fireplace at one end and some piles of rags in the corners for beds, a table, a chair, and some pots. On the walls snow-shoes, fishing-lines, dried fish in smellable bunches, a portrait of the Okapi from *Outing*, and a musical clock that played with

painful persistence the first three bars of "God Save the King." Everywhere else were rags, mud, and dirt.

"You see, I am joost like a white woman," said the swarthy queen. "I wear boots (she drew her bare brown feet and legs under her skirt) and. corsets. Zey are la," and she

Half-breed's kitchen, Fort Smith

pointed to the wall, where, in very truth, tied up with a bundle of dried fish, were the articles in question. Not simply boots and corsets, but high-heeled Louis Quinze slippers and French corsets. I learned afterward how they were worn. When she went shopping to the H. B. Co. store she had to cross the "parade" ground, the great open space; she crowded her brown broad feet into the slippers, then taking a final good long breath she strapped on the fearfully tight corsets outside of all. Now she hobbled painfully across the open, proudly conscious that the eyes of the world were upon her. Once in the store she would unhook the corsets and breathe comfortably till the agonized triumphant return parade was in order.

This, however, is aside; we are still in the home of the queen. She continued to adduce new evidences. "I am just like a white woman. I call my daughter darrr-leeng." Then turning to a fat, black-looking squaw by the fire, she said: "Darrr-leeng, go fetch a pail of vaw-taire."

But darling, if familiar with that form of address, must have been slumbering, for she never turned or moved a hair's-breadth or gave a symptom of intelligence.

Now, at length it transpired that the social leader wished to see me professionally.

"It is ze nairves," she explained. "Zere is too much going on in this village. I am fatiguée, very tired. I wish I could go away to some quiet place for a long rest."

It was difficult to think of a place, short of the silent tomb, that would be obviously quieter than Fort Smith. So I looked wise, worked on her faith with a pill, assured her that she would soon feel much better, and closed the blue door behind me.

With Chief Squirrel, who had been close by in most of this, I now walked back to my tent. He told me of many sick folk and sad lodges that needed me.

It seems that very few of these people are well. In spite of their healthy forest lives they are far less sound than an average white community. They have their own troubles, with the white man's maladies thrown in. I saw numberless other cases of dreadful, hopeless, devastating diseases, mostly of the white man's importation. It is heart-rending to see so much human misery and be able to do nothing at all for it, not even bring a gleam of hope. It made me feel like a murderer to tell one after another, who came to me covered with cankerous bone-eating sores, "I can do nothing"; and I was deeply touched by the simple statement of the Chief Pierre Squirrel, after a round of visits: "You see how unhappy we are, how miserable and sick. When I made this treaty with your government, I stipulated that we should have here a policeman and a doctor; instead of that you have sent nothing but missionaries."

Anemone patens, Slave River,
40 miles above Fort Smith, June 7, 1907
While sketching this a humming-bird moth visited the bloom

CHAPTER XIV

RABBITS AND LYNXES IN THE NORTH-WEST

THERE are no Rabbits in the north-west. This statement, far from final, is practically true to-day, but I saw plenty of Lynxes, and one cannot write of ducks without mentioning water.

All wild animals fluctuate greatly in their population, none more so than the Snowshoe or white-rabbit of the north-west. This is Rabbit history as far back as known: They are spread over some great area; conditions are favourable; some unknown influence endows the females with unusual fecundity; they bear not one, but two or three broods in a season, and these number not 2 or 3, but 8 or 10 each brood. The species increases far beyond the powers of predaceous birds or beasts to check, and the Rabbits after 7 or 8 years of this are multiplied into untold millions. On such occasions every little thicket has a Rabbit in it; they jump out at every 8 or 10 feet; they number not less than 100 to the acre on desirable ground, which means over 6,000 to the square mile, and a region as large as Alberta would contain not less than 100,000,000 fat white bunnies. At this time one man can readily kill 100 or 200 Rabbits in a day, and every bird and beast of prey is slaughtering Rabbits without restraint. Still they increase. Finally, they are so extraordina-

rily superabundant that they threaten their own food
supply as well as poison all the ground. A new influence appears on the scene; it is commonly called the
plague, though it is not one disease but many run
epidemic riot, and, in a few weeks usually, the Rabbits
are wiped out.

This is an outline of the established routine in Rabbit vital statistics. It, of course, varies greatly in every
detail, including time and extent of territory involved,
and when the destruction is complete it is an awful
thing for the carnivores that have lived on the bunny
millions and multiplied in ratio with their abundance.
Of all the northern creatures none are more dependent
on the Rabbits than is the Canada Lynx. It lives on
Rabbits, follows the Rabbits, thinks Rabbits, tastes
like Rabbits, increases with them, and on their failure
dies of starvation in the unrabbited woods.

It must have been a Hibernian familiar with the
north that said: "A Lynx is nothing but an animated
Rabbit anyway."

The Rabbits of the Mackenzie River Valley reached
their flood height in the winter of 1903–4. That
season, it seems, they actually reached billions.

Late the same winter the plague appeared, but did
not take them at one final swoop. Next winter they
were still numerous, but in 1907 there seemed not one
Rabbit left alive in the country. All that summer we
sought for them and inquired for them. We saw signs
of millions in the season gone by; everywhere were
acres of saplings barked at the snow-line; the floor of
the woods, in all parts visited, was pebbled over with

pellets; but *we saw not one Woodrabbit* and heard only a vague report of 3 that an Indian claimed he had seen in a remote part of the region late in the fall.

Then, since the Lynx is the logical apex of a pyramid of Rabbits, it naturally goes down when the Rabbits are removed.

These bobtailed cats are actually starving and ready to enter any kind of a trap or snare that carries a bait. The slaughter of Lynxes in its relation to the Rabbit supply is shown by the H. B. Company fur returns as follows:

In 1900, number of skins taken	. .	4,473
" 1901 " " " "	. .	5,781
" 1902 " " " "	. .	9,117
" 1903 " " " "	. .	19,267
" 1904 " " " "	. .	36,116
" 1905 " " " "	. .	58,850
" 1906 " " " "	. .	61,388
" 1907 " " " "	. .	36,201
" 1908 " " " "	. .	9,664

Remembering, then, that the last of the Rabbits were wiped out in the winter of 1906–7, it will be understood that there were thousands of starving Lynxes roaming about the country. The number that we saw, and their conditions, all helped to emphasise the dire story of plague and famine.

Some of my notes are as follows:

May 18th, Athabaska River, on roof of a trapper's hut found the bodies of 30 Lynxes.

May 19th, young Lynx shot to-day, female, very thin, weighed only 12½ lbs., should have weighed 25. In its stomach nothing but the tail of a white-footed mouse. Liver somewhat diseased. In its bowels at least one tapeworm.

June 3d, a young male Lynx shot to-day by one of the police boys, as previously recorded. Starving; it weighed only 15 lbs.

June 6th, adult female Lynx killed, weighed 15 lbs.; stomach contained a Redsquirrel, a Chipmunk, and a Bog-lemming. (*Synaptomys borealis.*)

June 18th, young male Lynx, weight 13 lbs., shot by Preble on Smith Landing; had in its stomach a Chipmunk (*borealis*) and 4 small young of the same, apparently a week old; also a score of pinworms. How did it get the Chipmunk family without digging them out?

June 26th, on Salt Mt. found the dried-up body of a Lynx firmly held in a Bear trap.

June 29th, one of the Jarvis bear-cub skins was destroyed by the dogs, except a dried-up paw, which he threw out yesterday. This morning one of the men shot a starving Lynx in camp. Its stomach contained nothing but the bear paw thrown out last night.

These are a few of my observations; they reflect the general condition—all were starving. Not one of them had any Rabbit in its stomach; not one had a bellyful; none of the females were bearing young this year.

To embellish these severe and skeletal notes, I add some incidents supplied by various hunters of the north.

Let us remember that the Lynx is a huge cat weighing 25 to 35 or even 40 lbs., that it is an ordinary cat multiplied by some 4 or 5 diameters, and we shall have a good foundation for comprehension.

Murdo McKay has often seen 2 or 3 Lynxes together in March, the mating season. They fight and caterwaul like a lot of tomcats.

The uncatlike readiness of the Lynx to take to water is well known; that it is not wholly at home there is shown by the fact that if one awaits a Lynx at the landing he is making for, he will not turn aside in the least, but come right on to land, fight, and usually perish.

The ancient feud between cat and dog is not forgotten in the north, for the Lynx is the deadly foe of the Fox and habitually kills it when there is soft snow and scarcity of easier prey. Its broad feet are snowshoes enabling it to trot over the surface on Reynard's trail. The latter easily runs away at first, but sinking deeply at each bound, his great speed is done in 5 or 6 miles; the Lynx keeps on the same steady trot and finally claims its victim.

John Bellecourt related that in the January of 1907, at a place 40 miles south of Smith Landing, he saw in the snow where a Lynx had run down and devoured a Fox.

A contribution by T. Anderson runs thus:

In late March, 1907, an Indian named Amil killed a Caribou near Fort Rae. During his absence a Lynx came along and gorged itself with the meat, then lay down alongside to sleep. A Silver Fox came next; but the Lynx sprang on him and killed him. When

Amil came back he found the Fox and got a large sum
for the skin; one shoulder was torn.   He did not see
the Lynx but saw the tracks.

The same old-timer is authority for a case in which
the tables were turned.

A Desert Indian on the headwaters of the Gatineau
went out in the early spring looking for Beaver.   At a
well-known pond he saw a Lynx crouching on a log,
watching the Beaver hole in the ice.   The Indian
waited.   At length a Beaver came up cautiously and
crawled out to a near bunch of willows; the Lynx
sprang, but the Beaver was well under way and dived
into the hole with the Lynx hanging to him.   After
a time the Indian took a crotched pole and fished
about under the ice; at last he found something soft
and got it out; it was the Lynx drowned.

Belalise ascribes another notable achievement to
this animal.

One winter when hunting Caribou near Fond du
Lac with an Indian named Tenahoo (human tooth),
they saw a Lynx sneaking along after some Caribou;
they saw it coming but had not sense enough to run
away.   It sprang on the neck of a young buck; the
buck bounded away with the Lynx riding, but soon fell
dead.   The hunters came up; the Lynx ran off.   There
was little blood and no large wound on the buck;
probably its neck was broken.   The Indian said the
Lynx always kills with its paw, and commonly kills
Deer.   David MacPherson corroborates this and maintains that on occasion it will even kill Moose.

In southern settlements, where the Lynx is little

known, it is painted as a fearsome beast of limitless
ferocity, strength, and activity.   In the north, where it
abounds and furnishes staple furs and meat, it is held
in no such awe.   It is never known to attack man.   It
often follows his trail out of curiosity, and often the
trapper who is so followed gets the Lynx by waiting

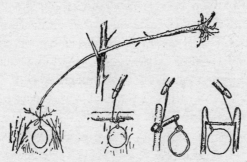

Pole for rabbit snare and various ways of
setting the noose

in ambush; then it is easily killed with a charge of
duck-shot.   When caught in a snare a very small club
is used to "add it to the list."   It seems tremendously
active among logs and brush piles, but on the level
ground its speed is poor, and a good runner can overtake one in a few hundred yards.

David MacPherson says that last summer he ran
down a Lynx on a prairie of Willow River (Mackenzie),
near Providence.   It had some 90 yards start; he ran
it down in about a mile, then it turned to fight and he
shot it.

Other instances have been recorded, and finally, as
noted later, I was eye-witness of one of these exploits.
Since the creature can be run down on hard ground, it

is not surprising to learn that men on snow-shoes commonly pursue it successfully. As long as it trots it is safe, but when it gets alarmed and bounds it sinks and becomes exhausted. It runs in a circle of about a mile, and at last takes to a tree where it is easily killed. At least one-third are taken in this way; it requires half an hour to an hour, there must be soft snow, and the Lynx must be scared so he leaps; then he sinks; if not scared he glides along on his hairy snow-shoes, refuses to tree, and escapes in thick woods, where the men cannot follow quickly.

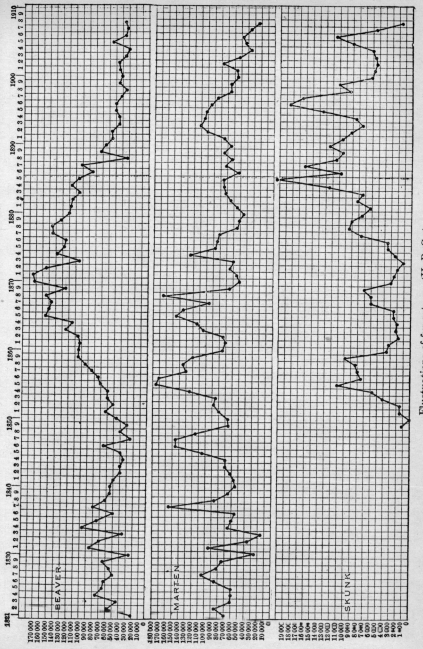

Fluctuations of fur returns (H. B. Co.)

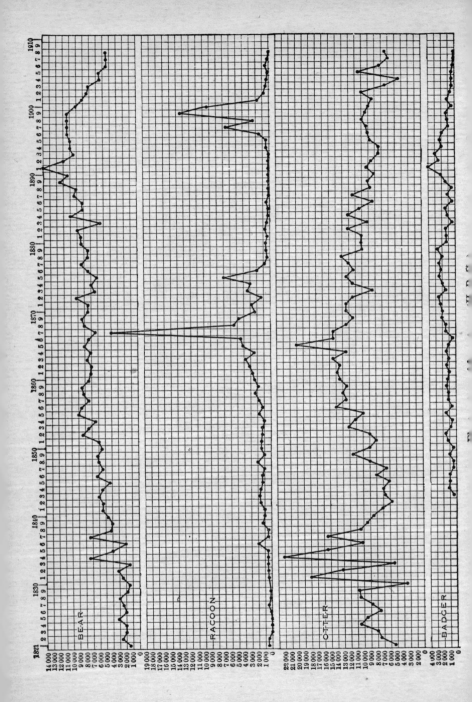

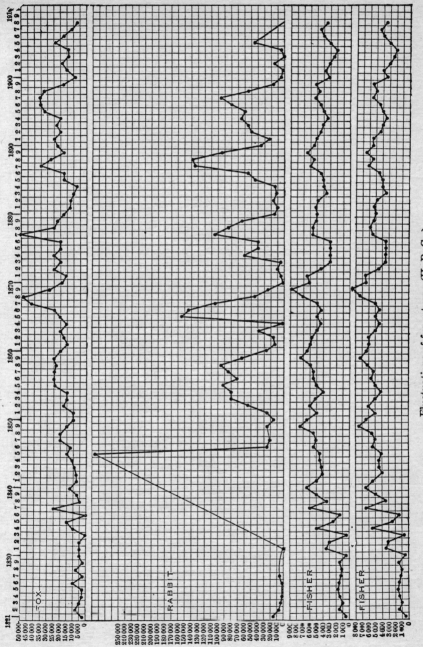

Fluctuations of fur returns (H. B. Co.)

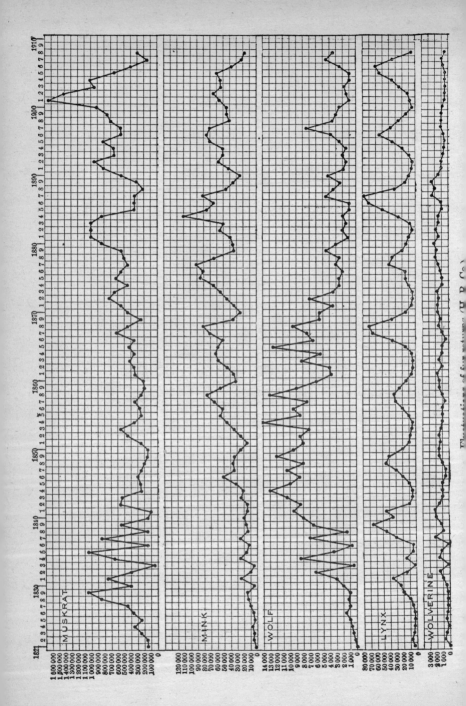

Fluctuations of fur-returns (H. B. Co.)

CHAPTER XV

EBB AND FLOW OF ANIMAL LIFE

THROUGHOUT this voyage we were struck by the rarity of some sorts of animals and the continual remarks that three, five, or six years ago these same sorts were extremely abundant; and in some few cases the conditions were reversed.

For example, during a week spent at Fort Smith, Preble had out a line of 50 mouse-traps every night and caught only one Shrew and one Meadowmouse in the week. Four years before he had trapped on exactly the same ground, catching 30 or 40 Meadowmice every night.

Again, in 1904 it was possible to see 100 Muskrats any fine evening. In 1907, though continually on the lookout, I saw less than a score in six months. Red-squirrels varied in the same way.

Of course, the Rabbits themselves were the extreme case, millions in 1904, none at all in 1907. The present, then, was a year of low ebb. The first task was to determine whether this related to all mammalian life. Apparently not, because Deermice, Lynxes, Beaver, and Caribou were abundant. Yet these are not their maximum years; the accounts show them to have been so much more numerous last year.

There is only one continuous statistical record of the abundance of animals, that is the returns of the

fur trade.   These have been kept for over 200 years,
and if we begin after the whole continent was covered
by fur-traders, they are an accurate gauge of the abundance of each species.   Obviously, this must be so, for
the whole country is trapped over every year, all the
furs are marketed, most of them through the Hudson's
Bay Company, and whatever falls into other hands

Drummond Vole or Fieldmouse

is about the same percentage each year, therefore the
H. B. Co. returns are an accurate gauge of the *relative*
rise and fall of the population.

Through the courtesy of its officials I have secured
the Company's returns for the 85 years—1821–1905 in-
clusive.   I take 1821 as the starting-point, as that was
the first year when the whole region was covered by
the Hudson's Bay Company to the exclusion of all
important rivals.

First, I have given these accounts graphic tabula-
tion, and at once many interesting facts are presented
to the eye.   The Rabbit line prior to 1845 is not reliable.
Its subsequent close coincidence with that of Lynx,
Marten, Skunk, and Fox is evidently cause and effect.

The Mink coincides fairly well with Skunk and
Marten.

The Muskrat's variation probably has relation chiefly to the amount of water, which, as is well known, is cyclic in the north-west.

The general resemblance of Beaver and Otter lines may not mean anything. If, as said, the Otter occasionally preys on the Beaver, these lines should in some degree correspond.

The Wolf line does not manifest any special relationship and seems to be in a class by itself. The great destruction from 1840 to 1870 was probably due to strychnine, newly introduced about then.

Microtus pocket hole.   Edmonton, May 10, 1907

The Bear, Badger, and Wolverine go along with little variation. Probably the Coon does the same; the enormous rise in 1867 from an average of 3,500 per annum to 24,000 was most likely a result of accidental accumulation and not representative of any special abundance. Finally, each and every line manifests extraordinary variability in the '30's. It is not to be supposed that the population fluctuated so enormously from one year to another, but rather that the facilities for export were irregular.

The case is further complicated by the fact that some of the totals represent part of this year and part of last; nevertheless, upon the whole, the following general principles are deducible:

(*a*) The high points for each species are with fair regularity 10 years apart.

(*b*) In the different species these are not exactly coincident.

(*c*) To explain the variations we must seek *not* the reason for the *increase*—that is normal—but for the destructive agency that *ended the increase*.

This is different in three different groups.

First. The group whose food and enemies fluctuate but little. The only examples of this on our list are the Muskrat and Beaver, more especially the Muskrat. Its destruction seems to be due to a sudden great rise of the water after the ice has formed, so that the Rats are drowned; or to a dry season followed by severe frost, freezing most ponds to the bottom, so that the Rats are imprisoned and starve to death, or are forced out to cross the country in winter, and so are brought within the power of innumerable enem'es.

How tremendously this operates may be judged by these facts. In 1900 along the Mackenzie I was assured one could shoot 20 Muskrats in an hour after sundown. Next winter the flood followed the frost and the Rats seemed to have been wiped out. In 1907 I spent 6 months outdoors in the region and saw only 17 Muskrats the whole time; in 1901 the H. B. Co. exported over $1\frac{1}{2}$ millions; in 1907, 407,472. The fact that they totalled as high was due, no doubt, to their abundance in eastern regions not affected by the disaster.

Second. The group that increases till epidemic disease attacks their excessively multiplied hordes. The Snowshoe-Rabbit is the only well-known case to-day, but there is reason for the belief that once the Beaver were subjected to a similar process. Concerning the Mice and Lemmings, I have not complete data, but they are believed to multiply and suffer in the same way.

Third. The purely carnivorous, whose existence is dependent on the Rabbits. This includes chiefly the Lynx and Fox, but in less degree all the small carnivores.

In some cases such as the Marten, over-feeding seems as inimical to multiplication as under-feeding, and it will be seen that each year of great increase for this species coincided with a medium year for Rabbits.

But the fundamental and phenomenal case is that of the Rabbits themselves. And in solving this we are confronted by the generally attested facts that when on the increase they have two or three broods each season and 8 to 10 in a brood; when they are decreasing they have but one brood and only 2 or 3 in that. This points to some obscure agency at work; whether it refers simply to the physical vigour of the fact, or to some uncomprehended magnetic or helio-logical cycle, is utterly unknown.

The practical consideration for the collecting natural-ist is this: Beaver, Muskrat, Otter, Fisher, Raccoon, Badger, Wolverine, Wolf, Marten, Fox reached the low ebb in 1904–5. All are on the up-grade; pre-sumably the same applies to the small rodents. Their decacycle will be complete in 1914–15, so that 1910–11 should be the years selected by the next collecting naturalist who would visit the north.

For those who will enter before that there is a rea-sonable prospect of all these species in fair numbers,

except perhaps the Lynx and the Caribou.   Evidently
the former must be near minimum now (1909) and the
latter would be scarce, if it is subject to the rule of the
decacycle, though it is not at all proven that such
is the case.

CHAPTER XVI

THE PELICAN TRIP

WE were still held back by the dilatory ways of our Indian friends, so to lose no time Preble and I determined to investigate a Pelican rookery.

Most persons associate the name Pelican with tropic lands and fish, but ornithologists have long known that in the interior of the continent the great white Pelican ranges nearly or quite to the Arctic circle. The northmost colony on record was found on an island of Great Slave Lake (see Preble, "N. A. Fauna," 27), but this is a very small one. The northmost large colony, and the one made famous by travellers from Alexander Mackenzie downward, is on the great island that splits the Smith Rapids above Fort Smith. Here, with a raging flood about their rocky citadel, they are safe from all spoilers that travel on the earth; only a few birds of the air need they fear, and these they have strength to repel.

On June 22 we set out to explore this. Preble, Billy, and myself, with our canoe on a wagon, drove 6 miles back on the landing trail and launched the canoe on the still water above Mountain Portage. Pelican Island must be approached exactly right, in the comparatively slow water above the rocky island, for 20 feet away on each side is an irresistible current leading into a sure-death cataract. But Billy was a river pilot and we made the point in safety.

Drifted like snow through the distant woods were the brooding birds, but they arose before we were near and sailed splendidly overhead in a sweeping, wide-fronted rank. As nearly as I could number them, there were 120, but evidently some were elsewhere, as this would not allow a pair to each nest.

We landed safely and found the nests scattered among the trees and fallen timbers. One or two mother birds ran off on foot, but took wing as soon as clear of the woods—none remained.

The nests numbered 77, and there was evidence of others long abandoned. There were 163 eggs, not counting 5 rotten ones, lying outside; nearly all had 2 eggs in the nest; 3 had 4; 5 had 3; 4 had 1. One or two shells were found in the woods, evidently sucked by Gulls or Ravens.

All in the nests were near hatching. One little one had his beak out and was uttering a hoarse chirping; a dozen blue-bottle flies around the hole in the shell were laying their eggs in it and on his beak. This led us to examine all the nests that the flies were buzzing around, and in each case (six) we found the same state of affairs, a young one with his beak out and the flies "blowing" around it. All of these were together in one corner, where were a dozen nests, probably another colony of earlier arrival.

We took about a dozen photos of the place (large and small). Then I set my camera with the long tube to get the old ones, and we went to lunch at the other end of the island. It was densely wooded and about an acre in extent, so we thought we should be forgotten. The old ones circled high overhead but at last dropped, I thought, back to the nests. After an hour and a half I returned to the ambush; not a Pelican was there. Two Ravens flew high over, but the Pelicans were far away, and all as when we went away, leaving the young to struggle or get a death-chill as they might. So much for the pious Pelican, the emblem of reckless devotion—a common, dirty little cock Sparrow would put them all to shame.

We brought away only the 5 rotten eggs. About half of the old Pelicans had horns on the bill.

On the island we saw a flock of White-winged Cross-bills and heard a Song-sparrow. Gulls were seen about. The white spruce cones littered the ground and were full of seed, showing that no Redsquirrel was on the island.

We left successfully by dashing out exactly as we came, between the two dangerous currents, and got well away.

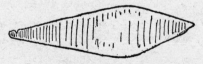

Spruce net-float 20 x 5 x ¼ inches

CHAPTER XVII

THE THIRD BUFFALO HUNT

THE Indians are subject to all kinds of mental revulsion, and no matter how reasonable your proposition, they take a long time to consider it. So we were lucky to get away from Fort Smith on July 4 with young François Bezkya as guide. He was a full-blooded Chipewyan Indian, so full that he had knowledge of no other tongue, and Billy had to be go-between.

Bezkya, the son of my old patient, came well recommended as *a good man and a moose-hunter*. A "good man" means a strong, steady worker, as canoeman or portager. He may be morally the vilest outcast unhung; that in no wise modifies the phrase "he is a good man." But more: the present was a moose-hunter; this is a wonderfully pregnant phrase. Moose-hunting by fair stalking is the pinnacle of woodcraft. The Crees alone, as a tribe, are supposed to be masters of the art; but many of the Chipewyans are highly successful. One must be a consummate trailer, a good shot, have tireless limbs and wind and a complete knowledge of the animal's habits and ways of moving and thinking. One must watch the wind, without ceasing, for no hunter has the slightest chance of success if once the Moose should scent him. This

last is fundamental, a three-times sacred principle.
Not long ago one of these Chipewyans went to con-
fessional. Although a year had passed since last he
got cleaned up, he could think of nothing to confess.
Oh! spotless soul! However, under pressure of the
priest, he at length remembered a black transgression.
The fall before, while hunting, he went to the wind-

Little Buffalo River looking north. July 8, 1907

ward of a thicket that seemed likely to hold his Moose,
because on the lee, the proper side, the footing happened to be very bad, and so he lost his Moose. Yes!
there was indeed a dark shadow on his recent past.

A man may be a good hunter, *i. e.*, an all-round
trapper and woodman, but not a moose-hunter. At
Fort Smith are two or three scores of hunters, and
yet I am told there are *only three moose-hunters*. The
phrase is not usually qualified; he *is*, or *is not*, a
moose-hunter. Just as a man is, or is not, an Oxford
M.A. The force, then, of the phrase appears, and
we were content to learn that young Bezkya, besides
knowing the Buffalo country, was also a good man
and a moose-hunter.

We set out in two canoes, Bezkya and Jarvis in the small one, Billy, Selig, Preble, and I in the large one, leaving the other police boys to make Fort Resolution in the H. B. steamer.

Being the 4th of July, the usual torrential rains set in. During the worst of it we put in at Salt River village. It was amusing to see the rubbish about the

Cornus canadensis

doors of these temporarily deserted cabins. The midden-heaps of the Cave-men are our principal sources of information about those by-gone races; the future ethnologist who discovers Salt River midden-heaps will find all the usual skulls, bones, jaws, teeth, flints, etc., mixed with moccasin beads from Venice, brass cartridges from New England, broken mirrors from France, Eley cap-boxes from London, copper rings, silver pins, lead bullets, and pewter spoons, and interpersed with them bits of telephone wires and the fragments of gramophone discs. I wonder what they will make of the last!

Eight miles farther we camped in the rain, reaching the Buffalo Portage next morning at 10, and had everything over its 5 miles by 7 o'clock at night.

It is easily set down on paper, but the uninitiated can scarcely realise the fearful toil of portaging. If you are an office man, suppose you take an angular box weighing 20 or 30 pounds; if a farmer, double the weight, poise it on your shoulders or otherwise, as you please, and carry it half a mile on a level pavement in cool, bright weather, and I am mistaken if you do not find yourself suffering horribly before the end of a quarter-mile; the last part of the trip will have been made in something like mortal agony. Remember, then, that each of these portagers was carrying 150 to 250 pounds

Ranunculus

of broken stuff, not half a mile, but several miles, not on level pavement, but over broken rocks, up banks, through quagmires and brush—in short, across ground that would be difficult walking without any burden, and not in cool, clear weather, but through stifling swamps with no free hand to ease the myriad punctures of his body, face, and limbs whenever unsufficiently protected from the stingers that roam in clouds. It is the hardest work I ever saw performed by human beings; the burdens are heavier than some men will allow their horses to carry.

Yet all this frightful labour was cheerfully gone through by white men, half-breeds, and Indians alike. They accept it as a part of their daily routine. This

Linnæa americana

fact alone is enough to guarantee the industrial future of the red-man when the hunter life is no longer possible.

Next day we embarked on the Little Buffalo River, beginning what should have been and would have been a trip of memorable joys but for the awful, awful, awful—see Chapter IX.

The Little Buffalo is the most beautiful river in the whole world except, perhaps, its affluent, the Nyarling.

This statement sounds like the exaggeration of mere impulsive utterance. Perhaps it is; but I am writing now after thinking the matter over for two and a half years, during which time I have seen a thousand others, including the upper Thames, the Afton, the Seine, the Arno, the Tiber, the Iser, the Spree, and the Rhine.

A hundred miles long is this uncharted stream; fifty feet its breadth of limpid tide; eight feet deep, crystal clear, calm, slow, and deep to the margin. A steamer could ply on its placid, unobstructed flood, a child could navigate it anywhere. The heavenly beauty of

Cranberry fruit and flowers

the shores, with virgin forest of fresh, green spruces towering a hundred feet on every side, or varied in open places with long rows and thick-set hedges of the gorgeous, wild, red, Athabaska rose, made a stream that most canoemen, woodmen, and naturalists would think without a fault or flaw, and with every river beauty in its highest possible degree. Not trees and flood alone had strenuous power to win our souls; at every point and bank, in every bend, were living creatures of the north, Beaver and Bear, not often seen but abundant; Moose tracks showed from time to time and birds were here in thousands. Rare winter birds, as we had long been taught to think them in our southern homes; here we found them in their native land and heard not a few sweet melodies, of which in faraway Ontario, New Jersey, and Maryland we had been

favoured only with promising scraps when wintry
clouds were broken by the sun. Nor were the old
familiar ones away—Flicker, Sapsucker, Hairy Woodpecker, Kingfisher, Least Flycatcher, Alder Flycatcher,
Robin, Crow, and Horned Owl were here to mingle
their noises with the stranger melodies
and calls of Lincoln Sparrow, Fox Sparrow, Olive-sided Flycatcher, Snipe, Rusty
Blackbird, and Bohemian Waxwing.

Never elsewhere have I seen Horned
Owls so plentiful. I did not know that
there were so many Bear and Beaver left;
I never was so much impressed by the inspiring raucous clamour of the Cranes,
the continual spatter of Ducks, the cries
of Gulls and Yellowlegs. Hour after hour
we paddled down that stately river ad-
ding our 3½ miles to its 1 mile speed;
each turn brought to view some new and
lovelier aspect of bird and forest life. I
never knew a land of balmier air; I never
felt the piney breeze more sweet; no-
where but in the higher mountains is there such a tonic
sense abroad; the bright woods and river reaches
were eloquent of a clime whose maladies are mostly
foreign-born. But alas! I had to view it all swaddled,
body, hands, and head, like a bee-man handling his
swarms. Songs were muffled, scenes were dimmed by
the thick, protecting, suffocating veil without which
men can scarcely live.

Ten billion dollars would be all too small reward,

Stellaria

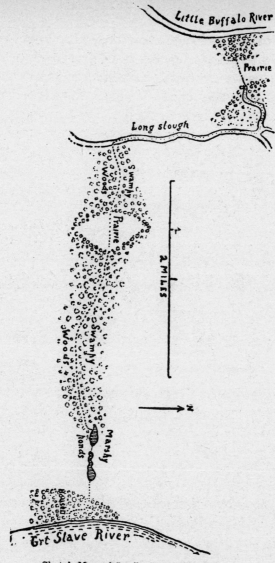

Sketch Map of 5-mile portage from Great
Slave River to Little Buffalo River

By E. T. Seton, June, 1907

a trifle totally inadequate to compensate, mere nominal
recognition of the man who shall invent and realise a
scheme to save this earthly paradise from this its damn-
ing pest and malediction.

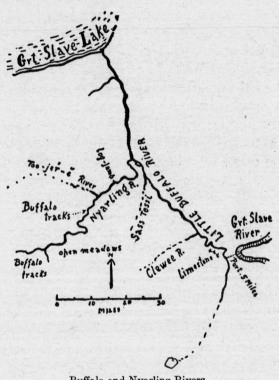

Buffalo and Nyarling Rivers

By E. T. Seton, July, 1907

CHAPTER XVIII

DOWN TO FUNDAMENTALS

At 8.30 a. m., 10 miles from the portage, we came to the Clew-ee, or White Fish River; at 6.30 p. m. made the Sass Tessi, or Bear River, and here camped, having covered fully 40 miles.

Now for the first time we were all together, with leisure to question our guide and plan in detail. But all our mirth and hopes were rudely checked by Corporal Selig, who had entire charge of the commissary, announcing that there were only two days' rations left.

In the dead calm that followed this bomb-shell we all did some thinking; then a rapid fire of questions demonstrated the danger of having a guide who does not speak our language.

It seems that when asked how many days' rations we should take on this Buffalo hunt he got the idea *how many days to the Buffalo.* He said five, meaning five days each way and as much time as we wished there. We were still two days from our goal. Now what should we do? Scurry back to the fort or go ahead and trust to luck? Every man present voted "go ahead on half rations."

We had good, healthy appetites; half rations was veritable hardship; but our hollow insides made hearty laughing. Preble disappeared as soon as we camped, and now at the right time he returned and silently threw at the cook's feet a big 6-pound Pike. It was just right, exactly as it happens in the most satisfactory books and plays. It seems that he always carried a spoon-hook, and went at once to what he rightly judged the best place, a pool at the junction of the two rivers. The first time he threw he captured the big fellow. Later he captured three smaller ones in the same place, but evidently there were no more.

That night we had a glorious feast; every one had as much as he could eat, chiefly fish. Next morning we went on 4½ miles farther, then came to the mouth of the Nyarling Tessi, or Underground River, that joins the Buffalo from the west. This was our stream; this was the highway to the Buffalo country. It was a miniature of the river we were leaving, but a little quicker in current. In about 2 miles we came to a rapid, but were able to paddle up. About 5 miles farther was an immense and ancient log-jamb that filled the stream from bank to bank for 190 yards. What will be the ultimate history of this jamb? It is added to each year, the floods have no power to move it, logs in water practically never rot, there is no prospect of it being removed by natural agencies. I suspect that at its head the river comes out of a succession of such things, whence its name Underground River.

Around this jamb is an easy portage. We were far now from the haunts of any but Indians on the winter hunt, so were surprised to see on this portage trail the deep imprints of a white man's boot. These were made apparently within a week, by whom I never

learned.   On the bank not far away we saw a Lynx
pursued overhead by two scolding Redsquirrels.

Lunch consisted of what remained of the Pike, but
that afternoon Bezkya saw two Brown Cranes on a
meadow, and manœuvring till they were in line killed
both with one shot of his rifle at over 100 yards, the
best shot I ever knew an Indian to make.   Still, two

Double lodge in bank 12 yards long, 4½ feet high.
July 7, 1907

Cranes totalling 16 pounds gross is not enough meat to
last five men a week, so we turned to our Moose-hunter.

"Yes, he could get a Moose."   He went on in the
small canoe with Billy; we were to follow, and if we
passed his canoe leave a note.   Seven miles above the
log-jamb, the river forked south and west; here a
note from the guide sent us up the South Fork; later
we passed his canoe on the bank and knew that he had
landed and was surely on his way "to market."   What
a comfortable feeling it was to remember that Bezkya
was a moose-hunter!   We left word and travelled till
7, having come 11 miles up from the river's mouth.
Our supper that night was Crane, a little piece of bread
each, some soup, and some tea.

At 10 the hunters came back empty-handed. Yes, they found a fresh Moose track, but the creature was so pestered by clouds of —— that he travelled continually as fast as he could against the wind. They followed all day but could not overtake him. They saw a Beaver but failed to get it. No other game was found.

Things were getting serious now, since all our food consisted of 1 Crane, 1 tin of brawn, 1 pound of bread, 2 pounds of pork, with some tea, coffee, and sugar, not more than one square meal for the crowd, and we were 5 men far from supplies, unless our hunting proved successful, and going farther every day.

Next morning (July 9) each man had coffee, one lady's finger of bread, and a single small slice of bacon. Hitherto from choice I had not eaten bacon in this country, although it was a regular staple served at each meal. But now, with proper human perversity, I developed an extraordinary appetite for bacon. It seemed quite the most delicious gift of God to man. Given bacon, and I was ready to forgo all other foods. Nevertheless, we had divided the last of it. I cut my slice in two, revelled in half, then secretly wrapped the other piece in paper and hid it in the watch-pocket of my vest, thinking "the time is in sight when the whole crowd will be thankful to have that scrap of bacon among them." (As a matter of fact, they never got it, for five days later we found a starving dog and he was so utterly miserable that he conjured that scrap from the pocket next my heart.)

We were face to face with something like starvation

now; the game seemed to shun us and our store of victuals was done. Yet no one talked of giving up or going back. We set out to reach the Buffalo country, and reach it we would.

That morning we got 7 little Teal, so our lunch was sure, but straight Teal without accompaniments is not very satisfying; we all went very hungry. And with one mind we all thought and talked about the good dinners or specially fine food we once had had. Selig's dream of bliss was a porterhouse steak with a glass of foaming beer; Jarvis thought champagne and roast turkey spelt heaven just then; I thought of my home breakfasts and the Beaux-Arts at New York; but Billy said he would he perfectly happy if he could have one whole bannock all to himself. Preble said nothing.

CHAPTER XIX

WHITE MAN AND RED. MEAT, BUT
NOTHING MORE

THERE was plenty of hollow hilarity but no word of turning back. But hold! yes, there was. There was one visage that darkened more each day, and finally the gloomy thoughts broke forth in words from the lips of—our Indian guide. His recent sullen silence was now changed to open and rebellious upbraiding. "He didn't come here to starve. He could do that at home. He was induced to come by a promise of plenty of flour." All of which was perfectly true. But, he went on, "We were still 1½ days from the Buffalo, and we were near the head of navigation; it was a case of tramp through the swamp with our beds and guns, living on the country as we went, and if we didn't have luck the Coyotes and Ravens would."

Before we had time to discuss this prospect, a deciding step was announced by Jarvis. He was under positive orders to catch the steamer *Wrigley* at Fort Resolution on the evening of July 10. It was now mid-day of July 9, and only by leaving at once and travelling all night could he cover the intervening 60 miles.

So then and there we divided the remnants of food *evenly*, for "Bezkya was a moose-hunter."

Then Major Jarvis and Corporal Selig boarded the smaller canoe. We shook hands warmly, and I at least had a lump in my throat; they were such good fellows in camp, and to part this way when we especially felt bound to stick together, going each of us on a journey of privation and peril, seemed especially hard; and we were so hungry. But we were living our lives. They rounded the bend, we waved good-bye, and I have never seen them since.

Hitherto I was a guest; now I was in sole command, and called a council of war. Billy was stanch and ready to go anywhere at any cost. So was Preble. Bezkya was sulky and rebellious. Physically, I had been at the point of a total breakdown when I left home; the outdoor life had been slowly restoring me, but the last few days had weakened me sadly and I was not fit for a long expedition on foot. But of one thing I was sure, we must halt till we got food. A high wind was blowing and promised some respite to the Moose from the little enemy that sings except when he stings, so I invited Bezkya to gird up his loins and make another try for Moose.

Nothing loath, he set off with Billy. I marked them well as they went, one lithe, sinewy, active, animal-eyed; the other solid and sturdy, following doggedly, keeping up by sheer blundering strength. I could not but admire them, each in his kind.

Two hours later I heard two shots, and toward evening the boys came back slowly, tired but happy, burdened with the meat, for Bezkya *was* a moose-hunter.

Many shekels and gladly would I have given to have been on that moose hunt. Had I seen it I could have told it. These men, that do it so well, never can tell it. Yet in the days that followed I picked up a few significant phrases that gave glimpses of its action.

Through the crooked land of endless swamp this son of the woods had set out "straightaway west." A big track appeared crossing a pool, seeming fresh. "No! he go by yesterday; water in track not muddy." Another track was found. "Yes, pretty good; see bite alder. Alder turn red in two hours; only half red." Follow long. "Look out, Billy; no go there; wrong wind. Yes, he pass one hour; see bit willow still white. Stop; he pass half-hour; see grass still bend. He lie down soon. How know? Oh, me know. Stand here, Billy. He sleep in thick willow there."

Then the slow crawl in absolute stillness, the long wait, the betrayal of the huge beast by the ear that wagged furiously to shake off the winged blood-suckers. The shot, the rush, the bloody trail, the pause in the opening to sense the foe, the shots from both hunters, and the death.

Next day we set out in the canoe for the Moose, which lay conveniently on the river bank. After pushing through the alders and poling up the dwindling stream for a couple of hours we reached the place two miles up, by the stream. It was a big bull with no bell, horns only two-thirds grown but 46 inches across; the tips soft and springy; one could stick a knife through them anywhere outside of the basal half.

Bezkya says they are good to eat in this stage; but we had about 700 pounds of good meat so did not try. The velvet on the horns is marked by a series of concentric curved lines of white hair, across the lines of growth; these, I take it, correspond with times of check by chill or hardship.

We loaded our canoe with meat and pushed on toward the Buffalo country for two miles more up the river. Navigation now became very difficult on account of alders in the stream. Bezkya says that only a few hundred yards farther and the river comes from underground. This did not prove quite correct, for I went half a mile farther by land and found no change.

Here, however, we did find some Buffalo tracks; one went through our camp, and farther on were many, but all dated from the spring and were evidently six weeks old.

There were no recent tracks, which was discouraging, and the air of gloom over our camp grew heavier. The weather had been bad ever since we left Fort Smith, cloudy or showery. This morning for the first time the day dawned with a clear sky, but by noon it was cloudy and soon again raining. Our diet consisted of nothing but Moose meat and tea; we had neither sugar nor salt, and the craving for farinaceous food was strong and growing. We were what the natives call "flour hungry"; our three-times-a-day prospect of Moose, Moose, Moose was becoming loathsome. Bezkya was openly rebellious once more, and even my two trusties were very, very glum. Still, the

thought of giving up was horrible, so I made a proposition: "Bezkya, you go out scouting on foot and
see if you can locate a band. I'll give you five dollars
extra if you show me one Buffalo."

At length he agreed to go provided I would set out
for Fort Resolution at once unless he found Buffalo
near. This was leaving it all in his hands. While I
was considering, Preble said: "I tell you this delay
is playing the mischief with our Barren-Ground trip;
we should have started for the north ten days ago,"
which was in truth enough to settle the matter.

I knew perfectly well beforehand what Bezkya's
report would be.

At 6.30 he returned to say he found nothing but old
tracks. There were no Buffalo nearer than two days'
travel on foot, and he should like to return at once to
Fort Resolution.

There was no further ground for debate; every one
and everything now was against me. Again I had to
swallow the nauseating draught of defeat and retreat.

"We start northward first thing in the morning,"
I said briefly, and our third Buffalo hunt was over.

These, then, were the results so far as Buffalo were
concerned: Old tracks as far down as last camp, plenty
of old tracks here and westward, but the Buffalo, as
before on so many occasions, were two days' travel
to the westward.

During all this time I had lost no good opportunity
of impressing on the men the sinfulness of leaving a
camp-fire burning and of taking life unnecessarily;
and now I learned of fruit from this seeding. That

night Bezkya was in a better humour, for obvious reasons; he talked freely and told me how that day he came on a large Blackbear which at once took to a tree. The Indian had his rifle, but thought, "I can kill him, yet I can't stop to skin him or use his meat," so left him in peace.

This is really a remarkable incident, almost unique. I am glad to believe that I had something to do with causing such unusual forbearance.

Blackfoot lodge, Calgary

CHAPTER XX

ON THE NYARLING

ALL night it rained; in the morning it was dull, foggy, and showery. Everything was very depressing, especially in view of this second defeat. The steady diet of Moose and tea was debilitating; my legs trembled under me. I fear I should be a poor one to stand starvation, if so slight a brunt should play such havoc with my strength.

We set out early to retrace the course of the Nyarling, which in spite of associated annoyances and disappointments will ever shine forth in my memory as the "Beautiful River."

It is hard, indeed, for words to do it justice. The charm of a stream is always within three feet of the surface and ten feet of the bank. The broad Slave, then, by its size wins in majesty but must lose most all its charm; the Buffalo, being fifty feet wide, has some waste water; but the Nyarling, half the size, has its birthright compounded and intensified in manifold degree. The water is clear, two or three feet deep at the edge of the grassy banks, seven to ten feet in mid-channel, without bars or obstructions except the two log-jambs noted, and these might easily be removed. The current is about one mile and a half an hour, so that canoes can readily pass up or down; the scenery

varies continually and is always beautiful. Everything that I have said of the Little Buffalo applies to
the Nyarling with fourfold force, because of its more
varied scenery and greater range of bird and other
life. Sometimes, like the
larger stream, it presents a
long, straight vista of a
quarter-mile through a sol-
emn aisle in the forest of
mighty spruce trees that
tower a hundred feet in
height, all black with
gloom, green with health,
and gray with moss.

Sometimes its channel
winds in and out of open
grassy meadows that are
dotted with clumps of
rounded trees, as in an
English park. Now it nar-
rows to a deep and sinu-
ous bed, through alders so
rank and reaching that
they meet overhead and
form a shade of golden

Senecio

green; and again it widens out into reedy lakes, the
summer home of countless Ducks, Geese, Tattlers
Terns, Peetweets, Gulls, Rails, Blackbirds, and half
a hundred of the lesser tribes. Sometimes the foreground is rounded masses of kinnikinnik in snowy
flower, or again a far-strung growth of the needle

bloom, richest and reddest of its tribe—the Athabaska rose. At times it is skirted by tall poplar woods where the claw-marks on the trunks are witness of the many

Cornel

Blackbears, or some tamarack swamp showing signs and proofs that hereabouts a family of Moose had fed to-day, or by a broad and broken trail that told of a Buffalo band passing weeks ago. And while we gazed at scribbled records, blots, and marks, the loud "slap plong" of a Beaver showed from time to time that the thrifty ones had dived at our approach.

On the way up Jarvis had gone first in the small canoe; he saw 2 Bears, 3 Beaver, and 1 Lynx; I saw nothing but birds. On the way down, being alone, the luck came my way.

At the first camp, after he left, we heard a loud

Ground Juniper, Juniperus sabina

"plong" in the water near the boat. Bezkya glided to the spot; I followed—here was a large Beaver swimming. The Indian fired, the Beaver plunged, and we saw nothing more of it. He told Billy, who told me, that it was dead, because it did not slap with its tail as it went down. Next night another splashed by our boat.

This morning as we paddled we saw a little stream, *very muddy*, trickling into the river. Bezkya said, "Beaver at work on his dam there." Now that we were really heading for flour, our Indian showed up well. He was a strong paddler, silent but apparently cheerful, ready at all times to work. As a hunter and guide he was of course first class.

About 10.30 we came on a large Beaver sunning himself on a perch built of mud just above the water. He looked like a huge chestnut Muskrat. He plunged at once but came up again 30 yards farther down,

Ledum groenlandicum

took another look, and dived, to be seen no more.

At noon we reached our old camp, the last where all had been together. Here we put up a monument on a tree, and were mortified to think we had not done so at our farthest camp.

There were numbers of Yellowlegs breeding here; we were surprised to see them resting on trees or flying from one branch to another.

A Great Gray-owl sitting on a stump was a conspicuous feature of our landscape view; his white choker shone like a parson's.

Early in the morning we saw a Kingbird. This was our northernmost record for the species.

We pressed on all day, stopping only for our usual supper of Moose and tea, and about 7 the boys were ready to go on again. They paddled till dark at 10. Camped in the rain, but every one was well pleased, for we had made 40 miles that day and were that much nearer to flour.

Two Robins chasing a Red-tail from its own nest.
July 12, 1907

This journey had brought us down the Nyarling and 15 miles down the Buffalo.

It rained all night; next morning the sun came out once or twice but gave it up, and clouds with rain sprinklings kept on. We had struck a long spell of wet; it was very trying, and fatal to photographic work.

After a delicious, appetising, and inspiring breakfast of straight Moose, without even salt, and raw tea, we pushed on along the line of least resistance, i.e., toward flour.

A flock of half a dozen Bohemian Waxwings were seen catching flies among the tall spruce tops; probably all were males enjoying a stag party while their wives were home tending eggs or young.

Billy shot a female Bufflehead Duck; she was so

small—only 8 inches in slack girth—that she could easily have entered an ordinary Woodpecker hole. So that it is likely the species nest in the abandoned holes of the Flicker. A Redtailed Hawk had its nest on a leaning spruce above the water. It was a most striking and picturesque object; doubtless the owner was very well pleased with it, but a pair of Robins militant attacked him whenever he tried to go near it.

A Beaver appeared swimming ahead; Bezkya seized his rifle and removed the top of its head, thereby spoil-

A windlass at the mouth of Little
Buffalo River. July 12, 1907

ing a splendid skull but securing a pelt and a new kind of meat. Although I was now paying his wages, the Beaver did not belong to me. According to the custom of the country it belonged to Bezkya. He owed me nothing but service as a guide. Next meal we had Beaver tail roasted and boiled; it was very delicious, but rather rich and heavy.

At 3.45 we reached Great Slave Lake, but found the sea so high that it would have been very dangerous to attempt crossing to Fort Resolution, faintly to be seen a dozen miles away.

We waited till 7, then ventured forth; it was only 11 miles across and we could send that canoe at $5\frac{1}{2}$

miles an hour, but the wind and waves against us were so strong that it took 3½ hours to make the passage. At 10.30 we landed at Resolution and pitched our tent among 30 teepees with 200 huge dogs that barked, scratched, howled, yelled, and fought around, in, and over the tent-ropes all night long. Oh, how different from the tranquil woods of the Nyarling!

Birch bark wavey quill rim

Pierre's water bucket, 10 in. high

Birch bark pail spruce root wrapping

Athabaska Rose

CHAPTER XXI

FORT RESOLUTION AND ITS FOLK

EARLY next morning Preble called on his old acquaintance, Chief Trader C. Harding, in charge of the post. Whenever we have gone to H. B. Co. officials to do business with them, as officers of the company, we have found them the keenest of the keen; but whenever it is their personal affair, they are hospitality out-hospitalled. They give without stint; they lavish their kindness on the stranger from the big world. In a few minutes Preble hastened back to say that we were to go to breakfast at once.

That breakfast, presided over by a charming woman and a genial, generous man, was one that will not be forgotten while I live. Think of it, after the hard scrabble on the Nyarling! We had real porridge and cream, coffee with veritable sugar and milk, and authentic butter, light rolls made of actual flour, unquestionable bacon and potatoes, with *jam* and *toast* —the really, truly things—and we had as much as we could eat! We behaved rather badly—intemperately, I fear—we stopped only when forced to do it, and yet both of us came away with appetites.

It was clear that I must get some larger craft than my canoe to cross the lake from Fort Resolution and take the 1,300 pounds of provisions that had come on the steamer. Harding kindly offered the loan of a

York boat, and with the help chiefly of Charlie McLeod
the white man, who is interpreter at the fort, I secured
a crew to man it. But oh, what worry and annoy-
ance it was!

One difficulty was that it became known that on the
Buffalo expedition Bezkya had received three dollars
a day, which is government emergency pay. I had
agreed to pay the regular maximum, two dollars a
day with presents and keep. All came and demanded
three dollars. I told them they could go at once in
search of the hottest place ever pictured by a diseased
and perfervid human imagination.

If they went there they decided not to stay, because
in an hour they were back offering to compromise. I
said I could run back to Fort Smith (it sounds like
nothing) and get all the men I needed at one dollar
and a half. (I should mortally have hated to try.)
One by one the crew resumed. Then another bomb-
shell. I had offended Chief Snuff by not calling and
consulting with him; he now gave it out that I was
here to take out live Musk-ox, which meant that all
the rest would follow to seek their lost relatives.
Again my crew resigned. I went to see Snuff. Every
man has his price. Snuff's price was half a pound of
tea; and the crew came back, bringing, however,
several new modifications in our contract.

Taking no account of several individuals that joined
a number of times but finally resigned, the following,
after they had received presents, provisions, and advance pay, were the crew secured to man the York boat
on the "3 or 4" days' run to Pike's Portage and then
carry my goods to the first lake.

Weeso. The Jesuits called him Louison d'Noire, but it has been corrupted into a simpler form. "Weeso" they call it, "Weeso" they write it, and for "Weeso" you must ask, or you will not find him. So I write it as I do "Sousi" and "Yum," with the true local colour.

He was a nice, kind, simple old rabbit, not much use and not over-strong, but he did his best, never murmuring, and in all the mutinies and rebellions that followed he remained staunch, saying simply, "I gave my word I would go, and I will go." He would make a safe guide for the next party headed for Aylmer Lake. He alone did not ask rations for his wife during his absence; he said, "It didn't matter about her, as they had been married for a long time now." He asked as presents a pair of my spectacles, as his eyes were failing, and a marble axe. The latter I sent him later, but he could not understand why glasses that helped me should not help him. He acted as pilot and guide, knowing next to nothing about either.

François d'Noire, son of Weeso, a quiet, steady, inoffensive chap, but not strong; nevertheless, having been there once with us, he is now a competent guide to take any other party as far as Pike's Portage.

C., a sulky brute and a mischief-maker. He joined and resigned a dozen times that day, coming back on each occasion with a new demand.

S., grandson of the chief, a sulky good-for-nothing; would not have him again at any price; besides the usual wages, tobacco, food, etc., he demanded extra to support his wife during his absence. The wife, I found, was a myth.

T., a sulky good-for-nothing.

Beaulieu, an alleged grandson of his grandfather. A perpetual breeder of trouble; never did a decent day's work the whole trip. Insolent, mutinous, and overbearing, till I went for him with intent to do bodily mischief; then he became extremely obsequious. Like the rest of the foregoing, he resigned and resumed at irregular intervals.

Yum (William) Freesay; the best of the lot; a bright, cheerful, intelligent, strong Indian boy. He and my old standby, Billy Loutit, did virtually all the handling of that big boat. Any one travelling in that country should secure Yum if they can. He was worth all the others put together.

Bess-hath or crooked knife. 10½ in. long.
Property of Weeso. Made of a file.
July 16, 1907

CHAPTER XXII

THE CHIPEWYANS, THEIR SPEECH AND WRITING

SWEEPING generalisations are always misleading, therefore I offer some now, and later will correct them by specific instances.

These Chipewyans are dirty, shiftless, improvident, and absolutely honest. Of the last we saw daily instances in crossing the country. Valuables hung in trees, protected only from weather, birds, and beasts, but never a suggestion that they needed protection from mankind. They are kind and hospitable among themselves, but grasping in their dealings with white men, as already set forth. While they are shiftless and lazy, they also undertake the frightful toil of hunting and portaging. Although improvident, they have learned to dry a stock of meat and put up a scaffold of white fish for winter use. As a tribe they are mild and inoffensive, although they are the original stock from which the Apaches broke away some hundreds of years ago before settling in the south.

They have suffered greatly from diseases imported by white men, but not from whiskey. The Hudson's Bay Company has always refused to supply liquor to the Indians. What little of the evil traffic there has been was the work of free-traders. But the Royal Mounted Police have most rigorously and effectually

suppressed this.   Nevertheless, Chief Trader Anderson
tells me that the Mackenzie Valley tribes have fallen
to less than half their numbers during the last century.

It is about ten years since they made the treaty
that surrendered their lands to the government.   They
have no reserves, but are free to hunt as their fathers
did.

I found several of the older men lamenting the
degeneracy of their people.   "Our fathers were hunters and our mothers made good moccasins, but the
young men are lazy loafers around the trading posts,
and the women get money in bad ways to buy what
they should make with their hands."

The Chipewyan dialects are peculiarly rasping, clicking, and guttural, especially when compared with Cree.

Every man and woman and most of the children
among them smoke.   They habitually appear with a
pipe in their mouth and speak without removing it,
so that the words gurgle out on each side of the pipe
while a thin stream goes sizzling through the stem.
This additional variant makes it hopeless to suggest on
paper any approach to their peculiar speech.

The Jesuits tell me that it was more clicked and
guttural fifty years ago, but that they are successfully
weeding out many of the more unpleasant catarrhal
sounds.

In noting down the names of animals, I was struck
by the fact that the more familiar the animal the
shorter its name.   Thus the Beaver, Muskrat, Rabbit,
and Marten, on which they live, are respectively Tsa,
Dthen, Ka, and Tha.   The less familiar (in a daily

sense) Red Fox and Weasel are Nak-ee-they, Noon-dee-a, Tel-ky-lay; and the comparatively scarce Musk-ox and little Weasel, At-huh-le-jer-ray and Tel-ky-lay-azzy. All of which is clear and logical, for the name originally is a description, but the softer parts and sharp angles are worn down by the attrition of use—

A. Typical teepee of Plains Indians. *B*. Chipewyan teepee with smoke flaps of a separate piece. *C*. Modern Chipewyan teepee with tent addition

the more use they have for a word the shorter it is bound to get. In this connection it is significant that "to-day" is To-ho-chin-nay, and "to-morrow" Kom-pay.

The Chipewyan teepee is very distinctive; fifty years ago all were of caribou leather, now most are of cotton; not for lack of caribou, but because the cotton does not need continual watching to save it from the dogs. Of the fifty teepees at Fort Chipewyan, one or two only were of caribou but many had caribou-skin tops, as these are less likely to burn than those of cotton.

The way they manage the smoke is very clever; in-stead of the two fixed flaps, as among the Plains River Indians, these have a separate hood which is easily set on any side (see III). Chief Squirrel lives in a lodge that is an admirable combination of the white men's tent with its weather-proof roof and the Indian teepee with its cosy fire.   (See cut, p. 149.)

Not one of these lodges that I saw, here or elsewhere, had the slightest suggestion of decoration.

For people who spend their whole life on or near the water these are the worst boatmen I ever saw. The narrow, thick paddle they make, compared with the broad, thin Iroquois paddle, exactly expressed the difference between the two as canoemen. The Chipewyan's mode of using it is to sit near the middle and make 2 or perhaps 3 strokes on one side, then change to the other side for the same, and so on. The line made by the canoes is an endless zigzag. The idea of paddling on one side so dexterously that the canoe goes straight is yet on an evolutionary pinnacle beyond their present horizon.

a. Chipewyan paddle.   *b.* Iroquois paddle

In rowing, their way is to stand up, reach forward with the 30-pound 16½-foot oar, throw all the weight on it, falling backward into the seat. After half an hour of this exhausting work they must rest 15 to 20 minutes. The long, steady, strong pull is unknown to them in every sense.

Their ideas of sailing a boat are childish. Tacking is like washing, merely a dim possibility of their very distant future. It's a sailing wind if behind; otherwise it's a case of furl and row.

By an ancient, unwritten law the whole country is roughly divided among the hunters. Each has his own recognised hunting ground, usually a given river valley, that is his exclusive and hereditary property; another hunter may follow a wounded animal into it, but not begin a hunt there or set a trap upon it.

Chipewyan canoe, Smith Landing

Most of their time is spent at the village, but the hunting ground is visited at proper seasons.

Fifty years ago they commonly went half naked. How they stood the insects I do not know, and when asked they merely grinned significantly; probably they doped themselves with grease.

This religious training has had one bad effect. Inspired with horror of being "naked" savages, they do not run any sinful risks, even to take a bath. In all

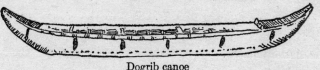

Dogrib canoe

the six months I was among them I never saw an Indian's bare arms, much less his legs. One day after the fly season was over I took advantage of the lovely weather and water to strip off and jump into a lake by our camp; my Indians modestly turned their backs until I had finished.

If this mock modesty worked for morality one might well accept it, but the old folks say that it operates quite the other way. It has at all events put an end to any possibility of them taking a bath.

Maybe as a consequence, but of this I am not sure, none of these Indians swim. A large canoe-load upset in crossing Great Slave Lake a month after we arrived and all were drowned.

Like most men who lead physical lives, and like all meat-eating savages, these are possessed of a natural proneness toward strong drink.

An interesting two-edged boomerang illustration of this was given by an unscrupulous whiskey trader. While travelling across country he ran short of provisions but fortunately came to a Chipewyan lodge. At first its owner had no meat to spare, but when he found that the visitor had a flask of whiskey he offered for it a large piece of Moose meat; when this was refused he doubled the amount, and after another refusal added some valuable furs and more meat till one hundred dollars worth was piled up.

Again the answer was "no."

Then did that Indian offer the lodge and everything he had in it, including his wife. But the trader was obdurate.

"Why didn't you take it," said the friend whom he told of the affair; "the stuff would have netted five hundred dollars, and all for one flask of whiskey."

"Not much," said the trader, "it was my last flask. I wouldn't 'a' had a drop for myself. But it just shows how fond these Indians are of whiskey."

While some of the Chipewyans show fine physique, and many do great feats of strength and endurance, they seem on the whole less powerful than whites.

Thus the strongest portager on the river is said to be Billy Loutit's brother George. At Athabaska Landing I was shown a house on a hill, half a mile away, to which he had carried on his back 450 pounds of flour without stopping. Some said it was only 350 pounds, but none made it less. As George is only three-quarters white, this is perhaps not a case in point. But during our stay at Fort Smith we had several athletic meets of Indians and whites, the latter represented by Preble and the police boys, and no matter whether in running, walking, high jumping, broad jumping, wrestling, or boxing, the whites were ahead.

As rifle-shots, also, the Indians seem far inferior. In the matter of moose-hunting only, as already noted, the red-man was master. This, of course, is a matter of life-long training.

These tribes are still in the hunting and fishing stage; they make no pretence of agriculture or stock-raising. Except that they wear white man's clothes and are most of them nominally Roman Catholics, they live as their fathers did 100 years ago. But there is one remarkable circumstance that impressed me more and more—practically every Chipewyan reads and writes his own language.

This miracle was inborn on me slowly. On the first Buffalo hunt we had found a smoothened pole stuck in the ground by the trail. It was inscribed as here-with.

"What is that Sousi?" "It's a notice from Chief William that Swiggert wants men on the portage," and he translated it literally: "The fat white man 5 scows, small white man 2 scows, gone down, men wanted for Rapids, Johnnie Bolette this letter for you. (Signed) Chief William."

Each of our guides in succession had shown a similar familiarity with the script of his people, and many

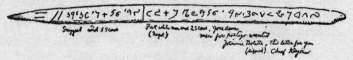

Chipewyan inscription with interpretation

times we found spideresque characters on tree or stone that supplied valuable information. They could, however, tell me nothing of its age or origin, simply "We all do it; it is easy."

At Fort Resolution I met the Jesuit fathers and got the desired chance of learning about the Chipewyan script.

First, it is not a true alphabet, but a syllabic; not letters, but syllables, are indicated by each character; 73 characters are all that are needed to express the whole language. It is so simple and stenographic that the fathers often use it as a rapid way of writing French. It has, however, the disadvantage of ambiguity at times. Any Indian boy can learn it in a week or two; practically all the Indians use it. What a commentary on our own cumbrous and illogical spelling, which takes even a bright child two or three years to learn!

Now, I already knew something of the Cree syllabic invented by the Rev. James Evans, Methodist missionary on Lake Winnipeg in the '40s, but Cree is a

◁ a	▽ e	△ i	▷ o	" Ʋⁿ"△
◁' an	▽' en	△' in	▷' on	⌐ Ɛ◁⌐
< ba	V be	∧ bi	> bo	⌐ ↪↩
⊂ da	∪ de	∩ di	⊃ do	⌐ ∪Ʋ◁ᑭ
ᑊ ka	ᕴ ke	ᑭ ki	ᑊ ko	⌐ Ʋᑐ⌐
ᑌ la	Ʋ le	ᒐ li	ᒡ lo	⌐ ᑐ▽
ᒣ ma	ᒉ me	ᒥ mi	ᒧ mo	⌐ ᒥↄ
ᑬ na	Ʋ ne	Ʋ ni	ᑌ no	⌐ ▽ᑐᑬ⌐
ᕒ ra	ᕯ re	ᕒ ri	ᕲ ro	⌐ ᕯᑬ
ᔕ sa	ᔆ se	↩ si	↩ so	⌐ Ʋ▷ˢↄ
ᕀ ya	◁ ye	↦ yi	↤ yo	⌐ ↦◁ᐟᑬ
ᓍ za	ᓬ ze	ᓯ zi	ᓵ zo	⌐ ↪↩ᐟᑌ
Ɛ cha	ᒐ che	ᒼ chi	ᒯ cho	⌐ ▷∪'ᕼ
∪ dha	ᑲ dhe	ᑭ dhi	∪ dho	⌐ ◁⌐ᑌ◁ᑔ
ᑔ tha	ᑐ the	ᑔ thi	ᑌ tho	⌐ ▽Ɛ⌐
⊂' tta	∪' tte	∩' tti	⊃' tto	⌐ ⌐▽⌐▽ᐟᑐ
Ɛ ttha	ᑌ tthe	ᑭ tthi	⊐ ttho	⌐ ⌐◁⊂
Ɛ tᶜa	ᑌ tᶜe	ᑭ tᶜi	ᑐ tᶜo	

▷ˢƐᑬ

Chipewyan syllabic alphabet

much less complex language; only 36 characters are needed, and these are so simple that an intelligent Cree can learn to write his own language in one day.

In support of this astounding statement I give, first, the 36 characters which cover every fundamental sound in their language and then a sample of application. While crude and inconcise, it was so logical and simple that in a few years the missionary had taught practically the whole Cree nation to read and write. And

SYLLABARIUM

A dot gives a "w" sound

EXAMPLES.

atokwa ▽⊃ᕐ· pimatisiw ∧ᒫᑎᕐᵒ

maskanaw ᒣᐣᑲᓇᵒ astumitik ◁ᐣᑕᒋ

ᑎᕐ makwach ᒣᕉᐧ ustootin ◁ᐣᒍᑎᐣ

pimachehewam ∧ᒫᑎ▽ᐧᒡ kakwi ᕉᕼ:

The syllabic alphabet of the Cree language

Lord Dufferin, when the matter came before him during his north-west tour, said enthusiastically: "There have been men buried in Westminster Abbey with national honours whose claims to fame were far less than those of this devoted missionary, the man who taught a whole nation to read and write."

These things I knew, and now followed up my Jesuit source of information.

"Who invented this?"

"I don't know for sure. It is in general use."

"Was it a native idea?"

"Oh, no; some white man made it."

"Where? Here or in the south?"

"It came originally from the Crees, as near as we can tell."

"Was it a Cree or a missionary that first thought of it?"

"I believe it was a missionary."

"Frankly, now, wasn't it invented in 1840 by Rev. James Evans, Methodist missionary to the Crees on Lake Winnipeg?"

Oh, how he hated to admit it, but he was too honest to deny it.

"Yes, it seems to me it was some name like that. 'Je ne sais pas.'"

Reader, take a map of North America, a large one, and mark off the vast area bounded by the Saskatchewan, the Rockies, the Hudson Bay, and the Arctic circle, and realise that in this region, as large as continental Europe outside of Russia and Spain, one simple, earnest man, inspired by the love of Him who alone is perfect love, invented and popularised a method of writing that in a few years—in less than a generation, indeed—has turned the whole native population from ignorant illiterates to a people who are proud to read and write their own language. This, I take it, is one of the greatest feats of a civiliser. The world has not yet heard of, much less comprehended, the magnitude of the achievement; when it does there will be no name on the Canadian roll of fame that will stand higher or be blazoned more brightly than that of James Evans the missionary.

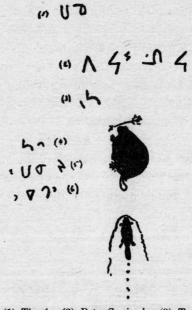

(1) Tinné. (2) Peter Squirrel. (3) Tsa or Beaver. (4) Sass or Bear. (5) Den-nee or Moose. (6) Et-then or Deer

CHAPTER XXIII

THE DOGS OF FORT RESOLUTION

It sounds like the opening of an epic poem but it is not.

The Chipewyan calender is divided in two seasons— dog season and canoe season. What the horse is to the Arab, what the Reindeer is to the Lap and the Yak to the Thibetan, the dog is to the Chipewyan for at least one-half of the year, until it is displaced by the canoe.

During dog season the canoes are piled away somewhat carelessly or guarded only from the sun. During canoe season the dogs are treated atrociously. Let us remember, first, that these are dogs in every doggy sense, the worshipping servants of man, asking nothing but a poor living in return for abject love and tireless service, as well as the relinquishment of all family ties and natural life. In winter, because they cannot serve without good food, they are well fed on fish that is hung on scaffolds in the fall in time to be frozen before wholly spoiled. The journeys they will make and the devoted service they render at this time is none too strongly set forth in Butler's "Cerf Vola" and London's "Call of the Wild." It is, indeed, the dog alone that makes life possible during the white half-year of the boreal calender. One cannot be many days in the north without hearing tales of dog prowess, devotion, and heroism. A typical incident was related as follows by Thomas Anderson:

Over thirty years ago, Chief Factor George McTavish and his driver, Jack Harvey, were travelling from East Main to Rupert's House (65 miles) in a blizzard so thick and fierce that they could scarcely see the leading dog. He was a splendid, vigorous creature, but all at once he lay down and refused to go. The driver struck him, but the factor reproved the man, as this dog had never needed the whip. The driver then went ahead and found open water only a few feet from the dogs, though out of sight. After that they gave the leader free rein, surrendered themselves to his guidance, and in spite of the blinding blizzard they struck the flagpole of Rupert's between 11 and 12 that night, only a little behind time.

Many of the wild Wolf traits still remain with them. They commonly pair; they bury surplus food; the mothers disgorge food for the young; they rally to defend one of their own clan against a stranger; and they punish failure with death.

A thousand incidents might be adduced to show that in the north there is little possibility of winter travel without dogs and little possibility of life without winter travel.

But April comes with melting snows and May with open rivers and brown earth everywhere; then, indeed, the reign of the dog is over. The long yellow-birch canoe is taken down from the shanty roof or from a sheltered scaffold, stitched, gummed, and launched;

and the dogs are turned loose to fend for themselves. Gratitude for past services or future does not enter into the owner's thoughts to secure a fair allowance of food. All their training and instinct prompts them to hang about camp, where, kicked, stoned, beaten, and starved, they steal and hunt as best they may, until the sad season of summer is worn away and merry winter with its toil and good food is back once more.

From leaving Fort MacMurray we saw daily the starving dog, and I fed them when I could. At Smith Landing the daily dog became a daily fifty. One big fellow annexed us. "I found them first," he seemed to say, and no other dog came about our camp without a fight.

Of course he fared well on our scraps, but many a time it made my heart ache and my food-store suffer to see the gaunt skeletons in the bushes, just beyond his sphere of influence, watching for a chance to rush in and secure a mouthful of—anything to stay the devastating pang. My journal of the time sets forth in full detail the diversity of their diet, not only every possible scrap of fish and meat or whatsoever smelled of fish or meat, but rawhide, leather, old boots, flour-bags, potato-peelings, soap, wooden fragments of meat-boxes, rags that have had enough animal contact to be odorous. An ancient dish-cloth, succulent with active service, was considered a treat to be bolted whole; and when in due course the cloth was returned to earth, it was intact, bleached, purged, and purified as by chemic fires and ready for a new round of benevolences.

In some seasons the dogs catch Rabbits enough to keep them up. But this year the Rabbits were gone. They are very clever at robbing fish-nets at times, but these were far from the fort. Reduced to such desperate straits for food, what wonder that cannibalism should be common! Not only the dead, but the sick or disabled of their own kind are torn to pieces and devoured. I was told of one case where a brutal driver disabled one of his dogs with heavy blows; its companions did not wait till it was dead before they feasted. It is hard to raise pups because the mothers so often devour their own young; and this is a charge I never heard laid to the Wolf, the ancestor of these dogs, which shows how sadly the creature has been deteriorated by contact with man. There seems no length to which they will not go for food. Politeness forbids my mentioning the final diet for which they scramble around the camp. Never in my life before have I seen such utter degradation by the power of the endless hunger pinch. Nevertheless—and here I expect the reader to doubt, even as I did when first I heard it, no matter how desperate their straits—these gormandisers of unmentionable filth, these starvelings, in their dire extremity will turn away in disgust from duck or any other web-footed water-fowl.

Billy Loutit had shot a Pelican; the skin was carefully preserved and the body guarded for the dogs, thinking that this big thing, weighing 6 or 7 pounds, would furnish a feast for one or two. The dogs knew me, and rushed like a pack of Wolves at sight of coming food. The bigger ones fought back the smaller.

I threw the prize, but, famished though they were, they turned away as a man might turn from a roasted human hand. One miserable creature, a mere skeleton, sneaked forward when the stronger ones were gone, pulled out the entrails at last, and devoured them as though he hated them.

I can offer no explanation. But the Hudson's Bay men tell me it is always so, and I am afraid the remembrance of the reception accorded my bounty that day hardened my heart somewhat in the days that followed.

On the Nyarling we were too far from mankind to be bothered with dogs, but at Fort Resolution we reentered their country. The following from my journal records the impression after our enforced three days' stay:

"*Tuesday, July* 16, 1907.—Fine day for the first time since July 3. At last we pulled out of Fort Resolution (9.40 A. M.). I never was so thankful to leave a place where every one was kind. I think the maddest cynophile would find a cure here. It is the worst dog-cursed spot I ever saw; not a square yard but is polluted by them; no article can be left on the ground but will be carried off, torn up, or defiled; the four corners of our tent have become regular stopping places for the countless canines, and are disfigured and made abominable, so that after our escape there will be needed many days of kindly rain for their purification.

"There certainly are several hundred dogs in the village; there are about 50 teepees and houses with 5 to 15 dogs at each, and 25 each at the mission and H. B. Co. In a short walk, about 200 yards, I passed 86 dogs.

"There is not an hour or ten minutes of day or night that is not made hideous with a dog-fight or chorus of yelps. There are about six different clans of dogs, divided as their owners are, and a Dogrib dog entering the Yellow-knife or Chipewyan part of the camp is immediately set upon by all the residents. Now the clansmen of the one in trouble rush to the rescue and there is a battle. Indians of both sides join in with clubs to belabour the fighters, and the yowling and yelping of those discomfited is painful to hear for long after the fight is over. It was a battle like this, I have been told, which caused the original split of the tribe, one part of which went south to become the Apaches of Arizona. The scenes go on all day and all night in different forms. A number of dogs are being broken in by being tied up to stakes. These keep up a heart-rending and peculiar crying, beginning with a short bark which melts into a yowl and dies away in a nerve-racking wail. This ceases not day or night, and half a dozen of these prisoners are within a stone's throw of our camp.

"The favourite place for the clan fights seems to be among the guy-ropes of our tent; at least half a dozen of these general engagements take place every night while we try to sleep.

"Everything must be put on the high racks eight feet up to be safe from them; even empty tins are carried off, boots, hats, soap, etc., are esteemed most toothsome morsels, and what they can neither eat, carry off, nor destroy, they defile with elaborate persistency and precision."

A common trick of the Indians when canoe season arrives is to put all the family and one or two of the best dogs in the canoes, then push away from the shore, leaving the rest behind. Those so abandoned come howling after the canoes, and in unmistakable pleadings beg the heartless owners to take them in. But the canoes push off toward the open sea, aiming to get out of sight. The dogs howl sadly on the shore, or swim after them till exhausted, then drift back to the nearest land to begin the summer of hardship.

If Rabbits are plentiful they get along; failing these they catch mice or fish; when the berry season comes they eat fruit; the weaker ones are devoured by their brethren; and when the autumn arrives their insensate owners generally manage to come back and pick up the survivors, feeding them so that they are ready for travel when dog-time begins, and the poor faithful brutes, bearing no grudge, resume at once the service of their unfeeling masters.

All through our voyage up Great Slave Lake we daily heard the sad howling of abandoned dogs, and nightly, we had to take steps to prevent them stealing our food and leathers. More than once in the dim light, I was awakened by a rustle, to see sneaking from my tent the gray, wolfish form of some prowling dog, and the resentment I felt at the loss inflicted, was never more than to make me shout or throw a pebble at him.

One day, as we voyaged eastward (July 23) in the Tal-thel-lay narrows of Great Slave Lake, we met 5 canoes and 2 York boats of Indians going west. A few hours afterward as we were nooning on an island (we were driven to the islands now) there came a long howling from the rugged main shore, a mile away to the east of us; then it increased to a chorus of wailing, and we knew that the Indians had that morning abandoned their dogs there. The wailing continued, then we saw a tiny black speck coming from the far shore. When it was half-way across the ice-cold bay we could hear the gasps of a tired swimmer. He got along fairly, dodging the cakes of ice, until within about 200 yards, when his course was barred by a long, thin, drifting floe. He tried to climb on it, but was too weak, then he raised his voice in melancholy howls of despair. I could not get to him, but he plucked up heart at length, and feebly paddling went around till he found an opening, swam through and came on, the slowest dog swimmer I ever saw. At last he struck bottom and crawled out. But he was too weak and ill to eat the meat that I had ready prepared for him. We left him with food for many days and sailed away.

Another of the dogs that tried to follow him across was lost in the ice; we heard his miserable wailing moans as he was carried away, but could not help him. My Indians thought nothing of it and were amused at my solicitude.

A couple of hours later we landed on the rugged east coast to study our course through the ice. At once we were met by four dogs that trotted along the shore to where we landed. They did not seem very gaunt; one, an old yellow female, carried something in her mouth; this she never laid down, and growled savagely when any of the others came near. It proved to be the blood-stained leg of a new-killed dog, yellow like herself.

As we pulled out a big black-and-white fellow looked at us wistfully from a rocky ledge; memories of Bingo, whom he resembled not a little, touched me. I threw him a large piece of dried meat. He ate it, but not ravenously. He seemed in need, not of food, but of company.

A few miles farther on we again landed to study the lake; as we came near we saw the dogs, not four but six, now racing to meet us. I said to Preble: "It seems to me it would be the part of mercy to shoot them all." He answered: "They are worth nothing now, but you shoot one and its value would at once jump up to one hundred dollars. Every one knows everything that is done in this country. You would have six hundred dollars' damages to pay when you got back to Fort Resolution."

I got out our stock of fresh fish. The Indians, seeing my purpose, said: "Throw it in the water and see them dive." I did so and found that they would dive into several feet of water and bring up the fish without fail. The yellow female was not here, so I suppose she had stayed to finish her bone.

When we came away, heading for the open lake, the dogs followed us as far as they could, then gathering on a flat rock, the end of a long point, they sat down, some with their backs to us; all raised their muzzles and howled to the sky a heart-rending dirge.

I was thankful to lose them in the distance.

Dog-toggle or clog, Smith Landing

CHAPTER XXIV

THE VOYAGE ACROSS THE LAKE

HITHERTO I have endeavoured to group my observations on each subject; I shall now for a change give part of the voyage across Great Slave Lake much as it appears in my journal.

"*July* 16, 1907.—Left Fort Resolution at 9.40 A. M. in the York boat manned by 7 Indians and Billy Loutit, besides Preble and myself, 10 in all; ready with mast and sail for fair wind, but also provided with heavy 16-foot oars for head-winds and calm. Harding says we should make Pike's Portage in 3 or 4 days.

"Reached Moose Island at 11.30 chiefly by rowing; camped. A large dog appeared on the bank. Freesay recognised it as his and went ashore with a club. We heard the dog yelping. Freesay came back saying: 'He'll go home now.'

"At 1.30 went on but stopped an unnecessary half-hour at a saw-mill getting plank for seats. Reached the Big, or Main, River at 4.10; stopped for tea again till 4.50, then rowed up the river till 5.40; rested 15 minutes, rowed till 6.30; rested 15 minutes, rowed till 7; then got into the down current of the north branch or mouth of the Slave; down then we drifted till 8, then landed and made another meal, the fourth to-day, and went on drifting at 8.30.

"At 9.30 we heard a Ruffed Grouse drumming, the last of the season, also a Bittern pumping, some Cranes trumpeting, and a Wood Frog croaking. Snipe were still whirring in the sky. Saw Common Tern.

"At 10.15, still light, we camped for the night and made another meal. The Indians went out and shot 2 Muskrats, making 7 the total of these I have seen in the country. This is the very lowest ebb. Why are they so scarce? Their low epoch agrees with that of the Rabbits.

"*July* 17.—Rose at 6 (it should have been 4, but the Indians would not rouse); sailed north through the marsh with a light east breeze. At noon this changed to a strong wind blowing from the north, as it has done with little variation ever since I came to the country. These Indians know little of handling a boat and resent any suggestion. They maintain their right to row or rest, as they please, and land when and where they think best. We camped on a sand-bar and waited till night; most exasperating when we are already behind time. The Indians set a net, using for tie-strings the bark of the willow (*Salix bebbiana*). They caught a Jack-fish. Reached Stony Island at night, after many stops and landings. The Indians land whenever in doubt and make a meal (at my expense), and are in doubt every two hours or so. They eat by themselves and have their own cook. Billy cooks for us, *i.e.*, Preble, Weeso, and myself. Among the crew I hear unmistakable grumblings about the food, which is puzzling, as it is the best they ever had in their lives; there is great variety and no limit to the quantity.

"Made 6 meals and 17 miles to-day, rowing 7, sailing 10.

"*July* 18.—Left Stony Island at 6.55; could not get the crew started sooner; sailing with a light breeze which soon died down and left us on a sea of glass. I never before realised how disgusting a calm could be.

"Camped at 9.15 on one of the countless, unnamed, uncharted islands of the lake. It is very beautiful in colour, red granite, spotted with orange and black lichen on its face, and carpeted with caribou moss and species of cetraria, great patches of tripe-de-roche, beds of saxifrage, long trailers, and masses of bearberry, empetrum, ground cedar, juniper, cryptograma, and many others; while the trees, willow, birch, and spruce are full of character and drawing. Sky and lake are in colour worthy of these rich details, the bird life is well represented and beautiful; there is beauty everywhere, and 'only man is vile.'

"I am more and more disgusted with my Indian crew; the leader in mischief seems to be young Beaulieu. Yesterday he fomented a mutiny because I did not give them 'beans,' though I had given them far more than promised, and beans were never mentioned. Still, he had discovered a bag of them among my next month's stores, and that started him.

"To-day, when sick of seeing them dawdling two hours over a meal when there are 6 meals a day, I gave the order to start. Beaulieu demanded insolently: 'Oh! who's boss?' My patience was worn out. I said: 'I am, and I'll show you right now,' and proceeded to do so, meaning to let him have my fist with all the steam I could get back of it. But he did not wait. At a safe distance he turned and in a totally different manner said: 'I only want to know; I thought maybe the old man (the guide). I'll do it, all ri, all ri,' and he smiled and smiled.

"Oh! why did I not heed Pike's warning to shun all Beaulieus; they rarely fail to breed trouble. If I had realised all this last night before coming to the open lake I would have taken the whole outfit back to Resolution and got rid of the crowd. We could do better with another canoe and two men, and at least make better time than this (17 miles a day).

"Yesterday the Indian boys borrowed my canoe, my line, and in my time, at my expense, caught a big fish, but sullenly disregarded the suggestion that I should have a piece of it.

"Each of them carries a Winchester and blazes away at every living thing that appears. They have volleyed all day at every creature big enough to afford a mouthful—Ducks, Gulls, Loons, Fish, Owls, Terns, etc.—but have hit nothing. Loons are abundant in the water and are on the Indians' list of Ducks, therefore good food. They are wonderfully expert at calling them. This morning a couple of Loons appeared flying far to the east. The Indians at once began to mimic their rolling *whoo-ooo-whoo-ooo;* doing it to the life. The Loons began to swing toward us, then to circle, each time nearer. Then all the callers stopped except Claw-hammer, the expert; he began to utter a peculiar cat-like wail. The Loons responded and dropped their feet as though to alight. Then at 40 yards the whole crew blazed away with their rifles, doing no damage whatever. The Loons turned away from these unholy callers, and were none the worse, but wiser.

"This scene was repeated many times during the voyage. When the Loons are on the water the Indians toll them by flashing a tin pan from the bushes behind which the toller hides till the bird is in range. I saw many clever tollings but I did not see a Loon killed.

"*July* 19.—I got up at 4, talked strong talk, so actually got away at 5.30. Plenty grumbling, many meals to-day, with many black looks and occasional remarks in English: 'Grub no good.' Three days ago these men were starving on one meal a day, of fish and bad flour; now they have bacon, dried venison, fresh fish, fresh game, potatoes, flour, baking powder, tea, coffee, milk, sugar, molasses, lard, cocoa, dried apples, rice, oatmeal, far more than was promised, all *ad libitum*, and the best that the H. B. Co. can supply, and yet they grumble. There is only one article of the food store to which they have not access; that is a bag of beans which I am reserving for our own trip in the north where weight counts for so much. Beaulieu smiles when I speak to him, but I know he is at the bottom of all this mischief. To day they made 6 meals and 17 miles—this is magnificent.

"About 7.30 a pair of Wild Geese (Canada) appeared on a bay. The boys let off a whoop of delight and rushed on them in canoe and in boat as though these were their deadliest enemies. I did not think much of it until I noticed that the Geese would not fly, and it dawned on me that they were protecting their young behind their own bodies. A volley of shot-guns and Winchesters and one noble head fell flat on the water, another volley and the gander fell, then a wild skurrying, yelling, and shooting for some minutes resulted in the death of the two downlings.

"I could do nothing to stop them. I have trouble enough in matters that *are* my business and this they consider solely their own. It is nothing but kill, kill, kill every living thing they meet. One cannot blame them in general, since they live by hunting, and in this case they certainly did eat every bit of all four birds, even to their digestive organs with contents; but it seemed hard to have the devotion of the parents made their death trap when, after all, we were not in need of meat.

"*July* 20.—Rose at 4; had trouble on my hands at once. The Indians would not get up till 5, so we did not get away till 6.20. Beaulieu was evidently instructing the crew, for at the third breakfast all together (but perhaps 2) shouted out in English, 'Grub no good.'

"I walked over to them, asked who spoke; no one answered; so I reviewed the bargain, pointed out that I had given more than agreed, and added: 'I did not promise you beans, but will say now that if you work well I'll give you a bean feast once in a while.'

"They all said in various tongues and ways, 'That's all ri.' Beaulieu said it several times, and smiled and smiled.

"If the mythical monster that dwells in the bottom of Great Slave Lake had reached up its long neck now and taken this same half-breed son of Belial, I should have said, 'Well done, good and faithful monster,' and the rest of our voyage would have been happier. Oh! what a lot of pother a beneficent little bean can make.

"At noon that day Billy announced that it was time to give me a lobstick; a spruce was selected on a slate island and trimmed to its proper style, then inscribed:

E. T. Seton
E. A. Preble
W. C. Loutit
20 July
1907

"Now I was in honour bound to treat the crew. I had neither the power nor the wish to give whiskey. Tobacco was already provided, so I seized the opportunity of smoothing things by announcing a feast of beans, and this, there was good reason to believe, went far in the cause of peace.

"At 1.30 for the first time a fair breeze sprang up or rather lazily got up. Joyfully then we raised our mast and sail. The boys curled up to sleep, except Beaulieu. He had his fiddle and now he proceeded to favour us with 'A Life on the Ocean Wave,' 'The Campbells are Coming,' etc., in a manner worthy of his social position and of his fiddle. When not in use this æsthetic instrument (in its box) knocks about on deck or underfoot, among pots and pans, exposed in all weather; no one seems to fear it will be injured.

"At 7 the usual dead calm was restored. We rowed till we reached Et-then Island at 8, covering two miles more or 32 in all to-day. I was unwilling to

Inscription on trunk

C. T. Seton
E. A. Preble
W. C. Loutit
20 July
1907

My Lobstick on a slate island,
Great Slave Lake

stop now, but the boys said they would row all day Sunday if I would camp here, and then added, 'And if the wind rises to-night we'll go on.'

"At 10 o'clock I was already in bed for the night, though of course it was broad daylight. Preble had put out a line of mouse-traps, when the cry was raised by the Indians now eating their 7th meal: 'Chim-pal-le! Hurra! Chilla quee!' ('Sailing wind! Hurra, boys!').

"The camp was all made, but after such a long calm a sailing wind was too good to miss. In 10 minutes every tent was torn down and bundled into the boat. At 10.10 we pulled out under a fine promising breeze; but alas! for its promise! at 10.30 the last vestige of it died away and we had to use the oars to make the nearest land, where we tied up at 11 P. M.

"That night old Weeso said to me, through Billy, the interpreter: 'To-morrow is Sunday, therefore he would like to have a prayer-meeting after breakfast.'

"'Tell him,' I said, 'that I quite approve of his prayer-meeting, but also it must be understood that if the good Lord sends us a sailing wind in the morning that is His way of letting us know we should sail.'

"This sounded so logical that Weeso meekly said, 'All right.'

"Sure enough, the morning dawned with a wind and we got away after the regular sullen grumbling. About 10.20 the usual glassy calm set in and Weeso asked me for a piece of paper and a pencil. He wrote something in Chipewyan on the sheet I gave, then returned the pencil and resumed his pilotic stare at the horizon, for his post was at the rudder. At length he rolled the paper into a ball, and when I seemed not observing dropped it behind him overboard.

"'What is the meaning of that, Billy?' I whispered.

"'He's sending a prayer to Jesus for wind.' Half an hour afterward a strong *head*-wind sprang up, and Weeso was severely criticised for not specifying clearly what was wanted.

"There could be no question now about the propriety of landing. Old Weeso took all the Indians off to a rock, where, bareheaded and in line, they kneeled facing the east, and for half an hour he led them in prayer, making often the sign of the cross. The head-wind died away as they came to the boat and again we resumed the weary rowing, a labour which all were supposed to share, but it did not need an expert to see that Beaulieu, Snuff, and Terchon merely dipped their oars and let them drift a while; the real rowing of that cumbrous old failure of a sailboat was done by Billy Loutit and Yum Freesay."

Platygobio gracilis

CHAPTER XXV

CROSSING THE LAKE—ITS NATURAL HISTORY

ALL day long here, as on the Nyarling, I busied myself with compass and sketch-book, making the field notes, sketches, and compass surveys from which my various maps were compiled; and Preble let no chance go by of noting the changing bird and plant life that told us we quit the Canadian fauna at Stony Island and now were in the Hudsonian zone.

This is the belt of dwindling trees, the last or northmost zone of the forest, and the spruce trees showed everywhere that they were living a life-long battle, growing and seeding, but dwarfed by frost and hardships. But sweet are the uses of adversity, and the stunted sprucelings were beautified, not uglified, by their troubles. I never before realised that a whole country could be such a series of charming little Japanese gardens, with tiny trees, tiny flowers, tiny fruits, and gorgeous oriental rugs upon the earth and rocks between.

I photographed one group of trees to illustrate their dainty elfish dwarfishness, but realising that no one could guess the height without a scale, I took a second of the same with a small Indian sitting next it.

Weeso is a kind old soul; so far as I could see he took no part in the various seditions, but he was not

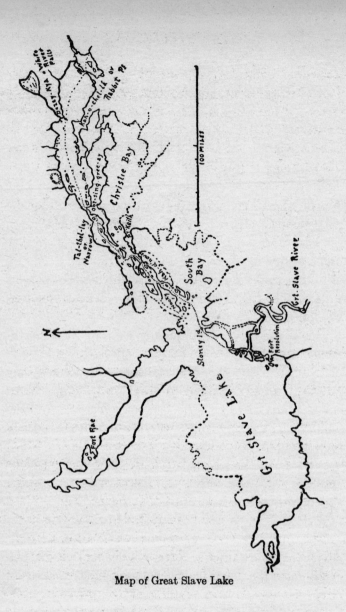

Map of Great Slave Lake

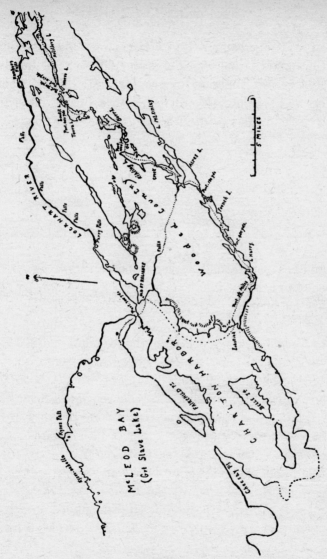

Pike's Portage

Founded chiefly on J. W. Tyrrell's map of 1900

an inspiring guide. One afternoon he did something
that made a final wreck of my confidence. A thunder-
storm was rumbling in the far east. Black clouds
began travelling toward us; with a line of dark and
troubled waters below, the faint breeze changed around

Oot-sing-gree-ay Island   Cliff on N. E. end of Et-then Island

and became a squall. Weeso looked scared and beck-
oned to Freesay, who came and took the helm. Nothing happened.

We were now running along the north shore of Et-
then, where are to be seen the wonderful 1,200-foot
cliffs described and figured by Captain George Back in
1834. They are glorious ramparts, wonderful in size
and in colour, marvellous in their geological display.

Flying, and evidently nesting among the dizzy tow-
ers, were a few Barn-swallows and Phœbe-birds.

This cliff is repeated on Oot-sing-gree-ay, the next
island, but there it is not on the water's edge. It gives
a wonderful echo which the Indians (not to mention
myself) played with, in childish fashion.

On Sunday, 21 July, we made a new record, 6 meals
and 20 miles.

On July 22 we made only 7 meals and 11 miles and
camped in the narrows Tal-thel-lay. These are a
quarter of a mile wide and have a strong current run-

ning westerly. This is the place which Back says is a
famous fishing ground and never freezes over, even in
the hardest winters. Here, as at all points, I noted
the Indian names, not only because they were appropriate, but in hopes of serving the next traveller. I
found an unexpected difficulty in writing them down,
viz.: no matter how I pronounced them, old Weeso
and Freesay, my informants, would say, "Yes, that
is right." This, I learned, was out of politeness; no
matter how you mispronounce their words it is good
form to say, "That's it; now you have it exactly."

The Indians were anxious to put out a net overnight
here, as they could count on getting a few Whitefish;
so we camped at 5.15. It is difficult to convey to
an outsider the charm of the word "whitefish." Any
northerner will tell you that it is the only fish that is
perfect human food, the only food that man or dog
never wearies of, the only lake food that conveys no
disorder no matter how long or freely it is used. It
is so delicious and nourishing that there is no fish in
the world that can even come second to it. It is as
far superior in all food qualities to the finest Salmon or
Trout as a first-prize, gold-medalled, nut-fed thorough-
bred Sussex bacon-hog is to the roughest, toughest,
boniest old razor-backed land-pike that ever ranged
the woods of Arkansas.

That night the net yielded 3 Whitefish and 3 Trout.
The latter, being 4 to 8 pounds each, would have been
reckoned great prizes in any other country, but now
all attention was on the Whitefish. They certainly
were radiantly white, celestial in color; their backs

were a dull frosted silver, with here and there a small
electric lamp behind the scales to make its jewels
sparkle. The lamps alternated with opals increased
on the side; the bellies were of a blazing mother-of-
pearl. It would be hard to imagine a less imaginative
name than "white" fish for such a shining, burning
opalescence. Indian names are usually descriptive,

Tha-sess San-dou-ay two miles away (Swallow Island)

but their name for this is simply "The Fish." All
others are mere dilutes and cheap imitations, but the
Coregonus is at all times and *par excellence* "The Fish."

Nevertheless, in looking at it I could not help feeling
that this is the fat swine, or the beef Durham of its
kind. The head, gills, fins, tail, vital organs and bones
all were reduced to a minimum and the meat parts
enlarged and solidified, as though they were the product of ages of careful breeding by man to produce a
perfect food fish, a breeding that has been crowned
with the crown of absolute success.

The Indians know, for the best of reasons, the just
value of every native food. When Rabbits abound
they live on them but do not prosper; they call it
"starving on rabbits." When Caribou meat is plenty
they eat it, but crave flour. When Moose is at hand
they eat it, and are strong. When Jack-fish, Sucker,
Conies, and Trout are there, they take them as a variant; but on Whitefish, as on Moose, they can live with-

out loathing, and be strong. The Indian who has his scaffold hung with Whitefish when winter comes, is accounted rich.

"And what," says the pessimist, "is the fly in all this precious ointment?" Alas! It is not a game fish; it will not take bait, spoon, or fly, and its finest properties vanish in a few hours after capture.

The Whitefish served in the marble palaces of other lands is as mere dish-water to champagne, when compared with the three times purified and ten times intensified dazzling silver *Coregonus* as it is landed on the bleak shores of those far-away icy lakes. So I could not say 'No' to the Indian boys when they wanted to wait here, the last point at which they could be sure of a catch.

That night (22d July) five canoes and two York boats of Indians landed at the narrows. These were Dogribs of Chief Vital's band; all told they numbered about thirty men, women, and children; with them were twenty-odd dogs, which immediately began to make trouble. When one is in Texas the topic of conversation is, "How are the cattle?" in the Klondike, "How is your claim panning out?" and in New York, "How are you getting on with your novel?" On Great Slave Lake you say, "Where are the Caribou?" The Indians could not tell; they had seen none for weeks, but there was still much ice in the east end of the lake which kept them from investigating. They had plenty of dried Caribou meat but were out of tea and tobacco. I had come prepared for this sort of situation, and soon we had a fine stock of dried venison.

These were the Indians whose abandoned dogs made so much trouble for us in the days that followed.

At 4 P. M. of 23d of July we were stopped by a long narrow floe of broken ice. Without consulting me the crew made for the shore.

It seemed they were full of fears: "What if they should get caught in that floe, and drift around for days? What if a wind should arise (it had been glassy calm for a week)? What if they could not get back?" etc., etc.

Preble and I climbed a hill for a view. The floe was but half a mile wide, very loose, with frequent lanes.

"Preble, is there any reason why we should not push through this floe using poles to move the cakes?"

"None whatever."

On descending, however, I found the boys preparing to camp for "a couple of days," while the ice melted or drifted away somewhere.

So I said, "You get right into this boat now and push off; we can easily work our way through." They made no reply, simply looked sulkier than ever, and proceeded to start a fire for meal No. 5.

"Weeso," I said, "get into your place and tell your men to follow."

The old man looked worried and did nothing. He wanted to do right, but he was in awe of his crew.

Then did I remember how John MacDonald settled the rebellion on the river.

"Get in there," I said to Preble and Billy. "Come on, Weeso." We four jumped into the boat and proceeded to push off *with all the supplies*.

Authorities differ as to the time it took for the crew to make up their minds. Two seconds and eleven seconds are perhaps the extremes of estimate. They came jumping aboard as fast as they could.

We attacked the floe, each with a lodge-pole; that is, Billy and Preble did in the bow, while Freesay and I did at the rear; and in thirty-five minutes we had pushed through and were sailing the open sea.

The next day we had the same scene repeated with less intensity, in this case because Freesay sided with me. What would I not give to have had a crew of white men. A couple of stout Norwegian sailors would have done far better than this whole outfit of reds.

When we stopped for supper No. 1 a tiny thimble-ful of down on two pink matches ran past, and at once the mother, a Peetweet, came running in distress to save her young. The brave Beaulieu fearlessly seized a big stick and ran to kill the little one. I shouted out, "Stop that," in tones that implied that I owned the heaven, the earth, the sea, and all that in them is, but could not have saved the downling had it not leaped into the water and dived out of sight. It came up two feet away and swam to a rock of safety, where it bobbed its latter end toward its adversaries and the open sea in turn.

I never before knew that they could dive.

About eight o'clock we began to look for a good place to camp and make meal No. 6. But the islands where usually we found refuge from the dogs were without wood, and the shores were too rugged and steep or had no dry timber, so we kept going on. After trying one or two places the Indians said it was only a mile to Indian Mountain River (Der-sheth Tessy), where was a camp of their friends. I was always glad of a reason for pushing on, so away we went. My crew seized their rifles and fired to let their village know we were coming. The camp came quickly into view, and volley after volley was fired and returned.

These Indians are extremely poor and the shots cost 5 and 6 cents each. So this demonstration totalled up about $2.00.

As we drew near the village of lodges the populace lined up on shore, and then our boys whispered, "Some white men." What a peculiar thrill it gave me! I had seen nothing but Indians along the route so far and expected nothing else. But here were some of my own people, folk with whom I could talk. They proved to be my American friend from Smith Landing, he whose hand I had lanced, and his companion, a young Englishman, who was here with him prospecting for gold and copper. "I'm all right now," he said, and held up the hand with *my* mark on it, and our greeting was that of white men meeting among strangers in a far foreign land.

As soon as we were ashore a number of Indians came to offer meat for tobacco. They seemed a lot of tobacco-maniacs. "Tzel-twee" at any price they must have. Food they could do without for a long time, but life without smoke was intolerable; and they offered their whole dried product of two Caribou, concentrated, nourishing food enough to last a family many days, in exchange for half a pound of nasty, stinking, poisonous tobacco.

Two weeks hence, they say, these hills will be alive with Caribou; alas! for them, it proved a wholly erroneous forecast.

Y.'s guide is Sousi King Beaulieu (for pedigree, see Warburton Pike); he knows all this country well and gave us much information about the route. He says that this year the Caribou cows went north as usual, but the bulls did not. The season was so late they did not think it worth while; they are abundant yet at Artillery Lake.

He recognised me as the medicine man, and took an early opportunity of telling me what a pain he had. Just where, he was not sure, but it was hard to bear; he would like some sort of a pain-killer. Evidently he craved a general exhilarator.

Next morning we got away at 7 A. M. after the usual painful scene about getting up in the middle of the night, which was absurd, as there was no night.

Next afternoon we passed the Great White Fall at the mouth of Hoar Frost River; the Indians call it Dezza Kya. If this is the Beverly Falls of Back, his illustrator was without information; the published picture bears not the slightest resemblance to it.

At three in the afternoon of July 27th, the twelfth day after we had set out on the "three or four day run" from Resolution, this exasperating and seemingly interminable voyage really did end, and we thankfully beached our York boat at the famous lobstick that marks the landing of Pike's Portage.

CHAPTER XXVI

THE LYNX AT BAY

ONE of the few rewarding episodes of this voyage took place on the last morning, July 27. We were half a mile from Charleston Harbour when one of the Indians said "Cheesay" (Lynx) and pointed to the south shore. There, on a bare point a quarter mile away, we saw a large Lynx walking quietly along. Every oar was dropped and every rifle seized, of course, to repeat the same old scene; probably it would have made no difference to the Lynx, but I called out: "Hold on there! I'm going after that Cheesay."

Calling my two reliables, Preble and Billy, we set out in the canoe, armed, respectively, with a shotgun, a club, and a camera.

When we landed the Lynx was gone. We hastily made a skirmishing line in the wood where the point joined the mainland, but saw no sign of him, so concluded that he must be hiding on the point. Billy took the right shore, Preble the left, I kept the middle. Then we marched toward the point but saw nothing. There were no bushes except a low thicket of spruce, some 20 feet across and 3 or 4 feet high. This was too dense to penetrate standing, so I lay down on my breast and proceeded to crawl in under the low boughs. I had not gone six feet before a savage growl warned me

back, and there, just ahead, crouched the Lynx. He
glared angrily, then rose up, and I saw, with a little
shock, that he had been crouching on the body of
another Lynx, eating it.   Photography was impossible
there, so I took a stick and poked at him; he growled,
struck at the stick, but went out, then dashed across
the open for the woods.   As he went I got photograph
No. 1.   Now I saw the incredible wonder I had heard
of—a good runner can outrun a Lynx.   Preble was
a sprinter, and before the timber 200 yards off was
reached that Lynx was headed and turned; and Preble
and Billy were driving him back into my studio.   He
made several dashes to escape, but was out-manœuvred
and driven onto the far point, where he was really
between the devils and the deep sea.   Here he faced
about at bay, growling furiously, thumping his little
bobtail from side to side, and pretending he was going
to spring on us.   I took photo No. 2 at 25 yards.   He
certainly did look very fierce, but I thought I knew the
creature, as well as the men who were backing me.   I
retired, put a new film in place, and said:

"Now, Preble, I'm going to walk up to that Lynx
and get a close photo.   If he jumps for me, and he
may, there is nothing can save my beauty but you
and that gun."

Preble with characteristic loquacity says, "Go
ahead."

Then I stopped and began slowly approaching the
desperate creature we held at bay.   His eyes were
glaring green, his ears were back, his small bobtail
kept twitching from side to side, and his growls grew

harder and hissier, as I neared him.   At 15 feet he gathered his legs under him as for a spring, and I pressed the button getting, No. 3.

Then did the demon of ambition enter into my heart and lead me into peril.   That Lynx at bay was starving and desperate.   He might spring at me, but I believed that if he did he never would reach me alive. I knew my man—this nerved me—and I said to him: "I'm not satisfied; I want him to fill the finder.   Are you ready?"

"Yep."

So I crouched lower and came still nearer, and at 12 feet made No. 4.   For some strange reason, now the Lynx seemed less angry than he had been.

"He didn't fill the finder; I'll try again," was my next.   Then on my knees I crawled up, watching the finder till it was full of Lynx.   I glanced at the beast; he was but 8 feet away.   I focused and fired.

And now, oh, wonder! that Lynx no longer seemed annoyed; he had ceased growling and simply looked *bored*.

Seeing it was over, Preble says, "Now where does he go?   To the Museum?"

"No, indeed!" was the reply.   "He surely has earned his keep; turn him loose.   It's back to the woods for him."   We stood aside; he saw his chance and dashed for the tall timber.   As he went I fired the last film, getting No. 6; and so far as I know that Lynx is alive and well and going yet.

CHAPTER XXVII

THE LAST OF THAT INDIAN CREW

CARVED on the lobstick of the Landing were many names famous in the annals of this region, Pike, Maltern, McKinley, Munn, Tyrrel among them. All about were evidences of an ancient and modern camp— lodge poles ready for the covers, relics and wrecks of all sorts, fragments of canoes and sleds, and the inevitable stray Indian dog.

First we made a meal, of course; then I explained to the crew that I wanted all the stuff carried over the portage, 3¼ miles, to the first lake. At once there was a row; I was used to that. There had been a row every morning over getting up, and one or two each day about other details. Now the evil face of Beaulieu showed that his tongue was at work again. But I knew my lesson.

"You were brought to man the boat and bring my stuff over this portage. So do it and start right now."

They started 3¼ miles with heavy loads, very heavy labour I must admit, back then in four hours to make another meal, and camp.

Next morning another row before they would get up and take each another load. But canoe and everything were over by noon. And then came the final scene.

In all the quarrels and mutinies, old Weeso had been faithful to me. Freesay had said little or nothing, and had always worked well and cheerfully. Weeso was old and weak, Freesay young and strong, and therefore he was the one for our canoe. I decided it would pay to subsidise Weeso to resign in favour of the younger man. But, to be sure, first asked Freesay if he would like to come with me to the land of the Musk-ox. His answer was short and final, "Yes," but he could not, as his uncle had told him not to go beyond this portage. That settled it. The childlike obedience to their elders is admirable, but embarrassing at times.

So Weeso went after all, and we got very well acquainted on that long trip. He was a nice old chap. He always meant well; grinned so happily when he was praised, and looked so glum when he was scolded. There was little of the latter to do; so far as he knew, he did his best, and it is a pleasure now to conjure up his face and ways. His cheery voice, at my tent door every morning, was the signal that Billy had the breakfast within ten minutes of ready.

"Okimow, To" (Chief, here is water), he would say as he set down the water for my bath and wondered what in the name of common sense should make the Okimow need washing every morning. He himself was of a cleaner kind, having needed no bath during the whole term of our acquaintance.

There were two peculiarities of the old man that should make him a good guide for the next party going northward. First, he never forgot a place once he had been there, and could afterward go to it direct from any other place. Second, he had the most wonderful nose for firewood; no keen-eyed raven or starving wolf could go more surely to a marrow-bone in cache, than could Weeso to the little sticks in far away hollows or granite clefts. Again and again, when we landed on the level or rocky shore and all hands set out to pick up the few pencil-thick stems of creeping birch, roots of annual plants, or wisps of grass to boil the kettle, old Weeso would wander off by himself and in five minutes return with an armful of the most amazingly acceptable firewood conjured out of the absolutely timberless, unpromising waste. I never yet saw the camp where he could not find wood. So he proved good stuff; I was glad we had brought him along.

And I was equally glad now to say good-bye to the rest of the crew. I gave them provisions for a week, added a boiling of beans, and finally the wonderful paper in which I stated the days they had worked for me, and the kind of service they had rendered, commended Freesay, and told the truth about Beaulieu.

"Dat paper tell about me," said that worthy suspiciously.

"Yes," I said, "and about the others; and it tells Harding to pay you as agreed."

We all shook hands and parted. I have not seen them since, nor do I wish to meet any of them again, except Freesay.

My advice to the next traveller would be: get one Indian for guide. When alone they are manageable, and some of them, as seen already, are quite satisfactory, but the more of them the worse. They combine, as Pike says, the meanest qualities of a savage and an unscrupulous money-lender. The worst one in the crowd seems most readily followed by the others.

CHAPTER XXVIII

GEOLOGICAL FORCES AT WORK

IT seems to me that never before have I seen the geological forces of nature so obviously at work. Elsewhere I have seen great valleys, cliffs, islands, etc., held on good evidence to be the results of such and such powers formerly very active; but here on the Athabaska I saw daily evidence of these powers in full blast, ripping, tearing, reconstructing, while we looked on.

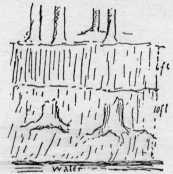

Bank exposing different levels, etc.
Showing how various floods and ice plowings have changed the level within recent years

All the way down the river we saw the process of undermining the bank, tearing down the trees to whirl them again on distant northern shores, thus widening the river channel until too wide for its normal flood, which in time drops into a deeper restricted channel, in the wide summer waste of gravel and sand.

Ten thousand landslides take place every spring, contributing their tons of mud to the millions that the river is deporting to the broad catch basins called the Athabaska and Great Slave Lakes.

Many a tree has happened to stand on the very crack that is the upmost limit of the slide and has in consequence been ripped in two.

Many an island is wiped out and many a one made in these annual floods. Again and again we saw the evidence of some island, continued long enough to raise a spruce forest, suddenly receive a 6-foot contribution from its erratic mother; so the trees were buried to the arm-pits.

Many times I saw where some frightful jam of ice had planed off all the trees; then a deep overwhelming layer of mud had buried the stumps and grown in time a new spruce forest. Now the mighty erratic river was tearing all this work away again, exposing all its history.

A 4½ inch birch split by a landslide. This is a common accident

In the delta of the Slave, near Fort Resolution, we saw the plan of delta work. Millions of tons of mud poured into the deep translucent lake have filled it for miles, so that it is scarcely deep enough to float a canoe; thousands of huge trees, stolen from the upper forest, are here stranded as wing-dams that check the current and hold more mud. Rushes grow on this and catch more mud. Then the willows bind it more, and the sawing down of the outlet into the Mackenzie results in all this mud being left dry land.

This is the process that has made all the lowlands at the mouth of Great Slave and Athabaska Rivers.

And the lines of tree trunks to-day, preparing for the next constructive annexation of the lake, are so regular that one's first thought is that this is the work of man. But these are things that my sketches and photographs will show better than words.

When later we got onto the treeless Barrens or Tundra, the process was equally evident, though at this time dormant, and the chief agent was not running water, but the giant Jack Frost.

CHAPTER XXIX

PIKE'S PORTAGE

PART of my plan was to leave a provision cache every hundred miles, with enough food to carry us 200 miles, and thus cover the possibility of considerable loss. I had left supplies at Chipewyan, Smith, and Resolution, but these were settlements; now we were pushing off into the absolute wilderness, where it was unlikely we should see any human beings but ourselves. Now, indeed, we were facing all primitive conditions. Other travellers have made similar plans for food stores, but there are three deadly enemies to a cache—weather, ravens, and wolverines. I was prepared for all three. Water-proof leatheroid cases were to turn the storm, dancing tins and lines will scare the ravens, and each cache tree was made unclimbable to Wolverines by the addition of a necklace of charms in the form of large fish-hooks, all nailed on with points downward. This idea, borrowed from Tyrrell, has always proved a success; and not one of our caches was touched or injured.

Tyrrell has done much for this region; his name will ever be linked with its geography and history. His map of the portage was a godsend, for now we found that our guide had been here only once, and that when he was a child, with many resultant lapses of memory and doubts about the trail. My only wonder was that he remembered as much as he did.

Here we had a sudden and unexpected onset of black flies; they appeared for the first time in numbers, and attacked us with a ferocity that made the mosquitoes seem like a lot of baby butterflies in comparison. However, much as we may dislike the latter, they at least do not poison us or convey disease (as yet), and are repelled by thick clothing. The black flies attack us like some awful pestilence walking in darkness, crawling in and forcing themselves under our clothing, stinging and poisoning as they go. They are, of course, worst near the openings in our armour, that is necks, wrists, and ankles. Soon each of us had a neck like an old fighting bull walrus; enormously swollen, corrugated with bloats and wrinkles, blotched, bumpy, and bloody, as disgusting as it was painful. All too closely it simulated the ravages of some frightful disease, and for a night or two the torture of this itching fire kept me from sleeping. Three days, fortunately, ended the black fly reign, and left us with a deeper sympathy for the poor Egyptians who on account of their own or some other bodies' sins were the victims of "plagues of flies."

But there was something in the camp that amply offset these annoyances; this was a spirit of kindness and confidence. Old Weeso was smiling and happy, ready at all times to do his best; his blundering about the way was not surprising, all things considered, but his mistakes did not matter, since I had Tyrrell's admirable maps. Billy, sturdy, strong, reliable, never needed to be called twice in the morning. No matter what the hour, he was up at once and cooking the break-

fast in the best of style, for an A 1 cook he was. And
when it came to the portages he would shoulder his
200 or 250 pounds each time. Preble combined the
mental force of the educated white man with the brawn
of the savage, and although not supposed to do it, he
took the same sort of loads as Billy did. Mine, for the
best of reasons, were small, and consisted chiefly of the
guns, cameras, and breakables, or occasionally, while
they were transporting the heavy stuff, I acted as
cook. But all were literally and figuratively in the
same boat, all paddled all day, ate the same food,
worked the same hours, and imbued with the same
spirit were eager to reach the same far goal. From
this on the trip was ideal.

We were $3\frac{1}{2}$ days covering the 8 small lakes and
9 portages (30 miles) that lie between the two great
highways, Great Slave Lake and Artillery Lake; and
camped on the shore of the latter on the night of July 31.

Two of these 9 lakes had not been named by the
original explorers. I therefore exercised my privilege
and named them, respectively, "Loutit" and "Weeso,"
in honour of my men.

The country here is cut up on every side with caribou
trails; deep worn like the buffalo trails on the plains,
with occasional horns and bones; these, however,
are not so plentiful as were the relics of the Buffalo.
This, it proved, was because the Caribou go far north
at horn-dropping time, and they have practically no
bones that the Wolves cannot crush with their teeth.

Although old tracks were myriad-many, there were
no new ones. Weeso said, however, "In about four

days the shores of this lake will be alive with Caribou."
It will show the erratic nature of these animals when
I say that the old man was all wrong; they did not
appear there in numbers until many weeks later,
probably not for two months.

Here, at the foot of Artillery Lake, we were near the
last of the timber, and, strange to say, we found some
trees of remarkably large growth. One, a tamarac,
was the largest and last seen; the other, a spruce—
Pike's Lobstick—was 55 inches in girth, 1 foot from
the ground.

At this camp Weeso complained that he was feeling
very sick; had pains in his back. I could not make
out what was the matter with him, but Billy said
sagaciously, "I think if you give him any kind of a pill
he will be all right. It doesn't matter what, so long
as it's a pill."

Of course "cathartic" is good blind play in case of
doubt. He got a big, fierce rhubarb, and all went well.

CHAPTER XXX

CARIBOU–LAND AT LAST

On the morning of August 1 we launched on Artillery
Lake, feeling, for the tenth time, that now we really
were on the crowning stretch of our journey, that at
last we were entering the land of the Caribou.

Over the deep, tranquil waters of the lake we went,
scanning the painted shores with their dwindling remnants of forest. There is something inspiring about the
profundity of transparency in these lakes, where they
are 15 feet deep their bottoms are no more obscured
than in an ordinary eastern brook at 6 inches. On
looking down into the far-below world, one gets the
sensation of flight as one skims overhead in the swift
canoe. And how swift that elegant canoe was in a
clear run I was only now finding out. All my previous
estimates had been too low. Here I had the absolute
gauge of Tyrrell's maps and found that we four pad-
dling could send her, not $3\frac{1}{2}$, but $4\frac{1}{2}$ or 5 miles an hour,
with a possibility of 6 when we made an effort. As we
spun along the south-east coast of the lake, the country
grew less rugged; the continuous steep granite hills
were replaced by lower buttes with long grassy plains
between; and as I took them in, I marvelled at their
name—*the Barrens;* bare of trees, yes, but the plains
were covered with rich, rank grass, more like New

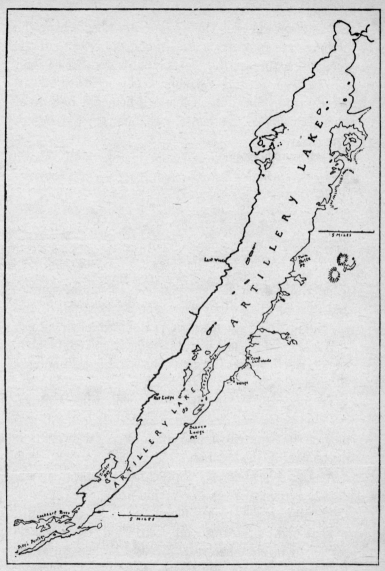

Artillery Lake

Founded chiefly on J. W. Tyrrell's map of 1900

England meadows.　There were stretches where the herbage was rank as on the Indiana prairies, and the average pasture of the bleaker parts was better than the best of central Wyoming.　A cattleman of the West would think himself made if he could be sure of such pastures on his range, yet these are the *Barren Grounds*.

At 3 we passed the splendid landmark of Beaver Lodge Mountain.　Its rosy-red granite cliffs contrast

Beaver Lodge Mountain.　Aug. 7, 1907

wonderfully with its emerald cap of verdant grass and mosses, that cover it in tropical luxuriance, and the rippling lake about it was of Mediterranean hues.

We covered the last 9 miles in 1 hour and 53 minutes, passed the deserted Indian village, and landed at Last Woods by 8.30 P. M.

The edge of the timber is the dividing line between the Hudsonian and the Arctic zones.　It is the beginning of the country we had come to see; we were now in the land of the Caribou.

At this point we were prepared to spend several days, leave a cache, gather a bundle of choice firewood, then enter on the treeless plains.

That night it stormed; all were tired; there was no reason to bestir ourselves; it was 10 when we arose. Half an hour later Billy came to my tent and said, "Mr. Seton, here's some deer."　I rushed to the door,

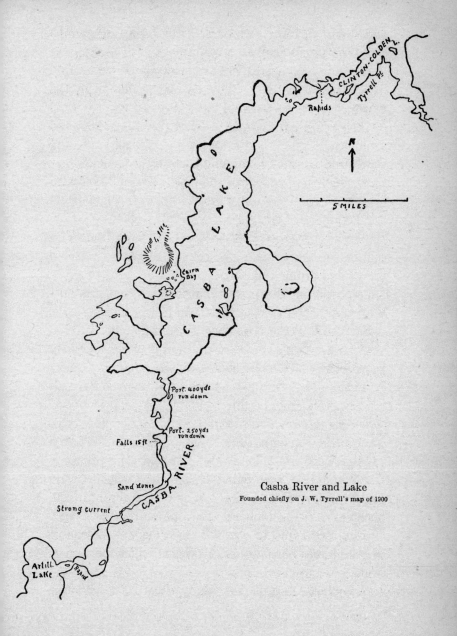

CLINTON-COLDEN L.

Tyrrell Pt

Rapids

CASBA LAKE

5 MILES

Cairn Bay

Port. 400 yds run down

Port. 250 yds run down

Falls 15 ft

CASBA RIVER

Sand dunes

Strong current

Artill. Lake

Casba River and Lake

Founded chiefly on J. W. Tyrrell's map of 1900

and there, with my own eyes, I saw on a ridge a mile away four great Caribou standing against the sky.

We made for a near hill and met Preble returning; he also had seen them. From a higher view-point the 4 proved part of a band of 20.

Then other bands came in view, 16, 61, 3, 200, and so on; each valley had a scattering few, all travelling slowly southward or standing to enjoy the cool breeze that ended the torment of the flies. About 1,000 were in sight. These were my first Caribou, the first fruits of 3,000 miles of travel.

Weeso got greatly excited; these were the forerunners of the vast herd. He said, "Plenty Caribou now," and grinned like a happy child.

I went in one direction, taking only my camera. At least 20 Caribou trotted within 50 feet of me.

Billy and Weeso took their rifles intent on venison, but the Caribou avoided them, and 6 or 8 shots were heard before they got a young buck.

All that day I revelled in Caribou, no enormous herds but always a few in sight.

The next day Weeso and I went to the top ridge eastward. He with rifle, I with camera. He has a vague idea of the camera's use, but told Billy privately that "the rifle was much better for Caribou." He could not understand why I should restrain him from blazing away as long as the ammunition held out. "Didn't we come to shoot?" But he was amenable to discipline, and did as I wished when he understood.

Now on the top of that windy ridge I sat with this

copper-coloured child of the spruce woods, to watch these cattle of the plains.

The Caribou is a travelsome beast, always in a hurry, going against the wind. When the wind is west, all travel west; when it veers, they veer. Now the wind was northerly, and all were going north, not walking, not galloping—the Caribou rarely gallops, and then only for a moment or two; his fast gait is a steady trot a 10-mile gait, making with stops about 6 miles an hour. But they are ever on the move; when you see a Caribou that does not move, you know at once it is not a Caribou; it's a rock.

We sat down on the hill at 3. In a few minutes a cow Caribou came trotting from the south, caught the wind at 50 yards, and dashed away.

In 5 minutes another, in 20 minutes a young buck, in 20 minutes more a big buck, in 10 minutes a great herd of about 500 appeared in the south. They came along at full trot, lined to pass us on the south-east. At half a mile they struck our scent and all recoiled as though we were among them. They scattered in alarm, rushed south again, then, gathered in solid body, came on as before, again to spring back and scatter as they caught the taint of man. After much and various running, scattering, and massing, they once more charged the fearsome odour and went right through it. Now they passed at 500 yards and gave the chance for a far camera shot.

The sound of their trampling was heard a long way off—half a mile—but at 300 yards I could not distinguish the clicking of the feet, whereas this clicking was very plainly to be heard from the band that passed within 50 yards of me in the morning.

They snort a good deal and grunt a little, and, notwithstanding their continual haste, I noticed that from time to time one or two would lie down, but at once jump up and rush on when they found they were being left behind. Many more single deer came that day, but no more large herds.

About 4.30 a fawn of this year ($2\frac{1}{2}$ or 3 months) came rushing up from the north, all alone. It charged up a hill for 200 yards, then changed its mind and charged down again, then raced to a bunch of tempting herbage, cropped it hastily, dashed to a knoll, left at an angle, darted toward us till within 40 yards, then dropped into a thick bed of grass, where it lay as though it had unlimited time.

I took one photograph, and as I crawled to get one nearer, a shot passed over my head, and the merry cackle told me that Weeso had yielded to temptation and had 'collected' that fawn.

A young buck now came trotting and grunting toward us till within 16 paces, which proved too much for Weeso, who then and there, in spite of repeated recent orders, started him on the first step toward my museum collection.

I scolded him angrily, and he looked glum and unhappy, like a naughty little boy caught in some indiscretion which he cannot understand. He said nothing to me then, but later complained to Billy, asking, "What *did* we come for?"

Next morning at dawn I dreamed I was back in

New York and that a couple of cats were wailing under my bedroom window. Their noise increased so that I awoke, and then I heard unaccountable caterwauls. They were very loud and near, at least one of the creatures was. At length I got up to see. Here on the lake a few yards from the tent was a loon swimming about, minutely inspecting the tent and uttering at intervals deep cat-like mews in expression of his curiosity.

The south wind had blown for some days before we arrived, and the result was to fill the country with Caribou coming from the north. The day after we came, the north wind set in, and continued for three days, so that soon there was not a Caribou to be found in the region.

In the afternoon I went up the hill to where Weeso left the offal of his deer. A large yellowish animal was there feeding. It disappeared over a rock and I could get no second view of it. It may have been a wolf, as I saw a fresh wolf trail near; I did not, however, see the animal's tail.

In the evening Preble and I went again, and again the creature was there, but disappeared as mysteriously as before when we were 200 yards away. Where it went we could not guess. The country was open and we scoured it with eye and glass, but saw nothing more of the prowler. It seemed to be a young Arctic wolf, yellowish white in colour, but tailless.

Next day at noon Preble and Billy returned bearing the illusive visitor; it was a large Lynx. It was very thin and yet, after bleeding, weighed 22 pounds. But why was it so far from the forest, 20 miles or more, and a couple of miles from this little grove that formed the last woods?

This is another evidence of the straits the Lynxes are put to for food, in this year of famine.

CHAPTER XXXI

GOOD-BYE TO THE WOODS

THE last woods is a wonderfully interesting biological point or line; this ultimate arm of the forest does not die away gradually with uncertain edges and in steadily dwindling trees. The latter have sent their stoutest champions to the front, or produced, as by a final effort, some giants for the line of battle. And that line, with its sentinels, is so marked that one can stand with a foot on the territory of each combatant, or, as scientists call them, the Arctic Region and the cold Temperate.

And each of the embattled kings, Jack-frost and Sombre-pine, has his children in abundance to possess the land as he wins it. Right up to the skirmish line are they.

The low thickets of the woods are swarming with Tree-sparrows, Redpolls, Robins, Hooded Sparrows, and the bare plains, a few yards away, are peopled and vocal with birds to whom a bush is an abomination. Lap-longspur, Snowbird, Shorelarks, and Pipits are here, soaring and singing, or among the barren rocks are Ptarmigan in garments that are painted in the patterns of their rocks.

There is one sombre fowl of ampler wing that knows no line—is at home in the open or in the woods. His

sonorous voice has a human sound that is uncanny;
his form is visible afar in the desert and sinister as a
gibbet; his plumage fits in with nothing but the night,
which he does not love.   This evil genius of the land is
the Raven of the north.   Its numbers increased as we

Cairn Bay, looking south.   August 7, 1907

reached the Barrens, and the morning after the first
Caribou was killed, no less than 28 were assembled
at its offal.

An even more interesting bird of the woods is the
Hooded Sparrow, interesting because so little known.

Here I found it on its breeding-grounds, a little late
for its vernal song, but in September we heard its
autumnal renewal like the notes of its kinsmen, White-
throat and White-crowned Sparrows, but with less
whistling, and more trilled.   In all the woods of the
Hudsonian Zone we found it evidently at home.   But
here I was privileged to find the first nest of the species
known to science.   The victory was robbed of its
crown, through the nest having fledglings instead of
eggs, but still it was the ample reward of hours of
search.

Of course it was on the ground, in the moss and creeping plants, under some bushes of dwarf birch, screened by spruces. The structure closely resembled that of the Whitethroat, was lined with grass and fibrous roots; no down, feathers, or fur were observable. The young numbered four.

The last woods was the limit of other interesting creatures—the Ants. Wherever one looks on the ground, in a high, dry place, throughout the forest country, from Athabaska Landing northward along our route, there is to be seen at least one Ant to the square foot, usually several. Three kinds seem common—one red-bodied, another a black one with brown thorax, and a third very small and all black. They seem to live chiefly in hollow logs and stumps, but are found also on marshes, where their hills are occasionally so numerous as to form dry bridges across.

I made many notes on the growth of timber here and all along the route; and for comparison will begin at the very beginning.

In March, 1907, at my home in Connecticut, I cut down an oak tree (*Q. palustris*) that was 110 feet high, 32 inches in diameter, and yet had only 76 rings of annual growth.

In the Bitterroot Mountains of Idaho, where I camped in September, 1902, a yellow pine 6 feet 6 inches high was $5\frac{1}{4}$ inches in circumference at base. It had 14 rings and 14 whorls of branches corresponding exactly with the rings.

At the same place I measured a balsam fir—84 feet high, 15 inches in diameter at 32 inches from the ground. It had 52 annual rings and 50 or possibly 52 whorls of branches. The most vigorous upward growth of the trunk corresponded exactly with the largest growth of wood in the stump. Thus ring No. 33 was ⅜ inch wide and whorl No. 33 had over 2 feet of growth, below it on the trunk were others which had but 6 inches.

On the stump most growth was on north-east side; there it was 9 inches, from pith to bark next on east 8½ inches, on south 8 inches, north 6½ inches, west 6½ inches, least on north-west side, 6 inches. The most light in this case came from the north-east. This was in the land of mighty timber.

On Great Slave River, the higher latitude is offset by lower altitude, and on June 2, 1907, while among the tall white spruce trees I measured one of average size—118 feet high, 11 feet 2 inches in girth a foot from the ground (3 feet 6½ inches in diameter), and many black poplars nearly as tall were 9 feet in girth.

But the stunting effect of the short summer became marked as we went northward. At Fort Smith, June 20, I cut down a jackpine that was 12 feet high, 1 inch in diameter, with 23 annual rings at the bottom; 6 feet up it had 12 rings and 20 whorls. In all it appeared to have 43 whorls, which is puzzling. Of these 20 were in the lower part. This tree grew in dense shade.

At Fort Resolution we left the Canadian region of large timber and entered the stunted spruce, as noted, and at length on the timber line we saw the final effort of the forests to combat Jack Frost in his own king-

dom. The individual history of each tree is in three
stages:

First, as a low, thick, creeping bush sometimes ten
feet across, but only a foot high. In this stage it continues until rooted enough and with capital enough to
send up a long central shoot; which is stage No. 2.

This central shoot is
like a Noah's Ark pine;
in time it becomes the
tree and finally the
basal thicket dies
away, leaving the spec-
imen in stage No. 3.

The three ages of the spruce

A stem of one of the low creepers was cut for ex-
amination; it was 1½ inches through and 25 years
old. Some of these low mats of spruce have stems 5
inches through. They must be fully 100 years old.

A tall, dead, white spruce at the camp was 30 feet
high and 11 inches in diameter at 4 feet from the
ground. Its 190 rings were hard to count, they were
so thin. The central ones were thickest, there being
16 to the inmost inch of radius; on the outside to the
north 50 rings made only ½ an inch and 86 made one
inch.

Numbers 42 and 43, counting from the outside, were
two or three times as thick as those outside of them
and much thicker than the next within; they must
have represented years of unusual summers. No. 99
also was of great size. What years these corresponded
with one could not guess, as the tree was a long time
dead.

Another, a dwarf but 8 feet high, was 12 inches through. It had 205 rings plus a 5-inch hollow which we reckoned at about 100 rings of growth; 64 rings made only 1⅜ inches; the outmost of the 64 was 2 inches in from the outside of the wood. Those on the outer two inches were even smaller, so as to be exceedingly difficult to count. This tree was at least 300 years old; our estimates varied, according to the data, from 300 to 325 years.

These, then, are the facts for extremes. In Idaho or Connecticut it took about 10 years to produce the same amount of timber as took 300 years on the edge of the Arctic Zone.

White spruce   Black spruce
(Like a red banana)   (Like a purple plum)

CHAPTER XXXII

THE TREELESS PLAINS

On August 7 we left Camp Last Woods. Our various specimens, with a stock of food, were secured, as usual, in a cache high in two trees, in this case those already used by Tyrrell seven years before, and guarded by the magic necklace of cod hooks.

By noon (in 3 hours) we made fifteen miles, camping far beyond Twin Buttes. All day long the boat shot through water crowded with drowned gnats. These were about 10 to the square inch near shore and for about twenty yards out, after that 10 to the square foot for two hundred or three hundred yards still farther from shore, and for a quarter mile wide they were 10 to the square yard.

This morning the wind turned and blew from the south. At 2 P. M. we saw a band of some 60 Caribou travelling southward; these were the first seen for two or three days. After this we saw many odd ones, and about 3 o'clock a band of 400 or 500. At night we camped on Casba River, having covered 36 miles in 7 hours and 45 minutes.

The place we had selected for camp proved to be a Caribou crossing. As we drew near a dozen of them came from the east and swam across. A second band of 8 now appeared. We gave chase. They spurted; so did we. Our canoe was going over 6 miles an hour, and yet was but slowly overtaking them. They made the water foam around them. Their heads, necks, shoulders, backs, rumps, and tails were out. I never before saw land animals move so fast in the water. A fawn in danger of being left behind reared up on its mother's back and hung on with forefeet. The leader was a doe or a young buck, I could not be sure which; the last was a big buck. They soon struck bottom and bounded along on the shore. It was too dark for a picture.

As we were turning in for the night 30 Caribou came trotting and snorting through the camp. Half of them crossed the water, but the rest turned back when Billy shouted.

Later a band of two hundred passed through and around our tents. In the morning Billy complained that he could not sleep all night for Caribou travelling by his tent and stumbling over the guy ropes. From this time on we were nearly always in sight of Caribou, small bands or scattering groups; one had the feeling that the whole land was like this, on and on and on, unlimited space with unlimited wild herds.

A year afterward, as I travelled in the fair State of Illinois, famous for its cattle, I was struck by the idea that one sees far more Caribou in the north than cattle in Illinois. This State has about 56,000 square miles of land and 3,000,000 cattle; the Arctic Plains have over 1,000,000 square miles of prairie, which, allowing for the fact that I saw the best of the range, would set the Caribou number at over 30,000,000. There is a good deal of evidence that this is not far from the truth.

The reader may recollect the original postulate of my plan. Other travellers have gone, relying on the abundant Caribou, yet saw none, so starved. I relied on no Caribou, I took plenty of groceries, and because I was independent, the Caribou walked into camp nearly every day, and we lived largely on their meat, saving our groceries for an emergency, which came in an unexpected form. One morning when we were grown accustomed to this condition I said to Billy:

"How is the meat?"

"Nearly gone. We'll need another Caribou about Thursday."

"You better get one now to be ready Thursday. I do not like it so steaming fresh. See, there's a nice little buck on that hillside."

"No, not him; why he is nearly half a mile off. I'd have to pack him in. Let's wait till one comes in camp."

Which we did, and usually got our meat delivered near the door.

Caribou meat fresh, and well prepared, has no superior, and the ideal way of cooking it is of course by roasting.

> Fried meat is dried meat,
> Boiled meat is spoiled meat,
> Roast meat is best meat.

How was it to be roasted at an open fire without continued vigilance? By a very simple contrivance that I invented at the time and now offer for the use of all campers.

A wire held the leg; on the top of the wire was a paddle or shingle of wood; above that, beyond the heat, was a cord.

The wind gives the paddle a push; it winds up the cord, which then unwinds itself. This goes on without fail and without effort, never still, and the roast is perfect.

Thus we were living on the fat of many lands and on the choicest fat of this.

And what a region it is for pasture. At this place it reminds one of Texas. Open, grassy plains, sparser reaches of sand, long slopes of mesquite, mesas dotted with cedars and stretches of chapparal and soapweed. Only, those vegetations here are willow, dwarf birch, tiny spruce, and ledum, and the country as a whole is far too green and rich. The emerald verdure of the shore, in not a few places, carried me back to the west coast of Ireland.

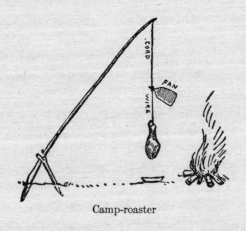

Camp-roaster

CHAPTER XXXIII

THE UNKNOWN

THE daily observations of route and landmark I can best leave for record on my maps. I had one great complaint against previous explorers (except Tyrrell); that is, they left no monuments. Aiming to give no ground of complaint against us, we made monuments at all important points. On the night of August 8 we camped at Cairn Bay on the west side of Casba Lake, so named because of the five remarkable glacial cairns or conical stone-piles about it. On the top of one of these I left a monument, a six-foot pillar of large stones.

On the afternoon of August 9 we passed the important headland that I have called "Tyrrell Point." Here we jumped off his map into the unknown. I had, of course, the small chart drawn by Sir George Back in 1834, but it was hastily made under great difficulties, and, with a few exceptions, it seemed impossible to recognize his landscape features. Next day I explored the east arm of Clinton-Colden and discovered the tributary that I have called "Laurier River," and near its mouth made a cairn enclosing a Caribou antler with inscription "E. T. Seton, 10 Aug., 1907."

Future travellers on this lake will find, as I did, that the Conical Butte in the eastern part is an important landmark. It is a glacial dump about 50 feet above the general level, which again is 100 feet above the water, visible and recognizable from nearly all parts of the lake.

Thus we went on day by day, sometimes detained by head or heavy winds, but making great progress in the calm, which nearly always came in the evening; 30

Ptarmigan Head from the east

and 35 miles a day we went, led on and stimulated by the thirst to see and know. "I must see what is over that ridge," "I must make sure that this is an island," or "Maybe from that lookout I shall see Lake Aylmer, or a band of Caribou, yes, or even a band of Musk-ox." Always there was some reward, and nearly always it was a surprise.

From time to time we came on Snowbirds with their young broods, evidently at home. Ptarmigan abounded. Parry's Groundsquirrel was found at nearly all points, including the large islands. The Laplongspur swarmed everywhere; their loud "*chee chups*" were the first sounds to greet us each time we neared the land. And out over all the lake were Loons, Loons, Loons. Four species abound here; they caterwaul and yodel all day and all night, each in its own particular speech. From time to time a wild hyena chorus from the tranquil water in the purple sunset haze suggested that a pack of goblin hounds were chivying a goblin buck, but it turned out always to be a family of Red-throated Loons, yodelling their inspiring marching song.

One day when at Gravel Mountain, old Weeso came to camp in evident fear—"*far off he had seen a man.*" In this country a man must mean an Eskimo; with them the Indian has a long feud; of them he is in terror. We never learned the truth; I think he was mistaken.

Once or twice the long howl of the White Wolf sounded from the shore, and every day we saw a few Caribou.

A great many of the single Caribou were on the small islands. In six cases that came under close observation the animal in question had a broken leg. A broken leg generally evidences recent inroads by hunters, but the nearest Indians were 200 miles to the south, and the nearest Eskimo 300 miles to the north. There was every reason to believe that we were the only human beings in that vast region, and certainly we had broken no legs. Every Caribou fired at (8) had been secured and used. There is only one dangerous large enemy common in this country; that is the White Wolf. And the more I pondered it, the more it seemed sure that the Wolves had broken the Caribous' legs.

How! This is the history of each case: The Caribou is so much swifter than the Wolves that the latter have no chance in open chase; they therefore adopt the stratagem of a sneaking surround and a drive over the rocks or a precipice, where the Caribou, if not actually killed, is more or less disabled. In some cases only a leg is broken, and then the Caribou knows his only

chance is to reach the water. Here his wonderful
powers of swimming make him easily safe, so much so
that the Wolves make no attempt to follow. The
crippled deer makes for some island sanctuary, where
he rests in peace till his leg is healed, or it may be, in
some cases, till the freezing of the lake brings him again
into the power of his foe.

These six, then, were the cripples in hospital, and
I hope our respectful behaviour did not inspire them
with a dangerously false notion of humanity.

On the island that I have called Owl-and-Hare, we
saw the first White Owl and the first Arctic Hare.

In this country when you see a tree, you know perfectly well it is not a tree; it's the horns of a Caribou.
An unusually large affair of branches appeared on an
island in the channel to Aylmer. I landed, camera in
hand; the Caribou was lying down in the open, but
there was a tuft of herbage 30 yards from him, another
at 20 yards. I crawled to the first and made a snap-
shot, then, flat as a rug, sneaked my way to the one estimated at 20 yards. The click of the camera, alarmed
the buck; he rose, tried the wind, then lay down again,
giving me another chance. Having used all the films,
I now stood up. The Caribou dashed away and by
a slight limp showed that he was in sanctuary. The
20-yard estimate proved too long; it was only 16 yards,
which put my picture a little out of focus.

There never was a day, and rarely an hour of each
day, that we did not see several Caribou. And yet
I never failed to get a thrill at each fresh one. "There's
a Caribou," one says with perennial intensity that is

evidence of perennial pleasure in the sight. There
never was one sighted that did not give us a happy sense
of satisfaction—the thought "This is what we came
for."

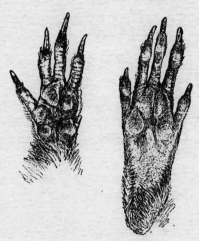

Feet of Groundsquirrel

CHAPTER XXXIV

AYLMER LAKE

ONE of my objects was to complete the ambiguous shore line of Aylmer Lake. The first task was to find the lake. So we left the narrows and pushed on and on, studying the Back map, vainly trying to identify points, etc. Once or twice we saw gaps ahead that seemed to open into the great inland sea of Aylmer. But each in turn proved a mere bay. On August 12 we left the narrows; on the 13th and 14th we journeyed westward seeking the open sea. On the morning of the 15th we ran into the final end of the farthest bay we could discover and camped at the mouth of a large river entering in.

As usual, we landed—Preble, Billy, and I—to study topography, Weeso to get firewood, and curiously enough, there was more firewood here than we had seen since leaving Artillery Lake. The reason of this appeared later.

I was utterly puzzled. We had not yet found Aylmer Lake, and had discovered an important river that did not seem to be down on any map.

We went a mile or two independently and studied the land from all the high hills; evidently we had crossed the only great sheet of water in the region. About noon, when all had assembled at camp, I said: "Preble,

BRITISH NORTH AMERICA

SKETCH MAP OF

AYLMER AND CLINTON-COLDEN LAKES

BY

ERNEST THOMPSON SETON

Scale of Miles

Canoe Route ·········
Heights in feet above level of Lakes

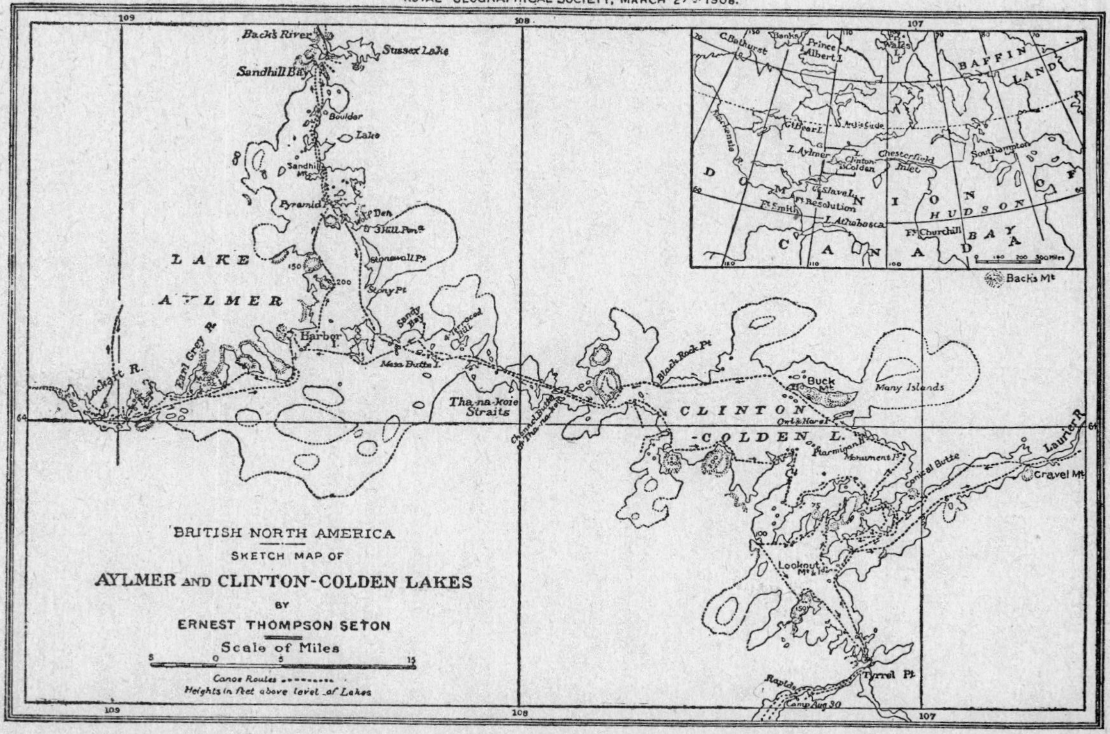

why, isn't *this* Lockhart's River, at the western extremity of Aylmer Lake?" The truth was dawning on me.

He also had been getting light and slowly replied: "I have forty-nine reasons why it is, and none at all why it isn't."

There could be no doubt of it now. The great open sea of Aylmer was a myth. Back never saw it; he passed in a fog, and put down with a query the vague information given him by the Indians. This little irregular lake, much like Clinton-Colden, was Aylmer. We had covered its length and were now at its farthest western end, at the mouth of Lockhart's River.

How I did wish that explorers would post up the names of the streets; it is almost as bad as in New York City. What a lot of time we might have saved had we known that Sandy Bay was in Back's three-fingered peninsula! Resolving to set a good example I left a monument at the mouth of the river. The kind of stone made it easy to form a cross on top. This will protect it from wandering Indians; I do not know of anything that will protect it from wandering white men.

Near mouth of Lockhart River

CHAPTER XXXV

THE MUSK-OX

In the afternoon, Preble, Billy, and I went northward on foot to look for Musk-ox. A couple of miles from camp I left the others and went more westerly.

After wandering on for an hour, disturbing Long-spurs, Snowbirds, Pipits, Groundsquirrel, and Caribou, I came on a creature that gave me new thrills of pleasure. It was only a Polar Hare, the second we had seen; but its very scarceness here, at least this year, gave it unusual interest, and the Hare itself helped the feeling by letting me get near it to study, sketch, and photograph.

It was exactly like a Prairie Hare in all its manners, even to the method of holding its tail in running, and this is one of the most marked and distinctive peculiarities of the different kinds.

On the 16th of August we left Lockhart's River, knowing now that the north arm of the lake was our way. We passed a narrow bay out of which there seemed to be a current, then, on the next high land, noted a large brown spot that moved rather quickly along. It was undoubtedly some animal with short legs, whether a Wolverine a mile away, or a Musk-ox two miles away, was doubtful. Now did that canoe put on its six-mile gait, and we soon knew for certain

231

that the brown thing was a Musk-ox. We were not yet in their country, but here was one of them to meet us. Quickly we landed. Guns and cameras were loaded.

"Don't fire till I get some pictures—unless he charges," were the orders. And then we raced after the great creature grazing from us.

Arctic Hare.   August 15, 1907

We had no idea whether he would run away or charge, but knew that our plan was to remain unseen as long as possible. So, hiding behind rocks when he looked around, and dashing forward when he grazed, we came unseen within two hundred yards, and had a good look at the huge woolly ox. He looked very much like an ordinary Buffalo, the same in colour, size, and action. I never was more astray in my preconcept of any animal, for I had expected to see something like a large brown sheep.

My first film was fired. Then, for some unknown reason, that Musk-ox took it into his head to travel fast away from us, not even stopping to graze; he would soon have been over a rocky ridge. I nodded to Preble. His rifle rang; the bull wheeled sharp about with an angry snort and came toward us. His head was up, his eye blazing, and he looked like a South African Buffalo and a Prairie Bison combined, and seemed to get bigger at every moment. We were safely hidden behind rocks, some fifty yards from him now, when I got my second snap.

Realising the occasion, and knowing my men, I said: "Now, Preble, I am going to walk up to that bull and get a close picture. He will certainly charge me,

Tracks of Musk-ox

as I shall be nearest and in full view. There is only one combination that can save my life: that is you and that rifle."

Then with characteristic loquacity did Preble reply: "Go ahead."

I fixed my camera for twenty yards and quit the sheltering rock. The bull snorted, shook his head, took aim, and just before the precious moment was to arrive a heavy shot behind me rang out, the bull staggered and fell, shot through the heart, and *Weeso* cackled aloud in triumph.

How I cursed the meddling old fool. He had not understood. He saw, as he supposed, "the Okimow in peril of his life,"and acted according to the dictates of his accursedly poor discretion. Never again shall he carry a rifle with me.

So the last scene came not, but we had the trophy

of a Musk-ox that weighed nine hundred pounds in
life and stood five feet high at the shoulders—a world's
record in point of size.

Now we must camp perforce to save the specimen.
Measurements, photos, sketches, and weights were
needed, then the skinning and preparing would be a
heavy task for all.   In the
many portages after-
wards the skull was part
of my burden; its weight
was actually forty pounds,
its heaviness was far
over a hundred.

Musk-ox tracks, male.
August 18, 1907

What extraordinary luck we were having. It was
impossible in our time limit to reach the summer haunt
of the Caribou on the Arctic Coast, therefore the Caribou came to us in their winter haunt on the Artillery
Lake.   We did not expect to reach the real Musk-ox
country on the Lower Back River, so the Musk-ox
sought us out on Aylmer Lake.   And yet one more
piece of luck is to be recorded.   That night something
came in our tent and stole meat.   The next night
Billy set a trap and secured the thief—an Arctic Fox
in summer coat.   We could not expect to go to him
in his summer home, so he came to us.

While the boys were finishing the dressing of the
bull's hide, I, remembering the current from the last
bay, set out on foot over the land to learn the reason.
A couple of miles brought me to a ridge from which I
made the most important geographical discovery of
the journey.   Stretching away before me to the far

dim north-west was a great, splendid river—broad, two hundred yards wide in places, but averaging seventy or eighty yards across—broken by white rapids and waterfalls, but blue deep in the smoother stretches and emptying into the bay we had noticed. So far as the record showed, I surely was the first

Left front foot of male Musk-ox

white man to behold it. I went to the margin; it was stocked with large trout. I followed it up a couple of miles and was filled with the delight of discovery. "Earl Grey River" I have been privileged to name it, after the distinguished statesman, now Governor-general of Canada.

Then and there I built a cairn, with a record of my visit, and sitting on a hill with the new river below me, I felt that there was no longer any question of the expedition's success. The entire programme was carried out. I had proved the existence of abundance of Caribou, had explored Aylmer Lake, had discovered two great rivers, and, finally, had reached the land of the Musk-ox and secured a record-breaker to bring away. This I felt was the supreme moment of the journey.

Realizing the farness of my camp from human abode—it could scarcely have been farther on the continent—my thoughts flew back to the dear ones at home, and my comrades, the men of the Camp-fire Club. I wondered if their thoughts were with me at the time. How they must envy me the chance of launching into the truly unknown wilderness, a land still marked on the maps as "unexplored!" How I enjoyed the thoughts of their sympathy over our probable perils and hardships, and imagined them crowding around me with hearty greetings on my safe return! Alas! for the rush of a great city's life and crowds, I found out later that these, my companions, did not even know that I had been away from New York.

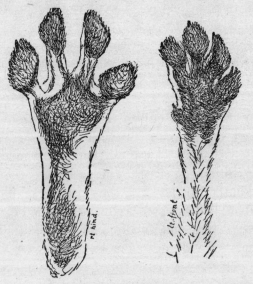

Feet of Polar Hare

CHAPTER XXXVI

THE ARCTIC PRAIRIES AND MY FARTHEST NORTH

CAMP MUSK-OX provided many other items of interest besides the Great River, the big Musk-ox, and the Arctic Fox. Here Preble secured a Groundsquirrel with its cheek-pouches full of mushrooms and shot a cock Ptarmigan whose crop was crammed with leaves of willow and birch, though the ground was bright with berries of many kinds. The last evening we were there a White Wolf followed Billy into camp, keeping just beyond reach of his shotgun; and, of course, we saw Caribou every hour or two.

"All aboard," was the cry on the morning of August 19, and once more we set out. We reached the north arm of the lake, then turned north-eastward. In the evening I got photos of a Polar Hare, the third we had seen. The following day (August 20), at noon, we camped in Sandhill Bay, the north point of Aylmer Lake and the northernmost point of our travels by canoe. It seems that we were the fourth party of white men to camp on this spot.

Captain George Back, 1833–34.
Stewart and Anderson, 1855.
Warburton Pike, 1890.
E. T. Seton, 1907.

All day long we had seen small bands of Caribou. A score now appeared on a sandhill half a mile away; another and another lone specimen trotted past our camp. One of these stopped and gave us an ex-

Our Cairn at Sand Hill Bay

traordinary exhibition of agility in a sort of St. Vitus's jig, jumping, kicking, and shaking its head; I suspect the nose-worms were annoying it. While we lunched, a fawn came and gazed curiously from a distance of 100 yards. In the afternoon Preble returned from a walk to say that the Caribou were visible in all directions, but not in great bands.

Next morning I was awakened by a Caribou clattering through camp within 30 feet of my tent.

After breakfast we set off on foot northward to seek for Musk-ox, keeping to the eastward of the Great Fish River. The country is rolling, with occasional rocky ridges and long, level meadows in the lowlands, practically all of it would be considered horse country; and nearly every meadow had two or three grazing Caribou.

About noon, when six or seven miles north of Aylmer, we halted for rest and lunch on the top of the long ridge of glacial dump that lies to the east of Great Fish River. And now we had a most complete and spectacular view of the immense open country that we had come so far to see. It was spread before us like a huge, minute, and wonderful chart, and plainly marked with the processes of its shaping-time.

Imagine a region of low archaean hills, extending one thousand miles each way, subjected for thousands of years to a continual succession of glaciers, crushing, grinding, planing, smoothing, ripping up and smoothing again, carrying off whole ranges of broken hills, in fragments, to dump them at some other point, grind them again while there, and then push and hustle them out of that region into some other a few hundred miles farther; there again to tumble and grind them together, pack them into the hollows, and dump them in pyramidal piles on plains and uplands. Imagine this going on for thousands of years, and we shall have the hills lowered and polished, the valleys more or less filled with broken rocks.

Now the glacial action is succeeded by a time of flood. For another age all is below water, dammed by the northern ice, and icebergs breaking from the parent sheet carry bedded in them countless boulders, with which they go travelling south on the open waters. As they melt the boulders are dropped; hill and hollow share equally in this age-long shower of erratics. Nor does it cease till the progress of the warmer day removes the northern ice-dam, sets free the flood, and the region of archaean rocks stands bare and dry.

It must have been a dreary spectacle at that time, low, bare hills of gneiss, granite, etc.; low valleys half-filled with broken rock and over everything a sprinkling of erratic boulders; no living thing in sight, nothing green, nothing growing, nothing but evidence of mighty power used only to destroy. A waste of shattered granite spotted with hundreds of lakes, thousands of lakelets, millions of ponds that are marvellously blue, clear, and lifeless.

But a new force is born on the scene; it attacks not this hill or rock, or that loose stone, but on every point of every stone and rock in the vast domain, it appears —the lowest form of lichen, a mere stain of gray. This spreads and by its own corrosive power eats foothold on the granite; it fructifies in little black velvet

Bugle moss   Lichens   Cetraria

spots. Then one of lilac flecks the pink tones of the granite, to help the effect. Soon another kind follows —a pale olive-green lichen that fruits in bumps of rich brown velvet; then another branching like a tiny tree —there is a ghostly kind like white chalk rubbed lightly on, and yet another of small green blots, and one like a sprinkling of scarlet snow; each, in turn, of a higher and larger type, which in due time prepares the way for mosses higher still.

In the less exposed places these come forth, seeking the shade, searching for moisture, they form like small sponges on a coral reef; but growing, spread and change to meet the changing contours of the land they win, and with every victory or upward move, adopt some new refined intensive tint that is the outward and visible sign of their diverse inner excellences and their triumph. Ever evolving they spread, until there are

great living rugs of strange textures and oriental tones;
broad carpets there are of gray and green; long luxuri-
ous lanes, with lilac mufflers under foot, great beds of
a moss so yellow chrome, so spangled with intense red
sprigs, that they might, in clumsy hands, look raw.
There are knee-deep breadths of polytrichum, which
blends in the denser shade into a moss of delicate crim-
son plush that baffles description.

Down between the broader masses are bronze-green
growths that run over each slight dip and follow down

Lichens and moss forms

the rock crannies like streams of molten brass. Thus
the whole land is overlaid with a living, corrosive
mantle of activities as varied as its hues.

For ages these toil on, improving themselves, and
improving the country by filing down the granite and
strewing the dust around each rock.

The frost, too, is at work, breaking up the granite
lumps; on every ridge there is evidence of that—low,
rounded piles of stone which plainly are the remnants
of a boulder, shattered by the cold. Thus, lichen, moss,
and frost are toiling to grind the granite surfaces to
dust.

Much of this powdered rock is washed by rain into
the lakes and ponds; in time these cut their exits

down, and drain, leaving each a broad mud-flat. The climate mildens and the south winds cease not, so that wind-borne grasses soon make green meadows of the broad lake-bottom flats.

The process climbs the hill-slopes; every little earthy foothold for a plant is claimed by some new settler, until each low hill is covered to the top with vegetation graded to its soil, and where the flowering kinds cannot establish themselves, the lichen pioneers still maintain their hold. Rarely, in the landscape, now, is any of the primitive colour of the rocks; even the tall, straight cliffs of Aylmer are painted and frescoed with lichens that flame and glitter with purple and orange, silver and gold. How precious and fertile the ground is made to seem, when every square foot of it is an exquisite elfin garden made by the

Saxifrage

little people, at infinite cost, filled with dainty flowers and still later embellished with delicate fruit.

One of the wonderful things about these children of the Barrens is the great size of fruit and flower compared with the plant. The cranberry, the crowberry, the cloudberry, etc., produce fruit any one of which might outweigh the herb itself.

Nowhere does one get the impression that these are

weeds, as often happens among the rank growths farther south. The flowers in the wildest profusion are
generally low, always delicate and mostly in beds of a
single species. The Lalique jewelry was the sensation
of the Paris Exposition of 1899. Yet here is Lalique
renewed and changed for every week in the season and
lavished on every square foot of a region
that is a million square miles in extent.

Not a cranny in a rock but is seized
on at once by the eager little gardeners in charge and made a bed of bloom,
as though every inch of room were priceless. And yet Nature here exemplifies
the law that our human gardeners are
only learning: "Mass your bloom, to
gain effect."

As I stood on that hill, the foreground   Cloudberry
was a broad stretch of old gold—the
shining sandy yellow of drying grass—but it was
patched with large scarlet mats of arctous that
would put red maple to its reddest blush. There was
no Highland heather here, but there were whole hillsides of purple red vaccinium, whose leaves were but
a shade less red than its luscious grape-hued fruit.

Here were white ledums in roods and acre beds;
purple mairanias by the hundred acres, and, framed in
lilac rocks, were rich, rank meadows of golden-green
by the mile.

There were leagues and leagues of caribou moss, pale
green or lilac, and a hundred others in clumps, that,
seeing here the glory of the painted mosses, were sim-

ulating their ways, though they themselves were the
not truly mosses at all.

I never before saw such a realm of exquisite flowers
so exquisitely displayed, and the effect at every turn
throughout the land was colour, colour, colour, to as
far outdo the finest autumn tints of New England as
the Colorado Canyon outdoes the Hoosac Gorge.
What Nature can do only in October, elsewhere, she
does here all season through, as though when she set
out to paint the world she began on the Barrens with
a full palette and when she reached the Tropics had
nothing left but green.

Thus at every step one is wading through lush grass
or crushing prairie blossoms and fruits. It is so on
and on; in every part of the scene, there are but few
square feet that do not bloom with flowers and throb
with life; yet this is the region called the *Barren Lands
of the North*.

And the colour is an index of its higher living forms,
for this is the chosen home of the Swans and Wild
Geese; many of the Ducks, the Ptarmigan, the Lap-
longspur and Snowbunting. The blue lakes echo with
the wailing of the Gulls and the eerie magic calling of
the Loons. Colonies of Lemmings, Voles, or Groundsquirrels are found on every sunny slope; the Wolverine and the White Wolf find this a land of plenty, for
on every side, as I stood on that high hill, were to be
seen small groups of Caribou.

This was the land and these the creatures I had
come to see. This was my Farthest North and this
was the culmination of years of dreaming. How very

good it seemed at the time, but how different and how·
infinitely more delicate and satisfying was the realisa-
tion than any of the day-dreams founded on my vision
through the eyes of other men.

Horns of the bull Musk-ox

CHAPTER XXXVII

FACING HOMEWARD

On this hill we divided, Preble and Billy going northward; Weeso and I eastward, all intent on finding a herd of Musk-ox; for this was the beginning of their range. There was one continual surprise as we journeyed—the willows that were mere twigs on Aylmer Lake increased in size and were now plentiful and as high as our heads, with stems two or three inches thick. This was due partly to the decreased altitude and partly to removal from the broad, cold sheet of Aylmer, which, with its July ice, must tend to lower the summer temperature.

For a long time we tramped eastward, among hills and meadows, with Caribou. Then, at length, turned south again and, after a 20-mile tramp, arrived in camp at 6.35, having seen no sign whatever of Musk-ox, although this is the region where Pike found them common; on July 1, 1890, at the little lake where we lunched, his party killed seven out of a considerable band.

At 9.30 that night Preble and Billy returned. They had been over Icy River, easily recognised by the thick ice still on its expansions, and on to Musk-ox Lake, without seeing any fresh tracks of a Musk-ox. As they came into camp a White Wolf sneaked away.

Rain began at 6 and continued a heavy storm all night. In the morning it was still in full blast, so no one rose until 9.30, when Billy, starved out of his warm bed, got up to make breakfast. Soon I heard him calling: "Mr. Seton, here's a big Wolf in camp!" "Bring him in here," I said. Then a rifle-shot was heard, another, and Billy appeared, dragging a huge White Wolf. (He is now to be seen in the American Museum.)

All that day and the next night the storm raged. Even the presence of Caribou bands did not stimulate us enough to face the sleet. Next day it was dry, but too windy to travel.

Billy now did something that illustrates at once the preciousness of firewood, and the pluck, strength, and reliability of my cook. During his recent tramp he found a low, rocky hollow full of large, dead willows. It was eight miles back; nevertheless he set out, of his own free will; tramped the eight miles, that wet, blustery day, and returned in five and one-half hours, bearing on his back a heavy load, over 100 pounds of most acceptable firewood. Sixteen miles afoot for a load of wood! But it seemed well worth it as we revelled in the blessed blaze.

Next day two interesting observations were made; down by the shore I found the midden-heap of a Lemming family. It contained about four hundred pellets: their colour and dryness, with the absence of grass, showed that they dated from winter.

In the evening the four of us witnessed the tragic end of a Lap-longspur. Pursued by a fierce Skua Gull, it unfortunately dashed out over the lake. In vain then it darted up and down, here and there, high and low; the Skua followed even more quickly. A second Skua came flying to help, but was not needed. With a falcon-like swoop, the pirate seized the Long-spur in his bill and bore it away to be devoured at the nearest perch.

At 7.30 A. M., August 24, 1907, surrounded by scattering Caribou, we pushed off from our camp at Sand Hill Bay and began the return journey.

At Wolf-den Point we discovered a large and ancient wolf-den in the rocks; also abundance of winter sign of Musk-ox. That day we made forty miles and camped for the night on the Sand Hill Mountain in Tha-

Tha-na-koie from south

na-koie, the channel that joins Aylmer and Clinton-Colden. Here we were detained by high winds until the 28th.

This island is a favourite Caribou crossing, and Billy and Weeso had pitched their tents right on the place selected by the Caribou for their highway. Next day, while scanning the country from the top of the mount, I saw three Caribou trotting along. They swam the river and came toward me. As Billy and Weeso were in their tents having an afternoon nap, I thought it would be a good joke to stampede the Caribou on top of them, so waited behind a rock, intending to jump out as soon as they were past me. They followed the main trail at a trot, and I leaped out with "horrid yells" when they passed my rock, but now the unexpected happened. "In case of doubt take to the water" is Caribou wisdom, so, instead of dashing madly into the tents, they made three desperate down leaps and plunged into the deep water, then calmly swam for the other shore, a quarter of a mile away.

This island proved a good place for small mammals. Here Preble got our first specimen of the White Lemming. Large islands usually prove better for small mammals than the mainland. They have the same conditions to support life, but being moated by the water are usually without the larger predatory quadrupeds.

The great central inland of Clinton-Colden proved the best place of all for Groundsquirrels. Here we actually found them in colonies.

On the 29th and 30th we paddled and surveyed without ceasing and camped beyond the rapid at the exit of Clinton-Colden. The next afternoon we made the exit rapids of Casba Lake. Preble was preparing to portage them, but asked Weeso, "Can we run them?"

Weeso landed, walked to a view-point, took a squinting look and said, "Ugh!" (Yes). Preble rejoined, "All right! If he says he can, he surely can. That's the Indian of it. A white man takes risks; an Indian will not; if it is risky he'll go around." So we ran the rapids in safety.

Lighter each day, as the food was consumed, our elegant canoe went faster. When not detained by heavy seas 30 or 40 miles a day was our journey. On August 30 we made our last 6 miles in one hour and $6\frac{1}{2}$ minutes. On September 2, in spite of head-winds, we made 36 miles in 8¼ hours and in the evening we skimmed over the glassy surface of Artillery Lake, among its many beautiful islands and once more landed at our old ground—the camp in the Last Woods.

Monument on Tha-na-Koie

CHAPTER XXXVIII

THE FIRST WOODS

How shall I set forth the feelings it stirred? None but the shipwrecked sailor, long drifting on the open sea, but come at last to land, can fully know the thrill it gave us. We were like starving Indians suddenly surrounded by Caribou. Wood—timber—fuel—galore! It was hard to realise—but there it was, all about us, and in the morning we were awakened by the sweet, sweet, home-like song of the Robins in the trees, singing their *"Cheerup, cheerily,"* just as they do it in Ontario and Connecticut. Our cache was all right; so our stock of luxuries was replenished. We now had unlimited food as well as unlimited firewood; what more could any one ask? Yet there was more. The weather was lovely; perfect summer days, and the mosquitoes were gone, yes, now actually nets and fly-bars were discarded for good. On every side was animal life in abundance; the shimmering lake with its Loons and islands would fit exactly the Indian's dream of the heavenly hunting-grounds. These were the happy halcyon days of the trip, and we stayed a week to rest and revel in the joys about us.

In the morning I took a long walk over the familiar hills; the various skeletons we had left were picked bare, evidently by Gulls and Ravens, as no bones were broken and even the sinews were left. There were many fresh

tracks of single Caribou going here and there, but no
trails of large bands. I sent Weeso off to the Indian
village, two miles south. He returned to say that it
was deserted and that, therefore, the folk had gone
after the Caribou, which doubtless were now in the
woods south of Artillery Lake. Again the old man was
wholly astray in his Caribou forecast.

That night there was a sharp frost; the first we had
had. It made nearly half an inch of ice in all kettles.
Why is ice always thickest on the kettles? No doubt
because they hold a small body of very still water surrounded by highly conductive metal.

Billy went "to market" yesterday, killing a nice,
fat little Caribou. This morning on returning to bring
in the rest of the meat we found that a Wolverine had
been there and lugged the most of it away. The
tracks show that it was an old one accompanied by one
or maybe two young ones. We followed them some
distance but lost all trace in a long range of rocks.

The Wolverine is one of the typical animals of the
far North. It has an unenviable reputation for being
the greatest plague that the hunter knows. Its habit
of following to destroy all traps for the sake of the bait
is the prime cause of man's hatred, and its cleverness
in eluding his efforts at retaliation give it still more
importance.

It is, above all, the dreaded enemy of a cache, and
as already seen, we took the extra precaution of putting our caches up trees that were protected by a
necklace of fishhooks. Most Northern travellers have
regaled us with tales of this animal's diabolical clever-

ness and wickedness. It is fair to say that the malice, at least, is not proven; and there is a good side to Wolverine character that should be emphasized; that is, its nearly ideal family life, coupled with the heroic bravery of the mother. I say "nearly" ideal, for so far as I can learn, the father does not assist in rearing the young. But all observers agree that the mother is absolutely fearless and devoted. More than one of the hunters have assured me that it is safer to molest a mother Bear than a mother Wolverine when accompanied by the cubs.

Bellalise, a half-breed of Chipewyan, told me that twice he had found Wolverine dens, and been seriously endangered by the mother. The first was in mid-May, 1904, near Fond du Lac, north side of Lake Athabaska. He went out with an Indian to bring in a skiff left some miles off on the shore. He had no gun, and was surprised by coming on an old Wolverine in a slight hollow under the boughs of a green spruce. She rushed at him, showing all her teeth, her eyes shining blue, and uttering sounds like those of a Bear. The Indian boy hit her once with a stick, then swung himself out of danger up a tree. Bellalise ran off after getting sight of the young ones; they were four in number, about the size of a Muskrat, and pure white. Their eyes were open. The nest was just such as a dog might make, only six inches deep and lined with a little dry grass. Scattered around were bones and fur, chiefly of Rabbits.

The second occasion was in 1905, within three miles of Chipewyan, and, as before, about the middle of May.

The nest was much like the first one; the mother saw him coming, and charged furiously, uttering a sort of coughing. He shot her dead; then captured the young and examined the nest; there were three young this time. They were white like the others.

Not far from this camp, we found a remarkable midden-yard of Lemmings. It was about 10 feet by 40 feet, the ground within the limits was thickly strewn with pellets, at the rate of 14 to the square inch, but nowhere were they piled up. At this reckoning, there

Foot of a Barren-Ground Caribou

were over 800,000, but there were also many outside, which probably raised the number to 1,000,000. Each pellet was long, brown, dry, and curved, *i.e.*, the winter type. The place, a high, dry, very sheltered hollow, was evidently the winter range of a colony of Lemmings that in summer went elsewhere, I suppose to lower, damper grounds.

After sunset, September 5, a bunch of three or four Caribou trotted past the tents between us and the Lake, 200 yards from us; Billy went after them, as, thanks to the Wolverine, we were out of meat, and at one shot secured a fine young buck.

His last winter's coat was all shed now, his ears were turning white and the white areas were expanding on feet and buttocks; his belly was pure white.

On his back and rump, chiefly the latter, were the

scars of 121 bots. I could not see that they affected the skin or hair in the least.

Although all of these Caribou seem to have the normal foot-click, Preble and I worked in vain with the feet of this dead one to make the sound; we could not by any combination of movement, or weight or simulation of natural conditions, produce anything like a "click."

That same day, as we sat on a hill, a cow Caribou came curiously toward us. At 100 yards she circled slowly, gazing till she got the wind 150 yards to one side, then up went her tail and off she trotted a quarter of a mile, but again drew nearer, then circled as before till a second time the wind warned her to flee. This she did three or four times before trotting away; the habit is often seen.

Next afternoon, Billy and I saw a very large buck; his neck was much swollen, his beard flowing and nearly white. He sighted us afar, and worked north-west away from us, in no great alarm. I got out of sight, ran a mile and a half, headed him off, then came on him from the north, but in spite of all I could do by running and yelling, he and his band (3 cows with 3 calves) rushed galloping between me and the lake, 75 yards away. He was too foxy to be driven back into that suspicious neighbourhood.

Thus we had fine opportunities for studying wild life. In all these days there was only one unfulfilled desire: I had not seen the great herd of Caribou returning to the woods that are their winter range.

This herd is said to rival in numbers the Buffalo herds of story, to reach farther than the eye can see,

and to be days in passing a given point; but it is utterly
erratic. It might arrive in early September. It was
not sure to arrive until late October, when the winter
had begun. This year all the indications were that it
would be late. If we were to wait for it, it would mean
going out on the ice. For this we were wholly unpre-
pared. There were no means of getting the necessary
dogs, sleds, and fur garments; my business was calling
me back to the East. It was useless to discuss the
matter, decision was forced on me. Therefore, without
having seen that great sight, one of the world's tremen-
dous zoological spectacles—the march in one body of
millions of Caribou—I reluctantly gave the order to
start. On September 8 we launched the *Ann Seton*
on her homeward voyage of 1,200 upstream miles.

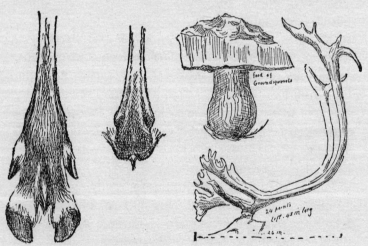

Front left foot of caribou showing
position of backward and forward
stroke when swimming

Food of groundsquirrels. Antlers
of Caribou

CHAPTER XXXIX

FAREWELL TO THE CARIBOU

ALL along the shore of Artillery Lake we saw small groups of Caribou. They were now in fine coat; the manes on the males were long and white and we saw two with cleaned antlers; in one these were of a brilliant red, which I suppose meant that they were cleaned that day and still bloody.

We arrived at the south end of Artillery Lake that night, and were now again in the continuous woods—what spindly little stuff it looked when we left it; what superb forest it looked now—and here we bade goodbye to the prairies and their Caribou.

Now, therefore, I shall briefly summarise the information I gained about this notable creature. The species ranges over all the treeless plains and islands of Arctic America. While the great body is migratory, there are scattered individuals in all parts at all seasons. The main body winters in the sheltered southern third of the range, to avoid the storms, and moves north in the late spring, to avoid the plagues of deer-flies and mosquitoes. The former are found chiefly in the woods, the latter are bad everywhere; by travelling against the wind a certain measure of relief is secured, northerly winds prevail, so the Caribou are kept travelling northward. When there is no wind, the instinctive habit of migration doubtless directs the general movement.

How are we to form an idea of their numbers? The only way seems to be by watching the great migration to its winter range. For the reasons already given this was impossible in my case, therefore, I array some of the known facts that will evidence the size of the herd.

Warburton Pike, who saw them at Mackay Lake, October 20, 1889, says: "I cannot believe that the herds [of Buffalo] on the prairie ever surpassed in size *La Foule* (the throng) of the Caribou. *La Foule* had really come, and during its passage of six days I was able to realize what an extraordinary number of these animals still roam the Barren Grounds."

From figures and facts given me by H. T. Munn, of Brandon, Manitoba, I reckon that in three weeks following July 25, 1892, he saw at Artillery Lake (N. latitude 62½°, W. Long. 112°) not less than 2,000,000 Caribou travelling southward; he calls this merely the advance guard of the great herd. Colonel Jones (Buffalo Jones), who saw the herd in October at Clinton-Colden, has given me personally a description that furnishes the basis for an interesting calculation of their numbers.

He stood on a hill in the middle of the passing throng, with a clear view ten miles each way and it was one army of Caribou. How much further they spread, he did not know. Sometimes they were bunched, so that a hundred were on a space one hundred feet square; but often there would be spaces equally large without any. They averaged at least one hundred Caribou to the acre; and they passed him at the rate of about three miles an hour. He did not know how long they were in passing this point; but at another place they were four days, and travelled day and night. The whole world seemed a moving mass of Caribou. He got the impression at last that they were standing still and he was on a rocky hill that was rapidly running through their hosts.

Even halving these figures, to keep on the safe side, we find that the number of Caribou in this army was over 25,000,000. Yet it is possible that there are several such armies. In which case they must indeed outnumber the Buffalo in their palmiest epoch. So much for their abundance to-day. To what extent are they being destroyed? I looked into this question with care.

First, of the Indian destruction. In 1812 the Chipewyan population, according to Kennicott, was 7,500. Thomas Anderson, of Fort Smith, showed me a census of the Mackenzie River Indians, which put them at 3,961 in 1884. Official returns of the Canadian government give them in 1905 at 3,411, as follows:

Peel	400
Arctic Red River	100
Good Hope	500
Norman	300
Wrigley	100
Simpson	300
Rae	800
Liard and Nelson	400
Yellowknives	151
Dogribs	123
Chipewyans	123
Hay River	114
	3,411

Of these the Hay River and Liard Indians, numbering about 500, can scarcely be considered Caribou-
eaters, so that the Indian population feeding on Caribou to-day is about 3,000, less than half what it was
100 years ago.

Of these not more than 600 are hunters. The traders
generally agree that the average annual kill of Caribou
is about 10 or 20 per man, not more. When George
Sanderson, of Fort Resolution, got 75 one year, it was
the talk of the country; many got none. Thus 20,000
per annum killed by the Indians is a liberal estimate
to-day.

There has been so much talk about destruction by
whalers that I was careful to gather all available information. Several travellers who had visited Hershell Island told me that four is the usual number
of whalers that winter in the north-east of Point Bar-
row. Sometimes, but rarely, the number is increased
to eight or ten, never more. They buy what Caribou
they can from Eskimo, sometimes aggregating 300 or
400 carcasses in a winter, and would use more if they
could get them, but they cannot, as the Caribou herds
are then far south. This, E. Sprake Jones, William
Hay, and others, are sure represents fairly the annual
destruction by whalers on the north coast. Only one
or two vessels of this traffic go into Hudson's Bay, and
these with those of Hershell are all that touch Caribou
country, so that the total destruction by whalers must
be under 1,000 head per annum.

The Eskimo kill for their own use. Franz Boas
("Handbook of American Indians") gives the number

of Eskimo in the central region at 1,100. Of these
not more than 300 are hunters. If we allow their destruction to equal that of the 600 Indians, it is liberal,
giving a total of 40,000 Caribou killed by native hunters. As the whites rarely enter the region, this is
practically all the destruction by man. The annual
increase of 30,000,000 Caribou must be several millions and would so far overbalance the hunter toll
that the latter cannot make any permanent difference.

There is, moreover, good evidence that the native
destruction has diminished. As already seen, the
tribes which hunt the Barren-Ground Caribou, number
less than one-half of what they did 100 years ago.
Since then, they have learned to use the rifle, and this,
I am assured by all the traders, has lessened the destruction. By the old method, with the spear in the
water, or in the pound trap, one native might kill 100
Caribou in one day, during the migrations; but these
methods called for woodcraft and were very laborious.
The rifle, being much easier, has displaced the spear;
but there is a limit to its destruction, especially with
cartridges at five cents to seven cents each, and, as
already seen, the hunters do not average 20 Caribou
each in a year.

Thus, all the known facts point to a greatly diminished slaughter to-day when compared with that of 100
years ago. This, then, is my summary of the Barren-
Ground Caribou between the Mackenzie River and
Hudson's Bay. They number over 30,000,000, and
may be double of that. They are in primitive conditions and probably never more numerous than now.

The native destruction is less now than formerly and never did make any perceptible difference.

Finally, the matter has by no means escaped the attention of the wide-awake Canadian government represented by the Minister of the Interior and the Royal North-west Mounted Police. It could not be in better hands; and there is no reason to fear in any degree a repetition of the Buffalo slaughter that disgraced the plains of the United States.

Barren-Ground Caribou

Old Fort Reliance in background, September 13, 1907

CHAPTER XL

OLD FORT RELIANCE TO FORT RESOLUTION

ALL night the storm of rain and snow raged around our camp on the south shore of Artillery Lake, but we were up and away in the morning in spite of it. That day we covered five portages (they took two days in coming out). Next day we crossed Lake Harry and camped three-quarters of a mile farther on the long portage. Next day, September 11, we camped (still in storm) at the Lobstick Landing of Great Slave Lake. How tropically rich all this vegetation looked after the "Land of little sticks." Rain we could face, but high winds on the big water were dangerous, so we were storm-bound until September 14, when we put off, and in two hours were at old Fort Reliance, the winter quarters of Sir George Back in 1833–4. In the Far North the word "old" means "abandoned" and the fort, abandoned long ago, had disappeared, except the great stone chimneys. Around one of these that intrepid explorer and hunter—Buffalo Jones—had built a shanty in 1897. There it stood in fairly good condition, a welcome shelter from the storm which now set in with redoubled fury. We soon had the big fireplace aglow and sitting there in comfort that we owed to him, and surrounded by the skeletons of the Wolves that he had killed about the door in that fierce winter time, we

drank in hot and copious tea the toast: "Long life
and prosperity to our host so far away, the brave old
hunter, Buffalo Jones."

The woods were beautiful and abounded with life,
and the three days we spent there were profitably
devoted to collecting, but on September 17 we

Old Fort Reliance from north

crossed the bay, made the short portage, and at night
camped 32 miles away, on the home track.

Next morning we found a camp of Indians down to
the last of their food. We supplied them with flour
and tobacco. They said that no Caribou had come to
the Lake, showing how erratic is the great migration.

In the afternoon we came across another band in
still harder luck. They had nothing whatever but
the precarious catch of the nets, and this was the off-
season. Again we supplied them, and these were
among the unexpected emergencies for which our carefully guarded supplies came in.

In spite of choppy seas we made from 30 to 35 miles
a day, and camped on Tal-thel-lay the evening of
September 20. That night as I sat by the fire the
moon rose in a clear sky and as I gazed on her calm
bright disc something seemed to tell me that at that

moment the dear ones far away were also looking on
that radiant face.

On the 21st we were storm-bound at Et-then Island,
but utilised the time collecting. I gathered a lot of
roots of *Pulsa-
tilla* and *Ca-
lypso*. Here
Billy amused
us by catching
Wiskajons in

Old Fort Reliance from east

an old-fashioned springle that dated from the days
when guns were unknown; but the captured birds
came back fearlessly each time after being released.

All that day we had to lie about camp, keeping under cover on account of the rain. It was dreary work
listening to the surf ceaselessly pounding the shore
and realising that all these precious hours were needed
to bring us to Fort
Resolution, where the
steamer was to meet
us on the 25th.

Old Fort Reliance from south

On the 23d it was
calmer and we got
away in the gray dawn
at 5.45. We were now in Weeso's country, and yet he
ran us into a singular pocket that I have called Weeso's
Trap—a straight glacial groove a mile long that came
to a sudden end and we had to go back that mile.

The old man was much mortified over his blunder,
but he did not feel half so badly about it as I did, for
every hour was precious now.

What a delight it was to feel our canoe skimming along under the four paddles. Three times as fast we trav lled now as when we came out with the bigger boat; 5½ miles an hour was frequently our rate and when we camped that night we had covered 47 miles since dawn.

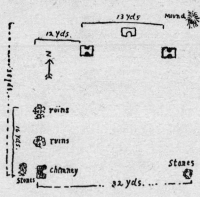

Plan of old Fort Reliance

On Kahdinouay we camped and again a storm arose to pound and bluster all night. In spite of a choppy sea next day we reached the last small island before the final crossing; and here, perforce, we stayed to await a calmer sea. Later we heard that during this very storm a canoe-load of Indians attempted the crossing and upset; none were swimmers, all were drowned.

We were not the only migrants hurrying southward. Here for the first time in my life I saw Wild Swans, six in a flock. They were heading southward and flew not in very orderly array, but ever changing, occasionally forming the triangle after the manner of Geese. They differ from Geese in flapping more slowly, from White Cranes in flapping faster, and seemed to vibrate only the tips of the wings. This was on the 23d. Next day we saw another flock of seven; I suppose that in each case it was the old one and young of the year.

As they flew they uttered three different notes: a deep horn-like *"too"* or *"coo,"* a higher pitched *"coo,"* and a warble-like *"tootle-tootle,"* or sometimes simply *"tee-tee."* Maybe the last did not come from the Swans, but no other birds were near; I suppose that these three styles of notes came from male, female, and young.

Next morning 7 flocks of Swans flew overhead toward the south-west. They totalled 46; 12 were the most in one flock. In this large flock I

Back's chimney in Buffalo Jones's cabin

saw a quarrel. No. 2 turned back and struck No. 3, his long neck bent and curled like a snake, both dropped downward several feet then 3, 4 and 5 left that flock. I suspect they were of another family.

But, later, as we entered the river mouth we had a thrilling glimpse of Swan life. Flock after flock came in view as we rounded the rush beds; 12 flocks in all we saw, none had less than 5 in it, nearly 100 Swans in sight at once, and all rose together with a mighty flapping of strong, white wings, and the chorus of the insignificant *"too-too-tees"* sailed farther southward, probably to make the great Swan tryst on Hay River.

No doubt these were the same 12 flocks as those observed on the previous days, but still it rejoiced my heart to see even that many. I had feared that the species was far gone on the trail of the Passenger Pigeon.

But this is anticipating. We were camped still on the island north of the traverse, waiting for possible water. All day we watched in vain, all night the surf kept booming, but at three in the morning the wind dropped, at four it was obviously calmer. I called the boys and we got away before six; dashing straight south in spite of rolling seas we crossed the 15-mile stretch in $3\frac{3}{4}$ hours, and turning westward reached Stony Island by noon. Thence southward through ever calmer water our gallant boat went spinning, reeling off the level miles up the river channel, and down again on its south-west branch, in a glorious red sunset, covering in one day the journeys of four during our outgoing, in the supposedly far speedier York boat. Faster and faster we seemed to fly, for we had the grand incentive that we must catch the steamer at any price that night. Weeso now, for the first time, showed up strong; knowing every yard of the way he took advantage of every swirl of the river; in and out among the larger islands we darted, and when we

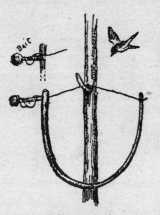

Billy's springle

should have stopped for the night no man said "Stop," but harder we paddled. We could smell the steamer smoke, we thought, and pictured her captain eagerly

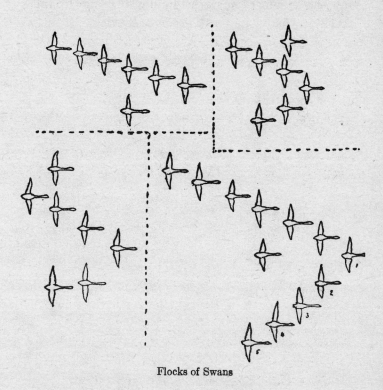

Flocks of Swans

scanning the offing for our flying canoe; it was most inspiring and the *Ann Seton* jumped up to 6 miles an hour for a time. So we went; the night came down, but far away were the glittering lights of Fort Resolution, and the steamer that should end our toil. How cheering. The skilly pilot and the lusty paddler slacked not—40 miles we had come that day—and when at last some 49, nearly 50, paddled miles brought us stiff and weary to the landing it was only to learn that the steamer, notwithstanding bargain set and agreed on, had gone south *two days before.*

CHAPTER XLI

GOING UP THE LOWER SLAVE

WHAT we thought about the steamboat official who was responsible for our dilemma we did not need to put into words; for every one knew of the bargain and its breach: nearly every one present had protested at the time, and the hardest things I felt like saying were mild compared with the things already said by that official's own colleagues. But these things were forgotten in the hearty greetings of friends and bundles of letters from home. It was eight o'clock, and of course black night when we landed; yet it was midnight when we thought of sleep.

Fort Resolution is always dog-town; and now it seemed at its worst. When the time came to roll up in our blankets, we were fully possessed of the camper's horror of sleeping indoors; but it was too dark to put up a tent and there was not a square foot of ground anywhere near that was not polluted and stinking of "dog-sign," so very unwillingly I broke my long spell of sleeping out, on this 131st day, and passed the night on the floor of the Hudson's Bay Company house. I had gone indoors to avoid the "dog-sign" and next morning found, alas, that I had been lying all night on "cat-sign."

I say lying; I did not sleep. The closeness of the room, in spite of an open window, the novelty, the

271

smells, combined with the excitement of letters from home, banished sleep until morning came, and, of course, I got a bad cold, the first I had had all summer.

Here I said "good-bye" to old Weeso. He grinned affably, and when I asked what he would like for a present said, "Send me an axe like yours." There were three things in my outfit that aroused the cupidity of nearly every Indian, the Winchester rifle, the Peterboro canoe and the Marble axe, "the axe that swallows its face." Weeso had a rifle, we could not spare or send him a canoe, so I promised to send him the axe. Post is slow, but it reached him six months later and I doubt not is even now doing active service.

Having missed the last steamer, we must go on by canoe. Canoeing up the river meant "tracking" all the way; that is, the canoe must be hauled up with a line, by a man walking on the banks; hard work needing not only a strong, active man, but one who knows the river. Through the kindness of J. McLeneghan, of the Swiggert Trading Company, I was spared the horrors of my previous efforts to secure help at Fort Resolution, and George Sanderson, a strong young half-breed, agreed to take me to Fort Smith for $2.00 a day and means of returning. George was a famous hunter and fisher, and a "good man" to travel. I marked his broad shoulders and sinewy, active form with joy, especially in view of his reputation. In one respect he was different from all other half-breeds that I ever knew—he always gave a straight answer. Ask an ordinary half-breed, or western white man, indeed, how far it is to such a point, his reply commonly is, "Oh, not so awful far," or "It is quite a piece," or "It aint such a hell of a ways," conveying to the stranger no shadow of idea whether it is a hundred yards, a mile, or a week's travel. Again and again when Sanderson was asked how far it was to a given place, he would pause and say, "Three miles and a half," or "Little more than eight miles," as the case might be. The usual half-breed when asked if we could make such a point by noon would say "Maybe. I don't know. It is quite a piece." Sanderson would say, "Yes," or "No, not by two miles," according to circumstances; and his information was always correct; he knew the river "like a book."

On the afternoon of September 27 we left "Dog-town" with Sanderson in Weeso's place and began our upward journey. George proved as good as his reputation. The way that active fellow would stride along the shore, over logs and brush, around fallen trees, hauling the canoe against stream some three or four miles an hour was perfectly fine; and each night my heart was glad and sang the old refrain, "A day's march nearer home."

The toil of this tracking is second only to that of portageing. The men usually relieve each other every 30 minutes. So Billy and George were the team. If I were going again into that country and had my choice these two again would be my crew.

Once or twice I took the track-line myself for a quarter of an hour, but it did not appeal to me as a permanent amusement. It taught me one thing that I did not suspect, namely, that it is much harder to haul a canoe with three inches of water under her keel than

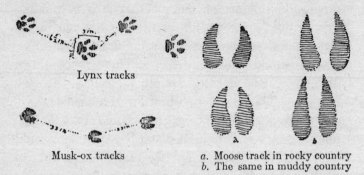

Lynx tracks

Musk-ox tracks

a. Moose track in rocky country
b. The same in muddy country

with three feet. In the former case, the attraction of the bottom is most powerful and evident. The experience also explained the old sailor phrase about the vessel feeling the bottom: this I had often heard, but never before comprehended.

All day we tracked, covering 20 to 25 miles between camps and hourly making observations on the wild life of the river. Small birds and mammals were evidently

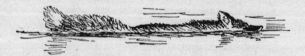

[Fox swimming Slave River.   October 4, 1907

much more abundant than in spring, and the broad, muddy, and sandy reaches of the margin were tracked over by Chipmunks, Weasels, Foxes, Lynxes, Bear, and Moose.

A Lynx, which we surprised on a sand-bar, took to the water without hesitation and swam to the mainland. It went as fast as a dog, but not nearly so fast as a Caribou. A large Fox that we saw crossing the river proved very inferior to the Lynx in swimming speed.

The two portages, Ennuyeux and Détour, were duly passed, and on the morning of October 3, as we travelled, a sailboat hove into sight. It held Messrs. Thomas Christy, C. Harding, and Stagg. We were now within 1½ days of Fort Smith, so I took advantage of the opportunity to send Sanderson back. On the evening of the 3d we came to Salt River, and there we saw Pierre Squirrel with his hundred dogs and at 1 P. M., October 4, arrived at Fort Smith.

Tracks of Blackbear, Athabaska River

CHAPTER XLII

FORT SMITH AND THE TUG

HERE again we had the unpleasant experience of sleeping indoors, a miserable, sleepless, stifling night, followed by the inevitable cold.

Next day we rode with our things over the portage to Smith Landing. I had secured the tug *Ariel* to give us a lift, and at 7 P. M., October 5, pulled out for the next stretch of the river, ourselves aboard the tug, the canoe with a cargo towed behind.

That night we slept at the saw-mill, perforce, and having had enough of indoors, I spread my blankets outside, with the result, as I was warned, that every one of the numerous dogs came again and again, and passed his opinion on my slumbering form. Next night we selected an island to camp on, the men did not want to stay on the mainland, for "the woods are full of mice and their feet are so cold when they run over your face as you sleep." We did not set up our tents that time but lay on the ground; next morning at dawn, when I looked around, the camp was like a country graveyard, for we were all covered with leaves, and each man was simply a long mound. The dawn came up an ominous rose-red. I love not the rosy dawn; a golden dawn or a chill-blue dawn is happy, but I fear the dawn of rose as the red head-light of a storm. It came; by 8.30 the rain had set in and steadily fell all day.

The following morning we had our first accident. The steamer with the loaded canoe behind was rushing up a rapid. A swirl of water upset the canoe, and all our large packs were afloat. All were quickly recovered except a bag of salted skins. These sank and were seen no more.

On October 9 we arrived at Fort Chipewyan. As we drew near that famous place of water-fowl, the long strings and massed flocks of various geese and ducks grew more and more plentiful; and at the Fort itself we found their metropolis. The Hudson's Bay Company had killed and salted about 600 Waveys or Snow Geese; each of the Loutit families, about 500; not less than 12,000 Waveys will be salted down this fall, besides Honkers, White-fronts and Ducks. Each year they reckon on about 10,000 Waveys, in poor years they take 5,000 to 6,000, in fat years 15,000. The Snow and White-fronted Geese all had the white parts of the head more or less stained with orange. Only one Blue Goose had been taken. This I got; it is a westernmost record. No Swans had been secured this year; in fact, I am told that they are never taken in the fall because they never come this way, though they visit the east end of the lake; in the spring they come by here and about 20 are taken each year. Chipewyan was Billy Loutit's home, and the family gave a dance in honour of the wanderer's return. Here I secured a tall half-breed, Gregoire Daniell, usually known as "Bellalise," to go with me as far as Athabaska Landing.

There was no good reason why we should not leave Chipewyan in three hours. But the engineer of my tug had run across an old friend; they wanted to have a jollification, as of course the engine was "hopelessly out of order." But we got away at 7 next day—my four men and the tug's three. At the wheel was a half-breed—David MacPherson—who is said to be a natural-born pilot, and the best in the country. Although he never was on the Upper Slave before, and it is an exceedingly difficult stream with its interminable, intricate, shifting shallows, crooked, narrow channels, and impenetrable muddy currents, his "nose for water" is so good that he brought us through at full speed without striking once. Next time he will be qualified to do it by night.

In the grove where we camped after sundown were the teepee and shack of an Indian (Chipewyan) Brayno (probably Brénaud). This is his hunting and trapping ground, and has been for years. No one poaches on it; that is unwritten law; a man may follow a wounded animal into his neighbour's territory, but not trap there. The nearest neighbour is 10 miles off. He gets 3 or 4 Silver Foxes every year, a few Lynx, Otter, Marten, etc.

Bellalise was somewhat of a character. About 6 feet 4 in height, with narrow, hollow chest, very large hands and feet and a nervous, restless way of flinging himself about. He struck me as a man who was killing himself with toil beyond his physical strength. He was strongly recommended by the Hudson's Bay Company people as a "good man." I liked his face and manners, he was an intelligent companion, and I was glad to have secured him.   At the first and second camps he worked hard.   At the next he ceased work suddenly and went aside; his stomach was upset.   A few hours afterwards he told me he was feeling ill.   The engineer, who wanted him to cut wood, said to me, "That man is shamming."   My reply was short: "You have known him for months, and think he is shamming; I have known him for hours and I know he is *not that kind of a man.*"

He told me next morning, "It's no use, I got my breast crushed by the tug a couple of weeks ago, I have no strength.   At Fort McKay is a good man named Jiarobia, he will go with you."

So when the tug left us Bellalise refunded his advance and returned to Chipewyan.   He was one of those that made me think well of his people; and his observations on the wild life of the country showed that he had a tongue to tell, as well as eyes to see.

That morning, besides the calls of Honkers and Waveys we heard the glorious trumpeting of the White Crane.   It has less rattling croak and more whoop than that of the Brown Crane.   Bellalise says that every year a few come to Chipewyan, then go north with the Waveys to breed.   In the fall they come back for a month; they are usually in flocks of three and four; two old ones and their offspring, the latter known by their brownish colour.   If you get the two old ones the young ones are easily killed, as they keep flying low over the place.

Is this then the secret of its disappearance? and is it

on these far breeding grounds that man has proved too hard?

At Lobstick Point, 2 P. M., October 13, the tug turned back and we three continued our journey as before, Preble and Billy taking turns at tracking the canoe.

Next day we reached Fort McKay and thus marked another important stage of the journey.

CHAPTER XLIII

FORT McKAY AND JIAROBIA

FORT McKAY was the last point at which we saw the Chipewyan style of teepee, and the first where the Cree appeared. But its chief interest to us lay in the fact that it was the home of Jiarobia, a capable river-man who wished to go to Athabaska Landing. The first thing that struck us about Jiarobia—whose dictionary name by the way is Elzear Robillard—was that his house had a good roof and a large pile of wood ready cut. These were extremely important indications in a land of improvidence. Robillard was a thin, active, half-breed of very dark skin. He was willing to go for $2.00 a day the round trip (18 days) plus food and a boat to return with. But a difficulty now appeared; Madame Robillard, a tall, dark half-breed woman, objected: "Elzear had been away all summer, he should stay home now." "If you go I will run off into the backwoods with the first wild Indian that wants a squaw," she threatened. "Now," said Rob, in choice English, "I am up against it." She did not understand English, but she could read looks and had some French, so I took a hand.

"If Madame will consent I will advance $15.00 of her husband's pay and will let her select the finest silk handkerchief in the Hudson's Bay store for a present."

In about three minutes her Cree eloquence died a

natural death; she put a shawl on her head and
stepped toward the door without looking at me. Rob
nodded to me, and signed to go to the Hudson's Bay
store; by which I inferred that the case was won;
we were going now to select the present. To my
amazement she turned from all the bright-coloured
goods and selected a large *black* silk handkerchief.

The men tell me it is always so now; fifty years ago
every woman wanted red things. Now all want black;
and the traders who made the mistake of importing
red have had to import dyes and dip them all.

Jiarobia, or, as we mostly call him, "Rob," proved a
most amusing character as well as a "good man" and
the reader will please note that nearly all of my single
help were "good men." Only when I had a crowd
was there trouble. His store of anecdote was un-
bounded and his sense of humour ever present, if
broad and simple. He talked in English, French, and
Cree, and knew a good deal of Chipewyan. Many of
his personal adventures would have fitted admirably
into the Decameron, but are scarcely suited for this
narrative. One evening he began to sing, I listened
intently, thinking maybe I should pick up some ancient *chanson* of the voyageurs or at least a woodman's "Come-all-ye." Alas! it proved to be nothing
but the "Whistling Coon."

Which reminds me of another curious experience
at the village of Fort Smith. I saw a crowd of the Indians about a lodge and strange noises proceeding
therefrom. When I went over the folk made way for
me. I entered, sat down, and found that they were

crowded around a cheap gramophone which was
hawking, spitting and screeching some awful rag-
time music. I could forgive the traders for bring-
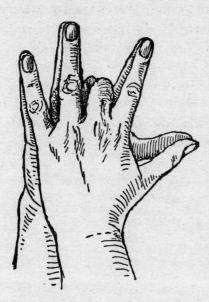
ing in the gramo-
phone, but why, oh,
why, did they not
bring some of the
simple world-wide
human songs which
could at least have
had an educational
effect? The Indian
group listened to this
weird instrument with
the profoundest grav-
ity. If there is any-
thing inherently com-
ic in our low comics
it was entirely lost on
them.

One of Rob's amusing fireside tricks was thus: He
put his hands together, so: (illustration). "Now de
tumbs is you and your fader, de first finger is you
and your mudder, ze next is you and your sister, ze
little finger is you and your brudder, ze ring finger is
you and your sweetheart. You and your fader separate easy, like dat; you and your brudder like dat, you
and your sister like dat, dat's easy; you and your
mudder like dat, dat's not so easy; but you and
your sweetheart cannot part widout all everything
go to hell first."

Later, as we passed the American who lives at Fort McMurray, Jiarobia said to me: "Dat man is the biggest awful liar on de river. You should hear him talk. 'One day,' he said, 'dere was a big stone floating up de muddy river and on it was tree men, and one was blind and one was plumb naked and one had no arms nor legs, and de blind man he looks down on bottom of river an see a gold watch, an de cripple he reach out and get it, and de naked man he put it in his pocket.' Now any man talk dat way he one most awful liar, it is not possible, any part, no how."

CHAPTER XLIV

THE RIVER

Now we resumed our daily life of tracking, eating, tracking, camping, tracking, sleeping. The weather had continued fine, with little change ever since we left Resolution, and we were so hardened to the life that it was pleasantly monotonous.

How different now were my thoughts compared with those of last Spring, as I first looked on this great river.

When we had embarked on the leaping, boiling, muddy Athabaska, in this frail canoe, it had seemed a foolhardy enterprise. How could such a craft ride such a stream for 2,000 miles? It was like a mouse mounting a monstrous, untamed, plunging and rearing horse. Now we set out each morning, familiar with stream and our boat, having no thought of danger, and viewing the water, the same turbid flood, as our servant. Even as a skilful tamer will turn the wildest horse into his willing slave, so have we conquered this river and made it the bearer of our burdens. So I thought and wrote at the time; but the wise tamer is ever alert, never lulled into false security. He knows that a heedless move may turn his steed into a deadly, dangerous monster. We had our lesson to learn.

That night (October 15) there was a dull yellow sunset. The morning came with a strong north wind and rain that turned to snow, and with it great flocks

of birds migrating from the Athabaska Lake. Many
rough-legged Hawks, hundreds of small land birds,
thousands of Snow-birds in flocks of 20 to 200, myriads
of Ducks and Geese, passed over our heads going southward before the frost.   About 8.30 the Geese began to
pass in ever-increasing flocks; between 9.45 and 10 I

Flocks of Snow-Geese passing southward

counted 114 flocks averaging about 30 each (5 to 300)
and they kept on at this rate till 2 P. M. This would give
a total of nearly 100,000 Geese.   It was a joyful thing
to see and hear them; their legions in flight array
went stringing high aloft, so high they looked not
like Geese, but threads across the sky, the cobwebs,
indeed, that Mother Carey was sweeping away with her
north-wind broom.   I sketched and counted flock after
flock with a sense of thankfulness that so many were
left alive. Most were White Geese, but a twentieth,
perhaps, were Honkers.

The Ducks began to pass over about noon, and became more numerous than the Geese as they went on.

In the midst of this myriad procession, as though they were the centre and cause of all, were two splendid White Cranes, bugling as they flew. Later that day we saw another band, of three, but these were all; their race is nearly run.

The full moon was on and all night the wild-fowl flew. The frost was close behind them, sharp and sudden. Next morning the ponds about us had ice an inch thick and we heard of it three inches at other places.

But the sun came out gloriously and when at ten we landed at Fort McMurray the day was warm and perfect in its autumnal peace.

Miss Gordon, the postmaster, did not recognise us at first. She said we all looked "so much older, it is always so with folks who go north."

Next morning we somehow left our tent behind. It was old and of little value, so we did not go back, and the fact that we never really needed it speaks much for the sort of weather we had to the end of the trip.

A couple of Moose (cow and calf) crossed the river ahead of us, and Billy went off in hot pursuit; but saw no more of them.

Tracks of animals were extremely abundant on the shore here. Large Wolves became quite numerous, evidently we were now in their country. Apparently they had killed a Moose, as their dung was full of Moose hair.

We were now in the Canyon of the Athabaska and from this on our journey was a fight with the rapids. One by one my skilful boatmen negotiated them; either we tracked up or half unloaded, or landed and portaged, but it was hard and weary work. My journal entry for the night of the 18th runs thus:

"I am tired of troubled waters. All day to-day and for five days back we have been fighting the rapids of this fierce river. My place is to sit in the canoe-bow with a long pole, glancing here and there, right, left, and ahead, watching ever the face of this snarling river; and when its curling green lips apart betray a yellow brown gleam of deadly teeth too near, it is my part to ply with might and main that pole, and push the frail canoe aside to where the stream is in milder, kindlier mood. Oh, I love not a brawling river any more than a brawling woman, and thoughts of the broad, calm Slave, with its majestic stretches of level flood, are now as happy halcyon memories of a bright and long-gone past."

My men were skilful and indefatigable. One by one we met the hard rapids in various ways, mostly by portaging, but on the morning of the 19th we came to one so small and short that all agreed the canoe could be forced by with poles and track-line. It looked an insignificant ripple, no more than a fish might make with its tail, and what happened in going up, is recorded as follows:

CHAPTER XLV

THE RIVER SHOWS ITS TEETH

"*Oct.* 20, 1907.—Athabaska River. In the Canyon. This has been a day of horrors and mercies. We left the camp early, 6.55—long before sunrise, and portaged the first rapid. About 9 we came to the middle rapid; this Billy thought we could track up, so with two ropes he and Rob were hauling us, I in bow, Preble in stern; but the strong waters of the middle part whirled the canoe around suddenly, and dashed her on a rock. There was a crash of breaking timber, a roar of the flood, and in a moment Preble and I and all the stuff were in the water.

"'My journals,' I shouted as I went down, and all the time the flood was boiling in my ears my thought was, 'My journals,'—'my journals.'

"The moment my mouth was up again above the water, I bubbled out, 'My journals,—save my journals,' then struck out for the shore. Now I saw Preble hanging on to the canoe and trying to right it. His face was calm and unchanged as when setting a mousetrap. 'Never mind that, save yourself,' I called out; he made no response, and, after all, it was safest to hang on to the canoe. I was swept into a shallow place at once, and got on my feet, then gained the shore.

" 'My journals—save them first!' I shouted to the
two boys, and now remembered with horror, how, this
very morning, on account of portaging, I had for the
first time put all three journals in the hand-bag that
had disappeared, whereas the telescope that used to
hold two of them, was floating high. It is the emergency that proves your man, and I learned that day
I had three of the best men that ever boarded a boat.
A glance showed Preble in shallow water coolly hauling in the canoe.

"Rob and Billy bounded along the rugged shores,
from one ice-covered rock to another, over piles of
drift logs and along steep ledges they went; like two
mountain goats; the flood was spotted with floating
things, but no sign of the precious journal-bag. Away
out was the grub-box; square and high afloat, it struck
a reef. 'You save the grub,' yelled Billy above the
roaring, pitiless flood, and dashed on. I knew Billy's
head was cool and clear, so I plunged into the water,
ice-cold and waist deep—and before the merciless one
could snatch it along, I had the grub-box safe. Mean-
while Rob and Billy had danced away out of sight
along that wild canyon bank. I set out after them. In
some eddies various articles were afloat, a cocoa tin,
a milk pot, a bag of rare orchids intended for a friend,
a half sack of flour, and many little things I saved at
cost of a fresh wetting each time, and on the bank,
thrown hastily up by the boys, were such bundles as
they had been able to rescue.

"I struggled on, but the pace was killing. They
were young men and dog-runners; I was left behind

and was getting so tired now I could not keep warm; there was a keen frost and I was wet to the skin. The chance to rescue other things came again and again. Twelve times did I plunge into that deadly cold river, and so gathered a lot of small truck. Then knowing I could do little more, and realising that everything man could do would be done without me, turned back reluctantly. Preble passed me at a run; he had left the canoe in a good place and had saved some bedding.

"'Have you seen my journal-bag?' He made a quick gesture down the river, then dashed away. Alas! I knew now, the one irreplaceable part of our cargo was deep in the treacherous flood, never to be seen again.

"At the canoe I set about making a fire; there was no axe to cut kindling-wood, but a birch tree was near, and a pile of shredded birch-bark with a lot of dry willow on it made a perfect fire-lay; then I opened my *waterproof* matchbox. Oh, horrors! the fifteen matches in it were damp and soggy. I tried to dry them by blowing on them; my frozen fingers could scarcely hold them. After a time I struck one. It was soft and useless; another and another at intervals, till thirteen; then, despairing, I laid the last two on a stone in the weak sunlight, and tried to warm myself by gathering firewood and moving quickly, but it seemed useless— a very death chill was on me. I have often lighted a fire with rubbing-sticks, but I needed an axe, as well as a buckskin thong for this, and I had neither. I looked through the baggage that was saved, no matches

and all things dripping wet. I might go three miles
down that frightful canyon to our last camp and maybe
get some living coals. But no! mindful of the forestry
laws, we had as usual most carefully extinguished the
fire with buckets of water, and the clothes were freezing
on my back. I was tired out, teeth chattering. Then
came the thought, Why despair while two matches
remain? I struck the first now, the fourteenth, and, in
spite of dead fingers and the sizzly, doubtful match,
it cracked, blazed, and then, oh blessed, blessed birch
bark!—with any other tinder my numbed hands had
surely failed—it blazed like a torch, and warmth at last
was mine, and outward comfort for a house of gloom.

"The boys, I knew, would work like heroes and do
their part as well as man could do it, my work was
right here. I gathered all the things along the beach,
made great racks for drying and a mighty blaze. I
had no pots or pans, but an aluminum bottle which
would serve as kettle; and thus I prepared a meal of
such things as were saved—a scrap of pork, some tea
and a soggy mass that once was pilot bread. Then sat
down by the fire to spend five hours of growing horror,
175 miles from a settlement, canoe smashed, guns gone,
pots and pans gone, specimens all gone, half our
bedding gone, our food gone; but all these things were
nothing, compared with the loss of my three precious
journals; 600 pages of observation and discovery,
geographical, botanical, and zoological, 500 drawings,
valuable records made under all sorts of trying circumstances, discovery and compass survey of the beautiful Nyarling River, compass survey of the two great

northern lakes, discovery of two great northern rivers, many lakes, a thousand things of interest to others and priceless to me—my summer's work—gone; yes, I could bear that, but the three chapters of life and thought irrevocably gone; the magnitude of this calamity was crushing. Oh, God, this is the most awful blow that could have fallen at the end of the six months' trip.

"The hours went by, and the gloom grew deeper, for there was no sign of the boys. Never till now did the thought of *danger* enter my mind. Had they been too foolhardy in their struggle with the terrible stream? Had they, too, been made to feel its power? My guess was near the truth; and yet there was that awful river unchanged, glittering, surging, beautiful, exactly as on so many days before, when life on it had seemed so bright.

"At three in the afternoon, I saw a fly crawl down the rocks a mile away. I fed the fire and heated up the food and tea. In twenty minutes I could see that it was Rob, but both his hands were empty. 'If they had found it,' I said to myself, 'they would send it back first thing, and if he had it, he would swing it aloft,' Yet no, nothing but a shiny tin was in his hands and the blow had fallen. The suspense was over, anyway. I bowed my head, 'We have done what we could.'

"Rob came slowly up, worn out. In his hand a tin of baking-powder. Across his breast was a canvas band. He tottered toward me, too tired to speak in answer to my unspoken question, but he turned and there on his back was the *canvas bag* that held the labour of all these long toilsome months.

"'I got 'em all right,' he managed to say, smiling in a weak way.

"'And the boys?'

"'All right now.'

"'Thank God!' I broke down, and wrung his hand; 'I won't forget,' was all I could say. Hot tea revived him, loosened his tongue, and I heard the story.

"'I knew,' he said, 'what was first to save when I seen you got ashore. Me and Billy we run like crazy, we see dat bag 'way out in the deep strong water. De odder tings came in de eddies, but dat bag it keep 'way out, but we run along de rocks; after a mile it came pretty near a point, and Billy, he climb on a rock and reach out, but he fall in deep water and was carried far, so he had to swim for his life. I jump on rocks anoder mile to anoder point; I got ahead of de bag, den I get two logs, and hold dem between my legs for raft, and push out; but dat dam river he take dem logs very slow, and dat bag very fast, so it pass by. But Billy he swim ashore, and run some more, and he make a raft; but de raft he stick on rock, and de bag he never stick, but go like hell.

"'Den I say, "Here, Billy, you give me yo' sash," and I run tree mile more, so far I loss sight of dat bag and make good raft. By'mebye Billy he come shouting and point, I push out in river, and paddle, and watch, and sure dere come dat bag. My, how he travel! far out now; but I paddle and push hard and bump he came at raft and I grab him. Oh! maybe I

warn't glad! ice on river, frost in air, 14 mile run on
snowy rocks, but I no care, I bet I make dat boss glad
when he see me."

"Glad! I never felt more thankful in my life! My
heart swelled with gratitude to the brave boys that
had leaped, scrambled, slidden, tumbled, fallen, swum
or climbed over those 14 perilous, horrible miles of
icy rocks and storm-piled timbers, to save the books
that, to them, seemed of so little value, but which
they yet knew were, to me, the most precious of all
my things. Guns, cameras, food, tents, bedding,
dishes, were trifling losses, and the horror of that day
was turned to joy by the crowning mercy of its close.

"'I won't forget you when we reach the Landing,
Rob!' were the meagre words that rose to my lips, but
the tone of voice supplied what the words might lack.
And I did not forget him or the others; and Robillard
said afterward, 'By Gar, dat de best day's work I ever
done, by Gar, de time I run down dat hell river after
dem dam books!'"

CHAPTER XLVI

BRIGHT AGAIN

In an hour the other men came back. The rest of the day we put in drying the things, especially our bedding. We used the aluminum bottle, and an old meat tin for kettle; some bacon, happily saved, was fried on sticks, and when we turned in that night it was with light and thankful hearts, in spite of our manifold minor losses.

Morning dawned bright and beautiful and keen. How glorious that surging river looked in its noble canyon; but we were learning thoroughly that noble scenery means dangerous travel—and there was much noble scenery ahead; and I, at least, felt much older than before this upset.

The boys put in a couple of hours repairing the canoe, then they studied the river in hopes of recovering the guns. How well the river-men seemed to know it! Its every ripple and curl told them a story of the bottom and the flood.

"There must be a ledge there," said Billy, "just where we upset. If the guns went down at once they are there. If they were carried at all, the bottom is smooth to the second ledge and they are there." He pointed a hundred yards away.

So they armed themselves with grappling-poles that had nails for claws. Then we lowered Rob in the canoe into the rapid and held on while he fished above the ledge.

"I tink I feel 'em," said Rob, again and again, but could not bring them up. Then Billy tried.

"Yes, they are there." But the current was too fierce and the hook too poor; he could not hold them.

Then I said: "There is only one thing to do. A man must go in at the end of the rope; maybe he can reach down. I'll never send any man into such a place, but I'll go myself."

So I stripped, padded the track-line with a towel and put it around my waist, then plunged in. Ouch! it was cold, and going seven miles an hour. The boys lowered me to the spot where I was supposed to dive or reach down. It was only five feet deep, but, struggle as I might, I could not get even my arm down. I ducked and dived, but I was held in the surface like a pennant on an air-blast. In a few minutes the icy flood had robbed me of all sensation in my limbs, and showed how impossible was the plan, so I gave the signal to haul me in; which they did, nearly cutting my body in two with the rope. And if ever there was a grovelling fire-worshipper, it was my frozen self when I landed.

Now we tried a new scheme. A tall spruce on the shore was leaning over the place; fifty feet out, barely showing, was the rock that wrecked us. We cut the spruce so it fell with its butt on the shore, and lodged against the rock. On this, now, Rob and Billy walked out and took turns grappling. Luck was with Rob.

In a few minutes he triumphantly hauled up the rifle and a little later the shotgun, none the worse.

Now, we had saved everything except the surplus provisions and my little camera, trifling matters, indeed; so it was with feelings of triumph that we went on south that day.

In the afternoon, as we were tracking up the last part of the Boiler Rapid, Billy at the bow, Rob on the shore, the line broke, and we were only saved from another

Gor-dn　ou-pa-que-se-Kan　ne-ma

Gordon　ʌ　flour　ʌ　his

dreadful disaster by Billy's nerve and quickness; for he fearlessly leaped overboard, had the luck to find bottom, and held the canoe's head with all his strength. The rope was mended and a safe way was found. That time I realized the force of an Indian reply to a trader who sought to sell him a cheap rope. "In the midst of a rapid one does not count the cost of the line."

At night we camped in a glorious red sunset, just above the Boiler Rapid. On the shore was a pile of flour in sacks, inscribed in Cree, "Gordon his flour."

Here it was, the most prized foreign product in the country, lying unprotected by the highway, and no man seemed to think the owner foolish. Whatever else these Indians are, they are absolutely honest.

The heavenly weather of the Indian Summer was now upon us. We had left all storms and frost behind, and the next day, our final trouble, the lack of food, was ended. A great steamer hove in sight—at least it looked like a steamer—but, steadily coming on, it proved a scow with an awning and a stove on it. The boys soon recognised the man at the bow as William Gordon, trader at Fort McMurray. We hailed him to stop when he was a quarter of a mile ahead, and he responded with his six sturdy oarsmen; but such was the force of the stream that he did not reach the shore till a quarter-mile below us.

"Hello, boys, what's up?" He shouted in the brotherly way that all white men seem to get when meeting another of their race in a savage land.

"Had an upset and lost all our food."

"Ho! that's easy fixed." Then did that generous man break open boxes, bales, and packages and freely gave without a stint, all the things we needed: kettles, pans, sugar, oatmeal, beans, jam, etc.

"How are you fixed for whiskey?" he asked, opening his own private, not-for-sale supply.

"We have none and we never use it," was the reply. Then I fear I fell very low in the eyes of my crew.

"Never use it! Don't want it! You must be pretty damn lonesome in a country like this," and he seemed quite unable to grasp the idea of travellers who would not drink.

Thus the last of our troubles was ended. Thenceforth the journey was one of warm, sunny weather and pleasant travel. Each night the sun went down in red and purple fire; and each morning rose in gold on a steel-blue sky. There was only one bad side to this, that was the constant danger of forest fire. On leaving each camp—we made four every day—I put the fire out with plenty of water, many buckets. Rob thought it unnecessary to take so much trouble. But great clouds of smoke were seen at several reaches of the river, to tell how dire it was that other campers had not done the same.

CHAPTER XLVII

WHEN NATURE SMILED

IT seems a law that every deep valley must be next a high mountain. Our sorrows ended when we quit the canyon, and then, as though in compensation, nature crammed the days with the small joys that seem so little and mean so much to the naturalist.

Those last few days, unmarred of the smallest hardship, were one long pearl-string of the things I came for —the chances to see and be among wild life.

Each night the Coyote and the Fox came rustling about our camp, or the Weasel and Woodmouse scrambled over our sleeping forms. Each morning at gray dawn, gray Wiskajon and his mate—always a pair— came wailing through the woods, to flirt about the camp and steal scraps of meat that needed not to be stolen, being theirs by right. Their small cousins, the Chicadees, came, too, at breakfast time, and in our daily travelling, Ruffed Grouse, Ravens, Pine Grosbeaks, Bohemian Chatterers, Hairy Woodpeckers, Shrikes, Tree-sparrows, Linnets, and Snowbirds enlivened the radiant sunlit scene.

One afternoon I heard a peculiar note, at first like the "*cheepy-teet-teet*" of the Pine Grosbeak, only louder and more broken, changing to the jingling of Blackbirds in spring, mixed with some Bluejay "*jay-jays*," and a Robin-like whistle; then I saw that it came from a Northern Shrike on the bushes just ahead of us. It flew off much after the manner of the Summer Shrike, with flight not truly undulatory nor yet straight, but flapping half a dozen times—then a pause and repeat. He would dive along down near the ground, then up with a fine display of wings and tail to the next perch selected, there to repeat with fresh variations and shrieks, the same strange song, and often indeed sang it on the wing, until at last he crossed the river.

Sometimes we rode in the canoe, sometimes tramped along the easy shore. Once I came across a Great Horned Owl in the grass by the water. He had a fish over a foot long, and flew with difficulty when he bore it off. Another time I saw a Horned Owl mobbed by two Wiskajons. Spruce Partridge as well as the Ruffed species became common: one morning some of the former marched into camp at breakfast time. Rob called them "Chickens"; farther south they are called "Fool Hens," which is descriptive and helps to distinguish them from their neighbours—the "Sage Hens." Frequently now we heard the toy-trumpeting and the clack of the Pileated Woodpecker or Cock-of the-Pines, a Canadian rather than a Hudsonian species. One day, at our three o'clock meal, a great splendid fellow of the kind gave us a thrill. "*Clack-clack-clack*," we heard him coming, and he bounded through the air into the trees over our camp. Still uttering his loud "*Clack-clack-clack*," he swung from tree to tree in one long festoon of flight, spread out on the up-swoop like an enormous black butterfly with white-starred wings. "*Clack-clack-clack*," he stirred the echoes from the other shore, and ignored us as he swooped and clanged. There was much in his song of the Woodpecker tang; it was very nearly the spring-time "*cluck-cluck*" of a magnified Flicker in black; and I gazed with open mouth until he thought fit to bound through the air to another woods. This was my first close meeting with the King of the Woodpeckers; I long to know him better.

Scatology of Wolf

Mammals, too, abounded, but we saw their signs rather than themselves, for most are noctur-nal. The Redsquirrels, so scarce last spring, were quite plentiful, and the beach at all soft places showed abundant trace of Weasels, Chipmunks, Foxes, Coyotes, Lynx, Wolves, Moose, Caribou, Deer. One Wolf track was of special interest. It was 5½ inches long and travelling with it was the track of a small Wolf; it vividly brought back the days of Lobo and Blanca, and I doubt not was an-other case of mates; we were evidently in the range of a giant Wolf who was travelling around with his wife. Another large Wolf track was lacking the two inner toes of the inner hind foot, and the hind foot pads were so faint as to be lost at times, although the toes were deeply impressed in the mud. This probably meant that he had been in a trap and was starved to a skeleton.

We did not see any of these, but we did see the post-graduate evidences of their diet, and were somewhat surprised to learn that it included much fruit, especially of the uva-ursi. We also saw proof that they had eaten part of a Moose; probably they had killed it.

Coyote abounded now, and these we saw from time to time. Once I tramped up within thirty feet of a

Bear-berry, or Uva-ursi

big fellow who was pursuing some zoological studies behind a log. But again the incontrovertible—post-mortem—evidence of their food habits was a surprise—the bulk of their sustenance now was berries, in one case this was mixed with the tail hairs—but no body hairs —of a Chipmunk. I suppose that Chipmunk escaped minus his tail. There was much evidence that all those creatures that can eat fruit were in good condition, but that flesh in its most accessible form—rabbits—was unknown, and even next best thing—the mice—were too scarce to count; this weighed with especial force on the Lynxes; they alone seemed unable to eke out with fruit. The few we saw were starving and at our camp of the 28th we found the wretched body of one that was dead of hunger.

On that same night we had a curious adventure with a Weasel.

All were sitting around the camp-fire at bed-time, when I heard a distinct patter on the leaves. "Something coming," I whispered. All held still, then out of the gloom came bounding a snow-white Weasel. Preble was lying on his back with his hands clasped behind his head and the Weasel fearlessly jumped on my colleague's broad chest, and stood peering about.

In a flash Preble's right elbow was down and held the Weasel prisoner, his left hand coming to assist. Now, it is pretty well known that if you and a Weasel grab each other at the same time he has choice of holds.

"I have got him," said Preble, then added feelingly, "but he got me first. Suffering Moses! the little cuss is grinding his teeth in deeper."

The muffled screaming of the small demon died away as Preble's strong left hand crushed out his life, but as long as there was a spark of it remaining, those desperate jaws were grinding deeper into his thumb. It seemed a remarkably long affair to us, and from time to time, as Preble let off some fierce ejaculation, one of us would ask, "Hello! Are you two still at it," or, "How are you and your friend these times, Preble?"

In a few minutes it was over, but that creature in his fury seemed to have inspired himself with lock-jaw, for his teeth were so driven in and double-locked, that I had to pry the jaws apart before the hand was free.

The Weasel may now be seen in the American Museum, and Preble in the Agricultural Department at Washington, the latter none the worse.

So wore away the month, the last night came, a night of fireside joy at home (for was it not Hallowe'en?), and our celebration took the form of washing, shaving, mending clothes, in preparation for our landing in the morning.

CHAPTER XLVIII

THE END

ALL that night of Hallowe'en, a Partridge drummed near my untented couch on the balsam boughs. What a glorious sound of woods and life triumphant it seemed; and why did he drum at night? Simply because he had more joy than the short fall day gave him time to express. He seemed to be beating our march of victory, for were we not in triumph coming home? The gray firstlight came through the trees and showed us lying each in his blanket, covered with leaves, like babes in the woods. The gray Jays came wailing through the gloom, a faroff Cock-of-the-Pines was trumpeting in the lovely, unplagued autumn woods; it seemed as though all the very best things in the land were assembled and the bad things all left out, so that our final memories should have no evil shade.

The scene comes brightly back again, the sheltering fir-clad shore, the staunch canoe skimming the river's tranquil reach, the water smiling round her bow, as we push from this, the last of full five hundred camps.

The dawn fog lifts, the river sparkles in the sun, we round the last of a thousand headlands. The little frontier town of the Landing swings into view once more—what a metropolis it seems to us now!—The *Ann Seton* lands at the spot where six months ago she had entered the water. Now in quick succession come the thrills of the larger life—the letters from home, the telegraph office, the hearty good-bye to the brave river-boys, and my long canoe-ride is over.

I had held in my heart the wanderlust till it swept me away, and sent me afar on the back trail of the north wind; I have lived in the mighty boreal forest, with its Red-men, its Buffalo, its Moose, and its Wolves; I have seen the Great Lone Land with its endless plains and prairies that do not know the face of man or the crack of a rifle; I have been with its count-less lakes that re-echo nothing but the wail and yodel of the Loons, or the mournful music of the Arctic Wolf. I have wandered on the plains of the Musk-ox, the home of the Snowbird and the Caribou. These were the things I had burned to do. *Was I content? Content!!* Is a man ever content with a single sip of joy long-dreamed of?

Four years have gone since then. The wanderlust was not stifled any more than a fire is stifled by giving it air. I have taken into my heart a longing, given shape to an ancient instinct. Have I not found for myself a kingdom and become a part of it? My reason and my heart say, "Go back to see it all." Grant only this, that I gather again the same brave men that manned my frail canoe, and as sure as life and strength continue *I shall go.*

APPENDICES

APPENDIX A

THE NEW NORTH-WEST

"Who cares for a few acres of snow?" said the flippant French statesman, when he found that through him Canada was lost to France; and our country has suffered ever since from this libellous jibe.

It was commonly said that no part of Canada was fit for agriculture except the extreme south of the Ontario Peninsula.

It was a surprise when the Ottawa Valley was found suitable for settlement. The Red River region was looked on as Arctic. It is not thirty years since wheat was considered a doubtful crop in what is now the banner grain-field of America. And all of this misconception was the result of a few malicious but far-reaching jeers.

How are we to get at the truth about our new North-west? How are we to make sure that we are leading none into disaster by unduly lauding a new region, and yet avoid the other extreme of ignoring a veritable Land of Promise?

There are three sure sources of light—the natural growth of the country; the scientific study of its climate and soil; the results of actual experiment.

1. The natural growth is nature's experimental farm. My notes, made while travelling through the northern part of the Peace River region, show that even near Great Slave Lake, White Poplar (*Populus tremuloides*), Balsam Poplar (*Populus balsamifera*), White Spruce (*Picea canadensis*), Black Spruce (*P. mariana*), Tamarac (*Larix americana*), Jackpine (*Pinus banksiana*) and Canoe-birch (*Betula papyrifera*) grow to perfection. Here, indeed, are great forest trees, affording the finest timber and a commercial asset of the highest importance.

Grasses of many kinds are so rich and rank on the prairies
of the Buffalo River that one may cut hay anywhere with a
horse mower. The characteristic flowers are the same as those
of central Manitoba; the Anemone, or Spring Crocus, is particularly abundant.

Early in July of 1907, while in the Salt River country, I rode
through hundreds of square miles of undulating country, which
was sparsely covered with poplar from a foot to two feet thick,
under which the ground was overgrown with pea-vine, two or
three feet high; the soil was clay loam, the land dry, and there
were brooks every mile or two; in other words, the most beautiful cattle range possible to conceive, and evidently suited
equally for agriculture.

2. A scientific study of the climate of internal America has
demonstrated the remarkable north-westward trend of the
summer isotherms, to which the north-westward trend of vegetation corresponds exactly.

The map (p. 4) shows these better than any description, and
we should remember that:

Where Balsam Poplar grows, we can grow potatoes.

Where White Poplar grows, we can grow barley.

Where Jackpine grows, we can grow wheat.

These terminal lines, it will be seen, are far beyond the
north-west part of the Peace River region. How remote,
then, from such limitation is the south part, five hundred miles
away.

Summer frost was the curse of the Ontario Peninsula at one
time, and of the Bruce Peninsula, and of southern Manitoba,
but now in these same regions, excepting in abnormal years
like 1907, it is unknown. With the opening of the country
the curse was removed. The theoretical reason is that the
ground, everywhere shaded by vegetation, cannot absorb much
of the sun's warmth and get thoroughly stored with the heat,
but ploughing the land gives it direct contact with the sun's rays
and enough heat is stored to raise the temperature a few de-
grees, enough to carry it over the danger point. This is the

theory, and, right or wrong, the fact is that in all wheat countries summer frost has fled before the plough. We are safe to
believe, therefore, that agriculture would have the effect of raising the summer temperature of this new Land of Promise.

So far as I can learn, the summer climate in general corresponds closely with that of Manitoba.

The soil is in most parts of the highest class, a rich clay loam,
of nearly level or slightly undulating surface. There are a few
small areas of sandy country and a considerable amount of
muskeg. The latter produces good timber and guarantees a
continual supply of water and range for cattle.

The length of the winter is a serious drawback—the most
serious—but I cannot learn that it differs materially from that of
Manitoba, lasting usually from the end of October to the first
of April. I make little account of the present extraordinary
season (1907)—if it damns this country, then it also damns
New England, and the whole northern tier of States, as unfit
for agriculture. Ordinarily, the rivers here are open and the
plough set free by the 20th of April.

In this lower Peace River region horses can and do, indeed,
run out all winter and dig through the snow for their food, but
no wise farmer will let them do it. All stock must be winter-
fed and housed to get satisfactory results, and in a country of
unlimited timber and hay, this is not a great difficulty.

There is another drawback, and we ought to point out and
honestly face these drawbacks as completely as we do the advantages, for the unscrupulous boomster is almost as mischiev-
ous as the unscrupulous libeller.

In summer there are mosquitoes and bull-dog flies; but they
are no worse here than in Manitoba and Minnesota, and those
who live in the country have learned to use the various expedients
of smudge and mosquito bar, and, I find, think but little about
these nuisances that force themselves so fully on the notice of
the newcomer. At other seasons there are no pests or special
diseases; the climate is, indeed, one of the most salubrious in
the world.

3. But the grand test of the country, the one that is looked to most trustfully by those agriculturally interested, is the practical one: *What has been done already?*

In travelling through this region I have made it a point to see for myself, as well as learn from all reliable sources, the results of agricultural experiments.

At Fort Resolution this year I saw potatoes, rhubarb, radishes, and other garden truck grown in perfection.

At Providence and Hay River, Bishop Breynat assured me that wheat is a regular and profitable crop. At the same place Elihu Stewart, on July 15th last, saw ripe wheat, potatoes in flower, and peas fit to use, as well as the usual garden truck.

Fort Providence is probably nearly the limit of wheat, but oats, barley, and potatoes grow much farther north. Barley was cut at Vermilion on the 24th of July, 1906. Potatoes are a good crop every year as far north as Good Hope, which is within the Arctic Circle, and everywhere the potato bug is unknown. E. A. Preble, the well-known naturalist and traveller, has given me much corroborative evidence of these statements. The result of the various testimonies I have tabulated in the most conservative manner, and present them in the accompanying map (p. 4), which, by the way, no one so far has challenged as too favourable. Messrs. Thomas Anderson and C. T. Christy, of the Hudson's Bay Company, think I have been wise and safely conservative. Bishop Breynat thinks I have been much too cautious, and that my wheat-line should be pushed up as far as the oat-line, with a corresponding advance of the others.

I do not doubt that wheat will grow in some localities even beyond the line given, as Bishop Breynat and many others say, but also there are localities within the present wheat-line where no wheat will grow. There are, indeed, places in Manitoba, Ontario, New York State, etc., not to say Peace River Valley, where for some local reason, elevation, slope, soil, etc., wheat will not grow, just as there are places in England and Ireland that cannot produce potatoes.

I think that both the Macouns are right in their descriptions of the country. Professor John Macoun says there is a great agricultural future for the Peace River Valley. James Macoun says: "True, but let us be frank about it; there are also areas on the high southern part of the Peace Uplands, where the elevation is too great for the successful growing of cereals. The northern part of the region is so low as to offset the high latitude, and offers a fine field for agriculture."

Doubtless wheat may be grown beyond the wheat-line, as I have drawn it, but there the unfavourable conditions become very frequent, and indeed the rule. There are obviously no hard and fast lines, but on the whole these shown do give us the broad facts. Each decade, however, is cutting down the time required for the growing of wheat, by providing us with hardier kinds, and thus they are extending its area.

This same is true not only of the other various staples of agriculture, but also of live stock. Breeds of cattle improved for our northern ranges have been produced, and a search of other lands has discovered two other creatures, the reindeer and the yak, whose natural habitat is a far colder region than the coldest part of that under discussion, and whose beef and other products have long been the principal wealth of other countries, where they are indigenous.

This great new province is abundantly supplied with minerals, water, timber, wild fruit, fish, fur, and game. It is, moreover, a white man's climate, one of the most salubrious in the world, and all that its detractors can say is—it is too far north, it is too cold. Which of us, they ask, would be willing to settle in a land that has admittedly four months of hard winter?

One may be sure of this: that no settler will readily leave a warm, sunny climate to go to a cold and frosty one. I do not expect that any Ontarian will cheerfully go to dwell in those northern climes. If a Floridian goes to live in Ontario, he thinks he is in a polar region, and suffers. So an Ontarian coming to Manitoba or Alberta thinks he is far enough north, and any farther would be too cold; but after a generation born to the region, their lives are adapted, and each thinks his own surroundings not only normal, but the best. I knew of a number of Ontarians that tried Manitoba for three or four years, then decided that it was too cold, and went off to Southern California, *but they all came back*, largely from the influence of the children who thought then, and still think, that the Manitoban climate is just right.

We do not, indeed, expect Manitobans to find paradise at the limit of trees, but there are in Europe thousands of Finns and Scandinavians, white men, that are familiar with a similar climate. They know the best ways of life for it—they have their summer way and their winter way—they know already how to be happy and prosperous under just such conditions, and can teach other settlers the same lesson. They would, indeed, find in the virgin possibilities of our new North-west the land of the New Hope they have so long dreamed of. How gladly they would come if only the way were opened!

And what does opening the way mean. The way for Europe is open. It is plain sailing to Edmonton. What is then needed, I think, is the railway rushed through at once. The way to open the Peace River Valley is to open the way to Peace River, and the steamboats will do the rest. Then it remains only for us to notify the man we need that we have cleared the way to the land of the New Hope.

And what is the ultimate race of the region to be? There is a zoological maxim that suggests the answer: An animal finds its highest development in the coldest part of its range where its food is abundant. How true this is of mankind! The giant races of America were from the North-west Buffalo Plains and from Patagonia. The giant race of Africa is the Zulu of the Cape; and the dwarf races the world over are from the tropics, where they are overhot, or the poles, where they are underfed. The highest product of civilisation we believe to have been the white man of northern Europe—a product indeed of the snow. This should help us to forecast the future of the North.

Henry Ward Beecher, who visited this country some twenty

years ago, said in his subsequent lectures on the Canadian North-west: "You note the class of men going in there—that means brains; you see the endless grain-lands—they mean wealth; you mark those long winter evenings—these mean time to think. There is a rare combination: brains, wealth, and time to think. I tell you there are great things coming out of the Canadian North-west. Keep your eye on Winnipeg."

Finally, if those who decry this Land of Promise would go to Europe and see there how much farther north, climatically, the arid soil is made to support a large population, they would quickly change their minds and see in their true light the possibilities of these fertile wooded plains. And they would be fortified in their new view by remembering that the words used to-day by those who condemn the Peace River, are the same as those used one hundred years ago to decry the Ontario Peninsula, and thirty years ago to condemn those parts of the North-west that are now producing the finest grain in the world.

APPENDIX B

BUFFALO SUMMARY

THE following is a summary of my observations on the Buffalo.

At Smith Landing, Thomas Kelly, purser of the *Grahame*, gave me an item from the southmost point of the range, as follows:

In October, 1903, he was camped at Rapid au Boyer on Peace River, with John Gullion and the crew of the steamer. During the night we heard the noise and trampling of a herd of Buffalo, coming to the water. It was too dark to see them, but next morning the men examined the track, and judged the herd to be about 50.

On our first Buffalo hunt we touched the extreme east point of their range, and saw 33.

On the Nyarling River we were at the north-west point of their range, and saw no Buffalo, and no fresh tracks, but plenty of signs a month old, representing, in the 3 localities, 2 Buffalo, 20, and perhaps 50, the last seen only by Bezkya.

The estimates of their numbers range from 50, by those who wish to underrate their importance, to 500, by those of the other mind.

In view of the extensive territory (100 miles by 100) on which they are scattered, and the number we saw on barely entering the range, I think 300 a safe estimate of the present number (1907).

The question is: "Why do they not increase, but rather dwindle?"

The answer, reiterated with questionable similarity, was: "The Wolves now kill all the calves, and occasionally take grownups," as though it were an entirely new habit of the Wolves to attack Buffalo.

And yet during all the days we spent in Buffalo country we found neither hair, hide, howl, nor track of a Wolf. Every river margin, every lake shore, and every mud bank did I and Jarvis and the guide search for track of a Wolf; not one did we see, and not a howl did we hear. Had there been wolves within 5 miles of us we surely would have heard them at night. At every opportunity among natives and among traders we made inquiries, and in artless contradiction of the much disseminated Wolf story, were assured that Wolves were exceedingly scarce in the region.

We saw the usual percentage of young calves of the year, so evidently the calves are not killed when very small, and to kill them when six months old, and with the herd, would take a large number of Wolves.

On the other hand, we found one ancient skeleton of Buffalo apparently not killed by hunters, and Sergeant R. Field, the Royal N. W. M. Policeman at Fort Chipewyan, believes that it is the Wolves that are keeping the Buffalo down. He is a capable man, and his opinion must receive attention. But he is 100 miles from the Buffalo country, and never has actually entered it.

Neither Major Jarvis nor Sergeant Field had such opportunity of learning from the natives as I had, *because they were officers*. These were the important points:

Sousi never dreamed of any one going to the range without killing Buffalo.

These Buffalo are as shy as a Moose. Why, if not hunted?

In January, 1900, J—— killed 5 Buffalo.

In January, 1905, S—— killed 2 by special permit.

In 1903, K—— killed 2 that he brought in, but was known to be after them all the time, and has undoubtedly killed many since.

All of the Indians whose territory includes Buffalo country, come from the hunt with plenty of pemmican; that is, neither Moose nor Caribou. But they bring no hides.

A trader at Fort Resolution, in answer to certain of my questions, said with a twinkle in his eye: "From where I now sit I see a big house where they had Buffalo tongues on the table all last winter."

Finally, when Jarvis and myself were discussing means of stopping the poaching, the chief of the tribe came out very frankly and said: "When our people made this treaty, there was nothing said about reserving the Buffalo. If you are going to take that hunting from us, we want a better treaty, more compensation, for that is part of our living."

These, then, are the conclusions I reach: There were about 300 Buffalo left in 1907; they are not increasing, partly because the Wolves kill a few calves every winter, and chiefly because the Indians pursue them regularly for food.

There are, I think, two things needed to enforce the existing law and save the remnants of Buffalo.

1st. Admit the justice of the Indians' plea and compensate them to let the Buffalo alone. On their own evidence, the value of the hunting is small.

2d. Have a Police Station on or near the Buffalo range. A Policeman 100 miles away cannot protect the Buffalo from poachers on the spot, especially when those poachers have in their favour the sentiment of the whole community.

P. S.—Since this was written (1907) I learn that the Mounted Police have demonstrated the existence of a much greater number of Buffalo than I supposed. They are chiefly about Caribou Mountain.

APPENDIX C

THE YAK—THE RANGE BEAST FOR THE NORTH-WEST

(This appeared first in *Country Life in America*, February, 1909.)

THERE exists in America a vast belt of unsettled country extending from Atlantic to Pacific, from Maine through Canada to Alaska—some four thousand miles, with an average width of more than five hundred miles, which is suited to cattle raising in every way but one—its winter is too severe.

With four months of hard frost and deep snow the ordinary range cattle cannot thrive, so that practically the north limit of cattle ranching, without winter-housing and feeding, is the south limit of the so-called Canadian fauna—not the south boundary of Canada, but a line crossing from the south end of Lake Winnipeg to the north Saskatchewan, then southward along the Rockies into the United States.

Reference to a map shows that this area is at least equal in size to all the cattle ranges hitherto utilised in America. At present, however, it is in a primitive condition, not turned to productive use, except on the edges, by lumbermen, and in general by a few trappers and Indians who need not be interfered with by any stock-raising enterprise.

Attempts to utilise this cold range have not been wanting. The American Buffalo and its various crosses with the long-haired cattle of the Highlands have been tried, but so far without satisfactory results, chiefly because of the unmanageable nature of the Buffalo. It is unreliable in temper, almost impossible to drive, and ever ready to stampede in the wrong direction.

A better solution of the problem is offered us ready-made in Asia, where they have precisely the same conditions to face. The

321

Yak or Woolly Ox (*Bos grunniens*, Linn.) has been formed by Nature for the northern ranges and has long been domesticated by man, so that the work of adapting and subduing it is already done.

Many authorities,[1] such as Prejevalsky, Kinloch, Blandford, Nott, Hooker, de Montigny, Huc, Smyth, etc., have written about the Yak, describing its many excellencies and asking why it has not been used in Europe. No one seems to have answered the question, and I venture to suggest it has not been used in Europe because there it offers no great advantages over the common cattle, cattle-ranching not being in vogue there. But in America, as we have seen, the differing conditions set a different value on the Yak.

Its native haunts are the snow-clad rocky hillsides and bare mountains of Thibet, even up to 20,000 feet above the sea, going higher, as some think, than any other animal. But experiments show that it thrives equally well near sea-level, as at Shanghai, Nice, Paris, Antwerp, and Woburn Park in England, as well as in the London Zoological Gardens.

Its native food is a coarse wiry grass (whence one of its names, *poëphagus*, or grass-eater), but the experiments at Woburn Abbey, and at the London Zoo show that it will eat anything that common cattle will eat, and that it thrives equally well on stuff that in the barnyard would be thought very poor fodder indeed.

In size the Yak resembles common cattle. Prejevalsky says the bulls are five to six feet high at the shoulder and weigh 1,000 to 1,200 pounds, but the accounts of various other authors would suggest a much greater weight. In build it is like a common ox with the hump of a Bison, but the distinguishing feature of this cold-ranger is its coat. On the upper parts generally it is three or four inches long and but little thicker than that of a well-furred Highland bull, but it lengthens on the sides, till the throat, shoulders, belly, and hams are covered with a dense hairy fringe that

---

[1] To these and the Duke of Bedford I am largely indebted for the information herein set forth.

reaches nearly to the ground. The tail is so enormously bushy, and with the hairy fringes is such a generous covering for the hocks, that it is difficult to see how any Wolf could hamstring a Yak. Thus its remarkable coat affords it an ample protection from flies in summer, frost in winter, and Wolves all the time. The coarser hair is used by the Thibetans to make strong cloth, while the finer wool is manufactured into shawls and soft carpets (*Hooker*). The wild Yak is usually brownish black; the tame ones are brown, black, piebald, or white.

Their breeding habits are like those of our range cattle. The bulls wander singly, or in groups of two or three, until the mating season, which is in winter, when they seek the cows, and after a certain amount of fuss and fighting each goes off with the half-dozen wives he has secured. When the rut is over, the cows and yearlings reunite in herds, and the bulls resume their unsociable life.

Gestation lasts nine and one-half months, as with common cattle. The calf is born in the fall and one at each birth is the rule. The cow reproduces every year, and continues to a much greater age than does the ordinary cow.

So far as is known, the Yak is not subject to any disease.

Living in a land of snow they are accustomed to eat snow in lieu of drinking water for at least half the year, but they drink much water when they can get it, and are fearless concerning rivers, etc.

Sven Hedin records that when his Yaks were attacked by a pack of dogs, which they probably took for Wolves, they promptly sprang into a pool too deep for the dogs to bottom, and there easily held their assailants at bay.

Another curious circumstance recorded in Huc's "Voyage dans la Tartare, etc., 1884–86," is thus referred to by Fortuné Nott:

"Messrs. Huc and Gabet, during their voyage, came to that river of many names, known to Europeans as Yang-tse-Kiang, or Blue River, and here a very strange sight presented itself. The river was frozen over and the party had from their encampment

observed dark, shapeless masses ranged across it, and when they
came to cross, they found these fantastic islets were nothing
more nor less than fifty wild cattle or Yak, which were absolutely
embedded in the ice. They had no doubt endeavored to swim
across the river, but it froze too quickly for them to do so, and
consequently they became hemmed in and were unable to extri-
cate themselves. Their fine heads, surmounted with their great
horns, were still above the surface, but the eagles and crows had
pecked out their eyes. The ice was so transparent that the por-
tions of their bodies which were enclosed therein were quite dis-
cernible, and the form and attitude of the unlucky beasts gave
them the appearance of still swimming." (p. 417, *Wild Animals
Described*.)

From all authorities we learn that the flesh of the Yak is
merely beef, differing, if at all, from the common cattle in being
finer grained. The veal in particular is described as excellent.

Different opinions are expressed about the milk. The Duchess of Bedford characterised what she got in India as "thin blue
stuff," but Fortuné Nott says: "Besides being good eating the
Yak yields the best of milk, for it is as rich as cream, and the
butter made from it is superior to all others." Possibly individual
differences may account for these two discrepant accounts. Or
it may be that the Duchess received her supply from the regular
milkman.

Sir J. D. Hooker is responsible for the statement that when the
calf is reduced to veal, the foot is always saved for the mother, as
she will not yield her milk unless she have at least the foot (failing
the entire stuffed skin of her young one) to lick and fondle.

The Yak is generally used as a beast of burden, and for the
saddle, in Thibet. As a pack animal it carries about the same
load as a horse of its weight. It is not liable to chafe, as its wool
protects it. It is slow, going only twenty miles a day, but is more
sure-footed than either horse or mule; indeed, in this respect it is
comparable to the goat or the mountain sheep. As a saddle
beast it presents few advantages, for besides being slow it has
usually to be led.

In its disposition it is much like the ordinary ox, which means that the cows are tractable, the steers manageable, and the bulls unreliable, sometimes dangerous. In general it seems to be an indolent, easy-going creature, ready to go slow and get fat.

Its temperamental contrast with the American Bison is illustrated by the arrangements at Woburn Park. There I saw the thirty-three American Bison in a separate, strongly fenced paddock, under ban as "dangerous," while we walked unarmed among the Yak as though among ordinary dairy cows.

The near affinity of this animal with the common cattle is shown by the fact that it can be readily crossed with any of the domestic breeds.[1] It is particularly fond of rugged hillside pastures, where it scrambles among the rocks like a goat, or grows fat on miserable wiry grass among which European stock would starve. The country along the north shore of Lake Superior would make a veritable Happyland for the Yak.

With these general facts of the country and of the beast before me, I found no difficulty in getting a sympathetic hearing on the Yak question from the very-much-alive authorities at Ottawa. I was asked to solve the question of getting a small herd to begin with, as well as full information on methods of management.

My opportunity for the last I recognized when on a visit to Woburn Abbey, where for so many years this animal has been successfully bred. The whole scheme was still further advanced when, on hearing the details of the proposed introduction, his Grace the Duke of Bedford, with characteristic generosity, presented to the Canadian Government a herd of six fine Yaks to be the breeding start for the enterprise.

These are to be handled first by the experimental farm at Ottawa. Their number will be increased by fresh importations as soon as experience shows that it is justified. Ultimately breed-

---

[1] Dr. W. T. Hornaday warns me that half-breeds are not desirable to breed from, and that all breeding stock should be of pure Asiatic blood. Hornless Yaks are either hybrids or degenerates. He says also that $200 or $300 a head would be a fair price for first-class stock.

ing stock will be sent to each of the Western and Northern state experimental stations, and thus in time we hope to effect a conquest of that great stock range which lies between the especial domains of the common cattle and the reindeer, and which at present is lying idle.

APPENDIX D

INSECTS COLLECTED BY SETON EXPEDITION, 1907

CHIEFLY ABOUT LAKE AYLMER

IDENTIFIED BY WILLIAM BEUTENMULLER, OF THE AMERICAN
MUSEUM OF NATURAL HISTORY, NEW YORK.

Thecla polios Wat.
Thecla augustus Kby.
Lycæna lygdamas Dbl.
Lycæna comyntas Godt.
Pieris sisymbri Bdv.
Pieris oleracea Harr. (winter form).
Colias elis Skrk.
Argynnis polaris Bdv.
Argynnis chariclea Schn.
Argynnis sp.
Erebia discoidalis Kby.
Chionobas macounii Edw.
Chionobas sp. (allied to *C. taygete*).
Papilio turnus L. (Arctic form).
Vanessa antiopa L.
Vanessa milberti Godt.
Pyrgus centaureæ Ramb.
Phyciodes Tharos Dru.
Drasterea erechtea (small form).

APPENDIX E

LIST OF PLANTS NOTED ON THE SETON EXPEDITION, 1907

The following list comprises only a small proportion of the plants inhabiting the region. A collection numbering about 60 species was brought back; of these, the species which are preceded by an asterisk (*) were identified by James M. Macoun, of the Canadian Geological Survey, Ottawa, Ont., and are named on his authority. Brief notes on a number of the more common species noted, but not collected, mainly trees and shrubs, are also incorporated in the list. For the names of these E. A. Preble is responsible.

Polypodium vulgare.

This widely spread fern is common on the rocks along the north shore of Kah-d'nouay Island, Great Slave Lake.

Dryopteris fragrans.

Common on the north shore of Kah-d'nouay Island, Great Slave Lake. Observed also on rocks on islands in Clinton-Colden Lake.

Cryptogramma acrostichoides.

Abundant on rocks on the island in eastern part of Great Slave Lake.

* *Carex physocarpa* Presl. Last woods, east shore, Artillery Lake, August 6.

* *Carex rigida* Good. Last woods, east shore, Artillery Lake, August 6.

* *Carex vaginata* Tausch. Last woods, east shore, Artillery Lake, August 6.

328

* *Luzula confusa* Lindeb. Last woods, east shore, Artillery Lake, August 6.

Pinus divaricata (Ait.). Du M. de C.

The Banksian pine is generally distributed in suitable places throughout the region north to Great Slave Lake. We observed it on Pike's Portage, a few miles east of the eastern extremity of this lake.

A tree near Smith Landing, 4 inches in diameter at the base, was 33 years old. Another near Fort Smith was 12 feet high, 1 inch thick at base, with 23 rings of annual growth.

Larix laricina (Du Roi) Koch.

Growing in swamps throughout the region nearly to the tree limit. One tree, at least a foot in diameter, was seen at the southern end of Artillery Lake.

On October 14, on the Athabaska below Fort McKay, we noted that the tamarack alone among the leaf shedders still bore its golden leaves.

Picea canadensis (Mill.). B. S. P.

The white spruce is generally distributed north to the tree limit. The height of one measured on an island below Fort McKay was 118 feet. A log measured near the same place was 22 inches thick at butt, 84 feet long, and 15 inches in diameter at the smaller end.

At the tree limit the white spruces, which form the bulk of the forest, attain a great age. A medium-sized one (8 feet high and 12 inches through at the butt), measured on the eastern shore of Artillery Lake at the "Last Woods," showed about 300 annual rings.

The northernmost point where we observed it was the northern shore of Aylmer Lake, near where Lockhart River enters the lake. The largest tree was about 4 inches in diameter and about the height of a man.

Picea mariana (Mill.) B. S. P.

The black spruce does not attain the size of the white spruce. It is more a tree of the muskegs, but has the same general distribution.

Populus tremuloides Michx.

The quaking aspen is common throughout the region to near the tree limit. We noted that its leaves were still green near Caribou Island, Great Slave Lake, on September 23.

Populus balsamifera Linn.

The balsam poplar attains a large size on the lower Athabaska and the Slave—at least 100 feet high. We observed it as far as the eastern extremity of Great Slave Lake, but there it is scarcely more than a shrub. Its leaves had partially turned color, near Caribou Island, on September 23.

* *Salix arctica* Pall. Last woods, east shore, Artillery Lake, August 6.

* *Salix alaxensis* (And.) Cov. Caribou Island, Great Slave Lake, July 21.

This is a widely spread species in the north, with decidedly woolly leaves and twigs.

* *Salix atra* Rydb. Caribou Island, Great Slave Lake, July 21.

* *Salix candida* Fleugge. Near Stone Island, 20 miles north of Fort Resolution, Great Slave Lake, July 17.

* *Salix chlorophylla* And. Near Stone Island, 20 miles north of Fort Resolution, Great Slave Lake, July 17.

A medium-sized willow with dark red twigs.

* *Salix myrtillifolia* And. Caribou Island, Great Slave Lake, July 21.

A species of Arctic and subarctic distribution, and especially abundant just south of the tree limit.

* *Salix niphoclada* Rydb. Last woods, east shore, Artillery Lake, August 6.

This is a medium-sized shrubby willow of quite extensive distribution

* *Salix reticulata* L. Last woods, east shore, Artillery Lake, August 6; Caribou Island, Great Slave Lake, July 21.

First seen on the subarctic islands in the eastern part of Great Slave Lake, and common from there to and beyond the tree limit.

* *Salix rostrata* Richards. Fort Smith, Mackenzie, June 22 and July 3; near Caribou Island, Great Slave Lake, July 21.

This is perhaps the commonest willow along the streams throughout the region. It is one of the several shrubs called by the natives "red willow." Its tough inner bark furnishes cordage, of which the Indians make nets and fish-lines.

Abies balsamea (Linn.). Mill.

The balsam poplar reaches a good size on the lower Athabaska, but was not observed north of the delta.

Juniperus sabina Linn.

The creeping juniper is common in suitable places, dry and usually rocky locations, throughout the wooded region. Noted at tree limit on Artillery Lake.

Juniperus nana Willd.

Similar in distribution and habit to the creeping juniper, and, like it, observed commonly at the tree limit.

Myrica gale Linn.

The sweet gale was common on the north shore of Great Slave Lake, near the Mountain Portage.

Calypso borealis Salisb. Noted on Little Buffalo River and abundant on Et-then Island in Great Slave Lake.

Betula papyrifera Marsh.

Common and of good size north to the Slave River delta, and occurring in a more or less dwarfed condition on the islands and shores of the eastern part of Great Slave Lake.

* *Betula nana* L. Last woods, east shore, Artillery Lake, August 6.

The dwarf birch was common on the islands of Great Slave Lake, as well as the large lakes to the north-eastward.

Alnus alnobetula (Ehrh.). Koch.

Common north to the tree limit. At our main camp on Artillery Lake, where this alder was common, the leaves were falling on September 4.

Alnus incana (Linn.). Willd.

Common north to Great Slave Lake. Observed at The Narrows, where it was only a few feet high. On the alluvial banks of the rivers it attains a good size. One examined on lower Slave River, 1½ inches in diameter and nearly 15 feet high, had ten rings of growth; another, 2 inches thick and 20 feet high, had 7 rings.

* *Stellaria longipes* Goldie. Fort Smith, Mackenzie, June 30; last woods, east shore, Artillery Lake, August 6.

* *Anemone multifida* Poir. Fort Smith, Mackenzie, June 30.

* *Anemone patens* L. var. *Wolfgangiana* (Bess.), Koch. Fort Smith, MacKenzie, June 30.

Common in dry situations throughout the region north at least to Great Slave Lake. It was abundant on Caribou Island.

Corydalis sempervirens (Linn.).

Common and in flower near Caribou Island on July 20.

* *Corydalis aurea* Willd. Fort Smith, Mackenzie, June 30.

This is a common plant nearly throughout the wooded country.

* *Corydalis lutea* Gilib. Fort Smith, Mackenzie, June 30.

* *Saxifrage tricuspidata* Rottb.   Last woods, east shore, Artillery Lake, August 6; near Caribou Island, Great Slave Lake, July 21.

Common on the dry banks and moss-clothed rocks of Great Slave Lake.

* *Ribes triste* Pall.   Fort Smith, Mackenzie, June 21.

* *Ribes hudsonianum* Richards.   Fort Smith, Mackenzie, June 21; near Caribou Island, Great Slave Lake, July 21.

* *Ribes setosum* Lindl.   Fort Smith, Mackenzie, June 21.

* *Rubus strigosus* Michx.   Near Caribou Islands, Great Slave Lake, July 19.

This species is quite generally distributed north to near the limit of trees.   It is of good size along the Athabaska, but is dwarfed toward its northern limit.

Rubus arcticus Linn.

This tiny single-fruited raspberry grows in the drier muskegs in the wooded country, but reaches its highest perfection on the Barren Grounds.   Some of the plants bore ripe berries on Artillery Lake on September 3, while others were still in flower.

Rubus chamœmorus Linn.

This baked-apple berry has a range similar to that of the preceding.   We noted it in flower on Caribou Island on July 20. Its fruit was ripe on Artillery Lake on September 2.

* *Potentilla multifida* L.   Fort Smith, Mackenzie, July 3.

* *Potentilla quinquefolia* Rydb.   Near Caribou Island, Great Slave Lake, July 18; Caribou Islands, Great Slave Lake, July 21.

* *Potentilla fruticosa* L.   Near Caribou Islands, Great Slave Lake, July 19.

Rather common in suitable places north to the limit of trees.

* *Amelanchier alnifolia* Nutt.   Fort Smith, Mackenzie, June 21.

We noted this shrub on Kah-d'nouay Island, Great Slave Lake.

* *Fragaria glauca* Rydb.   Fort Smith, Mackenzie, June 21.

A strawberry, apparently this species, was noted on Kah-d'nouay Island.

* *Dryas integrifolia* Vahl.   Last woods, east shore, Artillery Lake, August 6; Caribou Island, Great Slave Lake, July 21.

Found only toward the northern limit of the forest and on the Barren Grounds.

* *Rosa acicularis* Lindl.   Fort Smith, Mackenzie, July 2.

This rose reaches its perfection at the Slave River, and on the southern shores of Great Slave Lake.

* *Lathyrus ochroleucus* Hook.   Fort Smith, Mackenzie, July 2.

Prunus virginiana Linn.

Observed on the banks of the Athabaska near Fort McKay, which is near its northern limit.

* *Empetrum nigrum* L.   Last woods, east shore, Artillery Lake, August 6.

Common on Caribou Island, Great Slave Lake, where its fruit was still green on July 20.   The berries were thoroughly ripe at the eastern end of Great Slave Lake on September 11. The berries of this shrub furnish food for many species of birds and mammals.

Elæagnus argentea Pursh.

Observed in suitable places along the Athabaska, and common on Smith Portage.

* *Shepherdia canadensis* (L.), Nutt.   Fort Smith, Mackenzie, June 22; near Caribou Island, Great Slave Lake, July 19.

Common throughout the region north to near the limit of trees.

Shepherdia argentea Nutt.

A good sized thicket of this spiny shrub, still bearing the bright red fruit, was observed on the left bank of the Athabaska, below Brule Rapid, on October 22. This thicket represents, as far as I know, the most northerly station for the species. The Indians say that the berries are much relished by bears.

* *Epilobium latifolium* L. Last woods, east shore, Artillery Lake, August 6.

* *Cornus canadensis* L. Fort Smith, Mackenzie, June 30.

Cornus stolonifera Michx.

This shrub, usually called red willow, is common nearly to the tree limit. Especially common and luxuriant along the Athabaska.

* *Pyrola secunda* L., var. *pumila* Gr. Near Caribou Island, Great Slave Lake, July 19.

* *Pyrola grandiflora* Rad. Last woods, east shore, Artillery Lake, August 6; near Caribou Island, Great Slave Lake, July 19.

* *Ledum groenlandicum* Œder. Last woods, east shore, Artillery Lake, August 6; near Caribou Island, Great Slave Lake, July 19.

This shrub, the so-called Labrador tea, is common throughout the wooded country.

* *Ledum palustre* L. Last woods, east shore, Artillery Lake, August 6; near Caribou Island, Great Slave Lake, July 19.

Common on the islands of Great Slave Lake, and to and beyond the limit of trees.

* *Rhododendron lapponicum* Wahl. Last woods, east shore, Artillery Lake, August 6; near Caribou Island, Great Slave Lake, July 19.

This beautiful shrub is not found much south of the Barren Grounds, except on the exposed and wind swept islands of Great Slave Lake.

* *Loiseleuria procumbens* (L.), Desv. Last woods, east shore, Artillery Lake, August 6.

This is a characteristic Barren Ground species.

* *Andromeda Polifolia* L. Caribou Island, Great Slave Lake, July 21.

The tiny pink bells of this dainty species dot the mossy banks of most of the islands of Great Slave Lake, and of the treeless stretches to the northward.

* *Arctostaphylos Uva-ursi* (L.), Spreng. Fort Smith, Mackenzie, June 28.

Common throughout the region north at least to the limit of trees.

* *Arctostaphylos alpina* Spreng. Last woods, east shore, Artillery Lake, August 6.

This low herbaceous shrub, now usually referred to the genus *Arctous*, was common on the islands of Great Slave Lake, and northward as far as we penetrated. Its insipid fruit was full-grown, but still green, near Caribou Island on July 20; it was fully ripe on our return in early September. Its leaves had turned to a brilliant scarlet on Clinton-Colden Lake in late August.

Oxycoccus oxycoccus (Linn.).

Observed on Caribou Island on July 21.

* *Vaccinium uliginosum* L. Last woods, east shore, Artillery Lake, August 6.

This blueberry is common north to the tree limit. Its berries were ripe on Artillery Lake on September 2.

* *Vaccinium Vitis-Idœa* L.   Fort Smith, Mackenzie, June 30; Last woods, east shore, Artillery Lake, August 6.

This shrub was in flower on Caribou Island on July 21, and its fruit was ripe at Fort Reliance on September 11.

Menganthes trifoliata Linn.   Buckbean.

This aquatic plant, of wide distribution, was observed in a small pond near Big Stone Bay, Great Slave Lake.

* *Lappula Redowskii* (Hornem.)   Greene, var. *occidentale* (S. Wats.) Rydb.   Fort Smith, Mackenzie, June 22.

* *Mentha arvensis* L., var. *canadensis* (L.), Briquet.   Fort Smith, Mackenzie.

* *Castilleja pallida* (L.), Spreng. var. *septentrionalis* (Lindl.). Gray.   Fort Smith, Mackenzie, June 22; Caribou Island, Great Slave Lake, July 21.

* *Pedicularis euphrasioides* Steph.   Last woods, east shore, Artillery Lake, August 6.

* *Pinguicula villosa* L.   Caribou Island, Great Slave Lake, July 21.

This plant, which has a slight superficial resemblance to a violet, is common on the islands of Great Slave Lake.

* *Galium boreale* L.   Fort Smith, Mackenzie, June 30.

* *Lonicera glaucescens* Rydb.   Fort Smith, Mackenzie, June 30. This shrub was not observed much north of this point.

* *Linnœa borealis* L., var. *americanus* (Forbes), Rehder.   Near Caribou Island, Great Slave Lake, July 19.

This delicate species was observed on the northern shores of Aylmer Lake, where it was still in flower on August 17.

* *Viburnum pauciflorum* Raf.   Fort Smith, Mackenzie, June 21–30.

A very common shrub along the Athabaska and Slave Rivers.

Viburnum opulus. Linn.

This so-called high-bush cranberry is common along the Athabaska to Fort McKay. The Cree halfbreeds call it "Pembina," also "Saskatoon."

* *Aster Sibiricus* L.   Caribou Island, Great Slave Lake, July 19.

* *Arnica angustifolia* Vahl.   Fort Smith, Mackenzie, July 2.

* *Senecio cymbalarioides* Nutt.   Fort Smith, Mackenzie, July 2; near Caribou Island, Great Slave Lake, July 19.

* *Taraxacum ceretophorum* DC.   Fort Smith, Mackenzie, June 22.

APPENDIX F

A LIST OF THE MAMMALS NOTED ON THE SETON EXPEDITION OF 1907.[1]

Odocoileus hemionus (Rafinesque).   Mule Deer.

This species is called the jumping deer along the Athabaska. During our northward journey we were ashore so seldom that we collected no data on the species, but while returning we had a better opportunity to see its tracks, and to get information from hunters.   Our half-breed canoeman, Elzear Robillard, of Fort McKay, told us that there are now a great many jumping deer in that vicinity, but that they had come recently.   They now extend down the Athabaska as far as Point Brulé; last winter Aleck McDonald of Fort McMurray killed five or six near the Cascade Rapid.   They frequent the higher ground, evidently disliking the muskeg country, and are most numerous near the river. The Crees call the species Ah-pe-shee Moos-oos.

While tracking up the Athabaska above Grand Rapids, we saw many tracks along the banks, especially in the vicinity of Pelican Rapid, on October 26, and above there on the following day.   We also noted tracks near Calling River on October 29, and below Athabaska Landing October 31.   Later we saw a skin in the possession of W. E. Whiteley, about twenty miles south of Athabaska Landing.

Cervus canadensis Erxleben.   Canadian Wapiti.

E. Robillard told us that Elk, or, as he called them, Reindeer ("the size of a horse, and all brown with white rumps and round

---

[1] A catalogue of the actual specimens taken (270, representing 25 species) has already been published by Dr. J. A. Allen in the *Bulletin of the American Museum of Natural History*, New York, Jan. 5, 1910, under title, "Mammals from Athabaska-Mackenzie Region of Canada," vol. XXVIII, art. II, pp. 7–11.

horns"), were common in this country twenty years ago. The last he saw was sixteen or seventeen years ago, when he met one above the Boiler Rapid. The last he knew of being killed was between Fort McMurray and Fort McKay, 9 years ago, a buck. Maurice Bouchier, of McMurray, killed it. Point la Biche is named because there were plenty of them there in old days. Just above the Cascade Rapid is an island called La Biche, because there they killed some. The Cree call it *Wawaskesew*; the French, *La Biche*.

Alces americanus Jardine. Eastern Moose.

The moose is fairly common along the Athabaska and Slave Rivers, and is occasionally found on the shores of Great Slave Lake, east to its eastern extremity. The country drained by the Little Buffalo River and its tributary, the Nyarling, is a favorite haunt of the creature, and one was killed by our Indian canoeman near the head of the latter stream on July 9. This fortunate circumstance happening at a time when our provisions were nearly exhausted, saved us from some decidedly uncomfortable days.

While we were ascending the lower Slave River on our return trip we saw many tracks, on September 28 and 29, and near Point Brulé on October 1. We next noted the species on the Athabaska above Mountain Rapid on October 18, when a female, accompanied by her well-grown calf, crossed the river some distance above us. They were pursued by one of the canoemen, but without success. During the remainder of the month, between that point and Athabaska Landing, we saw tracks practically every day, but sighted no more of the animals. Robillard told us that moose calling is practiced regularly by many of the hunters, and he himself was evidently a proficient caller.

Rangifer caribou (Gmel.). Eastern Woodland Caribou.

We saw tracks of caribou on the Athabaska, below Iron Point, on October 28, and above there on the following day. The species is said by the natives to be of quite general distribution, but is nowhere common.

Rangifer arcticus (Richardson). Barren-Ground Caribou.

As will be seen from the narrative, this caribou was abundant in all the treeless region that we visited. Its habits, present numbers, etc., are sufficiently set forth in the various foregoing chapters, especially XXXIII and XXXIX.

Bison bison athabascæ Rhoads. Wood Bison or Buffalo.

According to Robillard, about sixteen years ago 3 cow Buffalo were killed near Fort McKay, by Chrysostom Pichee, during the month of August. These 3 had roamed in the region for three years at least, and never had a mate, as no calves were ever seen with them, and they were not with calf. These were the last ever seen there.

In Appendix B, Buffalo Summary, I have given all available evidence on the present numbers of wild Buffalo in the region.

Ovibos moschatus (Zimm.). Musk-ox.

Up to within a few years ago the musk-ox was frequently found in small numbers about Aylmer and Clinton-Colden Lakes, and occasionally about Artillery Lake, but persistent hunting by the Indians during recent years has resulted in their practical extermination about these points. The old bull taken by us on the north shore of Aylmer Lake on August 16 (see Chapter XXXV) was evidently a lone straggler from the herds to the northward, where the species is still fairly abundant. The fresh tracks of another very large one were seen on the shores of Sussex Lake, the head of Back River, which takes its rise within a very short distance of Sandhill Bay on Aylmer Lake. Unmistakable evidence of the presence of the species, undoubtedly made in winter, were seen on the shore of Aylmer Lake, a few miles south of Sandhill Bay, and on the southern shore of Clinton-Colden Lake a few miles south-east of its head, on August 24. A single horn, which had apparently been lying for a number of years on the tundra, was picked up on the eastern shore of Casba Lake during our return trip. These constitute our observations concerning the recent presence of this animal, so characteristic of the Arctic Prairies.

Measurements, etc., of the bull musk-ox:

Weight, after loss of blood, waste through one day's drying, etc., all cut up, 850½ pounds; therefore surely 900 pounds live weight.

Total length, 96 inches; tail, 4 inches; length of head, 23 inches; height at shoulders, 59 inches; hind-foot, 19 inches hock to toe; front hoof, width, 5¾ inches; hind hoof, width, 4 inches; girth of belly, 92 inches; length of each horn, 25 inches; width across base of horn, 9 inches.   Eye, golden brown like that of a sheep, with a linear horizontal pupil.

Marmota monax canadensis (Erxleben).   Canadian Woodchuck.

A female specimen was collected on the large island at Fort McMurray, on May 28.   It measured: Total length, 435 mm; tail, 125; hind-foot, 75; weight 3 pounds.   We learned from Robillard that the animal is fairly common near Fort McKay.

Citellus (*Colobotis*) *parryi* (Richardson).   Parry's Ground-
    Squirrel.

This fine species was first observed near our camp at the tree limit on Artillery Lake, on August 7.   The species was abundant from that point northward around the shores of Casba, Clinton-Colden, and Aylmer Lakes.   A large series was collected, but the skins, unfortunately, were lost by the upsetting of a canoe on our homeward trip.   The following description is of an adult female, collected at our camp on Artillery Lake in early September.

Adult female, length, 14½ in.; tail, 4 in.; hind-foot, $2\frac{3}{16}$ in.; weight, 1¾ lbs.   Head, legs, and under parts generally of a pale orange brown, or rich orange buff, darker on forehead, and nearly white on chin and eyelids; on the nape and sides this colour melts into the mantle of brownish gray, covered with little whitish spots, each as big as a small pea, each with a dusky edge above and below it.   The under side of the tail is deep orange, except the tip, which is black for 1½ in.; the upper side of tail is all black, except base and tipping at sides and end, which are buffy, the same as the body colour. The teeth are yellow (in the young they are white).

Citellus (*Ictidomys*) *tridecemlineatus* (Mitchill). Thirteen-lined
  Spermophile.

The little striped ground-squirrel is apparently not found farther north than the vicinity of Athabaska Landing. We found it common on the road about ten miles south of that point, on May 13.

Eutamias borealis (Allen). Liard River Chipmunk.

The chipmunk is generally distributed wherever there are suitable places throughout the region covered during our journey north to Great Slave Lake. We noted it on the Athabaska, a short distance below Athabaska Landing, on May 18. It was fairly abundant in the vicinity of Fort Smith, where a specimen was taken on June 15. It measured: length, 210; tail, 96; hindfoot, 30. At Fort Resolution, on September 27, Seton saw a chipmunk busily engaged in gathering the seeding of heads of a species of grass which grows abundantly about the post. One was noted on Slave River, near Point Ennuyeux, on September 29, and another, the last one seen on the Athabaska near Middle Rapid, on October 20.

Sciurus hudsonicus Erxleben. Hudson Bay Red-Squirrel.

The red-squirrel is quite generally distributed through the wooded country, excepting the extreme northern edge of the timber, where it is usually absent, or if found, is rare. During the summer of 1907, however, it was much less abundant than usual. It was occasionally noted during our northward journey, but was much less common in the fall during our homeward trip. The stomach of one taken at Fort Reliance, at the eastern extremity of Great Slave Lake, on September 16, contained the seeds of spruce and fragments of mushrooms. A male from Fort Reliance measured: length, 336; tail, 147; hind-foot, 53.

Sciuropterus sabrinus (Shaw).   Hudson Bay Flying Squirrel.

The flying squirrel was not observed by us during the trip, but the skin of one was given us by J. McLenaghen, of Fort Resolution.   He stated that the squirrels are occasionally taken in marten traps, but are rare.

Peromyscus arcticus (Mearns).   Arctic White-footed Mouse.

This species is quite generally distributed throughout the region north to Great Slave Lake, and a series of specimens was collected from the following localities: Grand Rapids and Fort McMurray, Athabaska River; Smith Landing, Fort Smith, Fort Resolution; Kah-d'nouay, Ootsingreeay, and Caribou Islands in Great Slave Lake; and Fort Reliance.

Specimens were taken at Fort Smith, between June 13 and July 1, comprising 5 adult females, containing embryos as follows: 7—7—7—5—4.

Evotomys gapperi athabascæ Preble.   Athabaska Red-backed Mouse.

This species, described from specimens taken at Fort Smith, is common north to Great Slave Lake.   We collected specimens at Grand Rapids, Fort McMurray, Fort Smith, Kah-d'nouay Island (a female, containing eight small embryos, July 19), and Caribou Island.   The last two localities represent extensions of the range of the animal, which were unrecorded previously to the eastward of Fort Resolution.

Evotomys dawsoni Merriam.   Dawson Red-backed Mouse.

This species replaces the Athabaska red-backed mouse, according to our observations, from the eastern extremity of Great Slave Lake, north at least to the northern shore of Aylmer Lake. Specimens were taken at the following points: Fort Reliance, Burr Lake on Pike's Portage, Artillery Lake at the tree limit, and at its head, head of Casba Lake, near the south end of Clinton-Colden Lake, outlet of Aylmer Lake, western end of Aylmer Lake, north shore of Aylmer Lake, and at Sandhill Bay.

Lemmus trimucronatus (Richardson).   Back Lemming.

This interesting species, which was described by Richardson from specimens taken at Point Lake, near the head of Coppermine River, was found by us near our camp at the tree limit on Artillery Lake, and was collected also at the following points to the northward: head of Casba Lake, outlet of Aylmer Lake, north shore of Aylmer Lake and Sandhill Bay. The series collected comprise the first specimens taken anywhere in the region of the type locality since the days of Richardson.

An adult male, taken on the north shore of Aylmer Lake, August 17, measured: length, 158; tail, 24; hind-foot, 20. An adult female, same place and date, contained four embryos.

Dicrostonyx richardsoni Merriam.   Richardson's Lemming.

A few specimens of this interesting species were collected from the following points: Artillery Lake at the tree limit and the outlet of Aylmer Lake.

Microtus (*Microtus*) *drummondi* (Aud. and Bach.).   Drummond Vole.

Specimens of this widely distributed species were taken at the following points: Near Fort McKay, Slave River, twenty miles below Peace River, Fort Smith, Fort Resolution, north shore of Great Slave Lake, near Mountain Portage, Fort Reliance, Burr Lake, on Pike's Portage, Artillery Lake at the tree limit, and Aylmer Lake (north shore and Sandhill Bay). Specimens containing embryos were obtained as follows: Fort McKay, May 31, five large embryos; Slave River, twenty miles below Peace River, 5—6—7 embryos, respectively; Fort Smith, June 14, nine large embryos.

Fiber zibethicus spatulatus Osgood.   Northwest Muskrat.

The muskrat is generally distributed throughout the region north to near the tree limit, but, like most of the small mammals, was unusually rare during the summer of 1907. The only place where we saw the animal in any numbers was the delta of the

Slave River. Here we saw one or two during the evening of July 17, and again noted several on our return trip on September 25. (See Chapter XV.)

The species multiplies in cycles as does the rabbit, reaching great numbers, and then dying, some think of a disease; but others say the mortality is due chiefly to weather conditions. Thus wet weather after the ice comes causes high water over the ice. The rats are forced out on the ice to wander in search of a new pond with available food and are exposed to countless dangers. T. Anderson has known 8 killed in one day as they were running on the ice; this was in February. Low water is equally dangerous, for the ponds then freeze to the bottom and the rats starve in their lodges, or, as before, are forced out to travel in search of water. G. Daniels found as many as 10 or 15 dead in the lodges in one colony during 1905. If overtaken when crossing the open country, the muskrat usually turns and fights desperately.

They are much preyed on by mink, but commonly escape by diving. A rat can swim 100 yards under water, a mink not more than a third as far.

Castor canadensis Kuhl.   Canadian Beaver.

The beaver is generally distributed throughout the region covered on our trip north to near the tree limit, but has been nearly exterminated from most of the region by persistent trapping. The only point where we found it at all common was the Nyarling, where we saw many burrows and houses and a number of the animals. We were told that the species is now increasing on the lower Athabaska.

Erethizon dorsatum (Linn.).   Canada Porcupine.

The porcupine, originally rather common throughout the region, has lately become rarer in most places. We saw none, but obtained a number of notes from Indians and others regarding its recent occurrence. Robillard told us that he had killed a porcupine at a point about twenty miles east of Fort McKay, where they were plentiful.   He described the country there as sandy and grown up to jackpine.   Gregoire Daniels of Fort Chipewyan informed us that the animals are still common on the south side of Lake Athabaska to the eastward of the mouth of the river.   He has seen three or four during a day's hunt there.   On one occasion he saw an old one accompanied by two young.   He describes them as being very small, jet black in color, with long thick tails.   George Sanderson of Fort Resolution, another of our canoemen, told us that he killed two porcupines in 1906 at Rocher River on the south side of Great Slave Lake, fifteen miles east of Stony Island.   At Fort Resolution we saw a skin in the possession of J. McLenaghen, which had been taken at The Narrows of Great Slave Lake.

Murdo McKay says he has often found bears with porcupine quills in paws and legs, but never saw much injury from them or heard of a bear killed by a porcupine.

Lepus americanus Erxleben. Hudson Bay Varying Hare. White Rabbit.

This species, which is found by thousands throughout the region during the years of its abundance, was so nearly absent during the season of 1907 that many natives, who had been in the woods daily during the summer, had not seen one, and we failed to observe a single rabbit during the six months we spent in the region.   Signs indicating abundance during recent years were observed on the shore of Great Slave Lake, near Mountain Portage, and near Fort Reliance.

Full details are given in the narrative, chapters XIV and XV.

Lepus arcticus canus Preble.   Keewatin Arctic Hare.

Although signs of Arctic hare were seen at a number of places from Artillery Lake northward, we observed only a very few of the animals.   We saw one on a large island, near the north shore of Clinton-Colden Lake, on August 11, and many tracks near the western end of the same lake on August 12.   An adult female was collected near the western extremity of Aylmer Lake on August 14. It measured: length, 625; tail, 76; hind-foot, 160. Another was seen at the western extremity of the same lake on the following day. We took another specimen, also a female, near Sandhill Bay on August 19. It measured: 570, 72, 142.

Lynx canadensis mollipilosus Stone. Northern Canada Lynx.

During our northward journey we saw lynxes on a number of occasions and collected several specimens. Although the animal was probably no more common than usual, the scarcity of the smaller animals which constitute its prey had evidently resulted in forcing the big cats to leave the depths of the woods and seek the clearings and river banks in search of food, so that they were more easily observed than usual. Several of those collected were evidently very weak from lack of food, and all were more or less emaciated. During the season at least two were found dead from starvation, one on the Athabaska, near Iron Point, and the other near the eastern extremity of Great Slave Lake. The stomach of one taken at Fort Smith on June 17 contained an adult chipmunk with four young ones a few days old; another one at Pelican Portage on May 19 had eaten a white-footed mouse (*Peromyscus arcticus*). The stomachs of most of the others were empty, or contained leather thongs, pieces of rope, or similar objects which the animals had swallowed to relieve the pangs of hunger. Full details are given in the narrative, chapter XIV.

Canis occidentalis Richardson. Gray Wolf.

The gray wolf is generally distributed throughout the wooded region but is seldom common in any locality. Judging by the tracks observed it was most common along the Athabaska between Athabaska Landing and Fort McMurray. During our return trip in the fall, tracks were seen at a number of points along this part of the river. We also noted the fresh tracks of a large wolf at Fort Reliance on September 13. The skull of a very large wolf was obtained near the mouth of Salt River.

The following are from Seton's note-book:

According to T. Anderson, wolves often kill moose on the Mackenzie. In February, 1905, he saw on the ice, thirty-four miles below Providence, the marks where a band of wolves had pulled down and devoured a moose.

Edmund Nagle, fur trader at Fort Smith, gives the two following items:

In January, 1907, at Fort Providence, a trapper named Baptiste Bouvier went out to look at his rabbit snares, when he came on the tracks of a band of half a dozen wolves, evidently attacking a cow moose. He followed half a mile and found the moose just killed; they had not begun to eat her. The wolves ran off and he brought the meat home on his dog sleigh.

Again last July (1906), when Bouvier was resting for lunch at a point twenty miles below Providence, he heard a crashing in the woods and a moose broke out of the woods and into the water, pursued by one wolf. He shot the moose but the wolf escaped. The wolves commonly kill moose by hamstringing them.

Last winter (March, 1907), on Steep-Bank River, E. Robillard says he saw a wolf running away. Then in the woods, near the bank, he found the body of a yearling cow moose fresh killed; its head was gone. He followed the back-track a long way and learned that the wolf was alone, had pursued the moose for miles, had finally disabled it by partly hamstringing it; but the moose was not overcome until at last driven over a high place where the fall crippled it. The trail had more and more blood up to the place of the kill. Here it seems the moose's throat was torn open, and the wolf had eaten until the head was off. The head was gone, he could not tell where, and did not understand why, or how; the "tripes" (entrails) of the moose were dragged for half a mile across the river.

About 1897 a large wolf appeared about Fort Smith and dogged the rabbit trappers. Wherever they went to operate, this wolf found the beat and stole their catch. At length he was poisoned by Sousi Beaulieu, and it was found that his under jaw was broken and stuck out at right angles to the upper; it was quite useless. It is supposed that he was kicked by a horse. The fall before a little white-faced sorrel mare belonging to Gerome Beaulieu had come running in with two gashes on her hip as though a wolf had tried to hamstring her, but she was very active and had known how to take care of herself; probably she broke that wolf's jaw.

The wolf was a very large one but very poor.

About 1886 E. Nagle knew of an immense wolf that ranged near Athabaska Landing. It used to travel from the Landing to the Sturgeon Creek in about ten days, and would then work back to the Landing, a distance of seventy miles; this was its regular beat. It was well known by the great size of its track and because there was no other wolf in the region.

In February, 1886, Nagle saw it on the ice (there were six inches of snow) of Athabaska River, a mile below the Landing; it was chasing a coyote. The track showed that the race had lasted for about a mile. When Nagle came up, the coyote was killed and partly devoured. He tried to shoot the wolf but it ran off. Knowing it would come back he put the coyote's body into the river, left a poisoned bait on the spot and got the wolf next morning. It was a male, 8 ft. 4 in. from nose to tail (skin). The natives said he had lived there for years making the same trip.

In February, 1907, at a place three miles west of Smith Landing, a wolf was trapped by the toes but escaped. In March he was trapped again, at a point beyond Fort Smith, fifteen miles from his first trapping, this time by the other foot, and again escaped. He had now lost toes on each foot and was well marked.

In the end of March, T. Anderson saw his fresh tracks near a house, eight miles north of Fort Smith. He was shot at Fort Smith about the last of May, this year, 1907.

In December, 1906, an Indian named Shirma shot a wolf near Smith Landing, breaking his hind leg. In the end of February Murdo Mackay trapped a wolf with a broken and healed hind leg at a place forty miles south of Smith Landing. As there is very little hunting done in this district they believe this to have been the same wolf.

T. Anderson believes that a wolf would haul in the set lines to get the fish, as described by B. R. Ross. It is well known that none but mad wolves attack man. These will even run into a tent. Mange is common at times.

Wolves were very common on Hay River last December. An Indian travelling there had a puppy dog trotting behind his sleigh; a wolf dashed out of the woods to seize the pup. The Indian fired, hitting the wolf somewhere in the head, but it ran off. The Indians went to see and found the wolf's teeth on the ice; he had hit it in the mouth blowing out all its teeth. T. Anderson believed this Indian to be telling the truth.

On the beach of the Athabaska River above Fort McMurray, October 19, I found many wolf tracks, one of immense size, 5½ x 5 wide; another smaller one, a female, by the water mark. There were also many moose tracks, and the wolves had killed a moose as their dung was full of moose hair. Not less than five wolves were in this band.

On October 30, about twenty miles below Athabaska Landing on the River, I saw a remarkable wolf track. It had lost the two inner toes of left front foot, and the hind-feet pads were so faint as to be lost at times, though the toes were deeply impressed in the mud. I took this to mean he was starved to a skeleton, probably had been in a trap.

The traders tell me that wolves are commonly tamed and used for sleigh dogs, but play out sooner than the regular train dog.

Canis occidentalis albus Sabine.   Barren-Ground Wolf.

The wolf of the Barren Grounds is referred to this form. We saw tracks on the shore of Artillery Lake, on Casba Lake, and on the north shore of Aylmer Lake. We once heard the howling of wolves on Clinton-Colden Lake, near its eastern end on August 10. At our camp at Sandhill Bay, Aylmer Lake, a large wolf was shot by William Loutit near the tent on the morning of August 22. Its length was about 5½ feet; the height at the shoulder, 28 inches; weight, 88 pounds; the color, a nearly uniform creamy white. He had been seen sneaking away from our camp at dark the evening before, and had probably remained about all night, attracted by our caribou meat.

The wolves of the Barrens are very subject to mange which kills them by leaving them naked in winter; it is supposed to be from eating too much reindeer flesh. At times also epidemic of rabies break out among them.

Canis latrans Say. Coyote.

The coyote has recently extended its range northward from the prairie country well into the woods. Ten years ago we were told that there were none of the species near Fort McKay. Five or six years ago they first appeared, and now are abundant along the Athabaska nearly down to Athabaska Lake, and extend in less numbers for some distance farther north. E. Nagle got one coyote from Fort Simpson last year, and one from Fort Liard. Inspector A. M. Jarvis of the R.N.W.M. Police, got one at Grand Détour, Great Slave River, and saw another on Salt River ten miles west of Smith Landing. It is usually called the "brush wolf." During our northward trip we collected a number of skulls from trappers' cabins along the Athabaska, and while returning up the river we saw its tracks almost daily, and frequently caught sight of the animals themselves. Signs observed along this part of the Athabaska showed that the animals had been feeding on the berries of *Arctostaphylos uva-ursi*, *Rosa*, sarsaparilla, and water insects.

Vulpes alascensis abietorum Merriam. British Columbia Red Fox.

The red fox with its colour phases, the cross, silver and black varieties, is found throughout the region north to the tree limit, being most common probably about the lower Athabaska and along Slave River. We frequently saw the tracks of foxes, and several times caught sight of one on the river banks. Besides a number of skulls we collected a fine red fox, which was swimming the Slave, below Fort Smith, on October 4. It did not see us

till quite close. It swam very slowly, head back, and tail out.
Was not nearly so fast as the Lynx, was slower even than a dog.

It was an adult male: weight, 15½lbs.; length, 3 ft. 7¾ in.;
tail, 16½; hind-foot, 7½; height at shoulder, 16 in.; snout, to ear
tip, 10 in.; tip to tip of ears when wide set, 7½ in; eye to snout,
3¼ in.; fat; no tape-worm; stomach contained quantity of fish;
legs and feathers of ruffed grouse, and a mass of hairs of mice,
and apparently of squirrel.

The following are from Seton's note-book:

Belalise says foxes are scarce this year, owing to the high water and floods all spring. The young probably were drowned. A
few years ago we could see 9 or 10 foxes a day on the open country. This year only one, or maybe none, and no young ones.

He once saw a silver fox on a small island, and landed to give
chase, though armed only with a hatchet. After a short pursuit
the fox got into a hole. He stopped up the hole with a bag, also
four others near by, and went home. Next day he returned with
spade and crowbar and dug out the fox. Its pelt brought $150.
The ground was hard frozen, and there was an inch of snow.

As interesting evidence on the life-history of the fox, I collected
the following:

Belalise says that about the 1st November, 1904, about five
miles from Chipewyan, he was out hunting when he came on
two big foxes, one a silver, one a cross, hunting mice together;
they were less than a yard apart at times, and occasionally seemed
to unite in hunting the same mouse.

George Sanderson says that he has seen *two adult foxes* travelling together in early fall.

According to T. Anderson, foxes are well known to cache eggs
when they are plentiful. They bury them in the sand, and
mark the place by urination.

Vulpes lagopus innuitus Merriam.   Continental Arctic Fox.

The Arctic fox inhabits the Barren Grounds exclusively in
summer, but in winter migrates some distance into the wooded
country. We took a specimen on the north shore of Aylmer

Lake on August 18, and a number of skulls left by trappers were picked up at Fort Reliance, at the eastern extremity of Great Slave Lake. We learned from Thomas Anderson, of Fort Smith, that the species is often taken at Fort Chipewyan, as well as at Fond du Lac, near the eastern extremity of Athabaska Lake. He stated also that the species often reaches as far south as Cree Lake, southward of Athabaska Lake.

Ursus americanus Pallas. Black Bear.

Black bears are rather common throughout the wooded part of the country. We frequently saw tracks on the muddy margins of the rivers during the summer and early fall. At Athabaska Landing, a young cub of a yellowish color was seen. It had been taken from a den which contained the mother—a black bear—and three cubs, one of which was black, and the other two yellowish. An old bear and two cubs were killed by Sousie Beaulieau, south-east of Smith Landing, about the middle of June. The mother had a large white patch on her breast, as had also each of the young. Their muzzles were brown. Both the cubs were males. Their stomachs were crammed with the buds and leaves of poplar, and the leaves and berries of *Arctostaphylos uva-ursi*.

The red berries of *Shepherdia argentea*, which we found growing on the banks of the Athabaska, below Brulé Rapid, are said to be much sought for by bears. Last year Robillard roused a bear in this thicket.

Ursus horribilis Ord. Grizzly Bear.

We learned from Thomas Anderson that a grizzly was killed two years before our visit near the Birch Mountains, fifty or sixty miles north-west of Fort McKay. They are considered very scarce in this region, though plentiful at times along Peace River.

Lutra canadensis (Schreber). The Canada Otter.

This species is of general distribution, though rare. We did not meet with it in the flesh, but saw a fine skin in possession of the Indian at Salt River village, on the Great Slave River.

G. Daniels tells me that he has seen five full grown otters together on Athabaska River, about November 15. Either this represented a large family of four young, or the father had been re-admitted to the group.

Mephitis hudsonica Richardson. Northern Plains Skunk.

We saw no skunks, but saw a portion of a skin hanging in a bush on the bank of the lower Athabaska. Gregoire Daniels, of Fort Chipewyan, informed us that the skunk is fairly common near that place. He has known as many as forty to be taken in one winter by a single trapper. He told us that when a skunk enters an Indian teepee, a not uncommon occurrence, the Indians let him alone, and keep perfectly quiet. The skunk satisfies his hunger and departs in peace. The Indians say it is better so. C. Harding, of Fort Resolution, informed us that during the autumn of 1906 a good many skunks were taken about that place, where it was formerly very rare. A few at least are now taken there every year, also at Providence.

Lutreola vison energumenos (Bangs). Western Mink.

We saw the tracks of mink on the banks of Slave River on one or two occasions, and obtained a skull on the Nyarling River. The species is generally distributed, but persistent trapping keeps it from becoming common.

Putorius cicognanii (Bonaparte). Bonaparte Weasel.

This little weasel is found only in the southern part of the region covered by our trip. A specimen, still in nearly complete summer pelage, was seen on the Athabaska, near Calling River, on October 30. Another, in complete winter pelage, was taken on the Athabaska on October 28, as recorded in the narrative, Chapter XLVII. This was a male; length, 12 in.; tail $3\frac{1}{2}$ in.; hind-foot, $1\frac{3}{4}$ in. Pure white, except that the ears were half brown, upper part of tail and a few hairs on rump were brown and of course the black tail tip. (There had been no snow whatever here this season.) The white fur around anus and penis was tinged yellow, no doubt from the glands. I doubt not the yellow stain often seen on cheeks, is from sleeping curled, with head against glands of rear.

The stomach was empty, its interior perfectly healthy, no tape-worms.

Ermine skins are now down to 12½ cents each, but about the time of King Edward's coronation they went up to 50 cents and even $1.

Putorius cicognanii richardsoni (Bonaparte). Richardson Weasel.

A skull of this weasel was picked up at a trapper's cabin at Fort McMurray. The species was elsewhere observed on but one occasion—on September 3, when we saw one on a small island, near the northern shore of Kah-d'nouay Island, Great Slave Lake.

Putorius arcticus Merriam. Tundra Weasel.

A specimen was shot among glacial boulders on the southern shore of Clinton-Colden Lake on August 29. It measured: Length, 365 mm.; tail, 110; hind-foot, 50. Male.

Near Sandhill Bay, Lake Aylmer, August 20, we found the pellet of a white owl, with the skull of a weasel in it.

Putorius rixosus Bangs. Least Weasel.

This diminutive species was met with but once. An adult female was trapped at Fort Reliance on September 15. It measured: length, 172; tail, 32; hind-foot, 21. It was taken at the corner of the old cabin in which we were camping. Following is the description of the fresh specimen:

All the upper parts, even umber brown; all below, pure white; no black on tail. The brown is much darker and grayer than that of *Putorius arcticus*; the white is without any yellow tinge. The tail is of the same brown, without any hint of a dark tip. On the face the white runs to the base of the ear and borders the upper lip; the legs are white within, brown without; the feet are white, except on the soles, where the hair is brown; eyes, black and beady; the rear view is all brown, except the narrow white lining of thighs which ends at the anus. This one was apparently young and had not borne young this year, or at all. Its body after skinning was three-fourths of an inch through the deepest part, but through the chest it was only one-half an inch. Its stomach was empty. It had come on one of our mouse-traps containing a mouse, had torn the head of it and taken it some twenty feet away, when another mouse-trap killed it. As its stomach was empty, maybe there were two weasels.

Weeso calls it Tel-ky-lay-azzy, *i. e., Little Weasel.*

Mustela americana abieticola Preble.   Hudson Bay Marten.

The marten is still taken by trappers along the Athabaska although it is much less common than formerly. We collected skulls at a deserted cabin of a trapper at Fort McMurray.

The following account of the taming of young martens was related by E. Robillard:

One year, in the early spring, near Lac la Biche, his brother-in-law, Ben Edwards, saw a marten come out of a hole under a stump. He dug in and got two little martens; these he brought up; they were as tame and playful as kittens. He had them a year and a half before they were killed by the dogs. They had a box of sand and ashes; in this they always buried their dung. They would sleep in bed with the children, under the blankets, and never got cross. They were male and female. They were cleaner than cats. They were never seen to cache food. They ate only meat and fish, or perhaps bread with grease on it. They caught mice, hunted day and night, but chiefly by night. They were free of the country, often went to the woods, but always came back. They curled up together to sleep, never quarrelled, uttered sometimes a shrill screech, and were so tame that they often crawled into one's pocket to sleep.

Mustela pennanti Erxleben.   Fisher.

The fisher is generally distributed throughout the region north to Great Slave Lake, but is nowhere common. According to

Robillard it is very rare about Fort McKay. Two, however, were taken there during the autumn of 1906. C. Harding told us that about a dozen were taken each year in the country tributary to Fort Resolution. Thomas Anderson of Fort Smith informed us that the fishers were very rare in that vicinity. An occasional one is traded from the Liard River, and in November, 1905, a small female was trapped near the mouth of the North Nahanni where it enters the MacKenzie. This was the northernmost record known to the natives to whom it was a new animal.

Gulo luscus (Linn.).   Hudson Bay Wolverene.

The wolverene was stated by Robillard, our half-breed canoeman, to be rather common in the vicinity of Fort McKay. We obtained skulls at Fort Reliance, and saw the tracks of a female and her young on several occasions near our camp at the tree limit on Artillery Lake.

Joseph Hoole, interpreter at Smith Landing, told us that he had seen the tracks of a wolverene following the track of a moose, near Moose Lake, sixty miles west of Smith Landing. The Indians say that wolverene will kill moose, following them till they begin to run in circles and go sort of crazy.

Some interesting anecdotes of the wolverene mother are given in the narrative, pages 252–254.

Sorex personatus I. Geoffroy.   Common Eastern Shrew.

A specimen of this small species was taken at Fort Smith on June 17. It is common throughout the region north to the limit of trees.

Lasiurus cinereus (Beauvois).   Hoary Bat.

This large bat was seen on but one occasion—at Fort Resolution, during the late evening of July 12. This is apparently the northernmost record for the species in this region.

APPENDIX G

LIST OF BIRDS NOTED ON THE SETON EXPEDITION OF 1907[1] BY E. T. SETON AND E. A. PREBLE.

Colymbus holbœlli (Reinhardt). Holbœll's Grebe.

This grebe was first observed at Edmonton on May 10, and several were seen and one was collected at Athabaska Landing on May 17. Next observed on October 16 on the Athabaska, near Fort McKay, during our return trip.

Colymbus auritus Linn. Horned Grebe.

The horned grebe was observed on a small pond near Sandy Creek, south of Athabaska Landing, on May 12. It was next observed on the Athabaska, near Fort McKay, May 30, and again below Fort Chipewyan on June 5. It was also noted a few miles below Fort Smith on June 24.

Gavia immer (Brunn.). Loon.

The common loon was first observed near Edmonton on May 11, and during our northward voyage was seen on the Athabaska, near Athabaska Landing, on May 13 and 15, and near Brulé Rapid, May 26. It was common on Great Slave Lake, being noted almost daily, June 18 to 26, between Fort Resolution and the eastern extremity of the lake. It was seen also on Clinton-Colden Lake, near its southern shore, on August 28. On our return trip it was seen on Great Slave Lake, near Caribou Island, on September 20 and 21, and one was observed on the Athabaska, near Calling River, on October 30. Chr. Harding informed us that numbers of loons are caught in fish nets at Fort Resolution in the spring.

[1] See also "Bird Record from Great Slave Lake Region," by E. T. Seton. "Auk," Jan., 1908, pp. 68–74.

Gavia adamsi (Gray).　Yellow-billed Loon.

The yellow-billed loon was first observed on Great Slave Lake to the eastward of Mountain Portage on July 24.　It was next seen on Artillery Lake, near its southern end, on August 1, and was again noted near the head of the lake August 7.　It was also seen on Casba Lake on August 8, and was common on Clinton-Colden Lake August 9 to 12.　We found it abundant on Aylmer Lake, noting it nearly every day, August 13 to 24.　On our return trip we again observed it on Clinton-Colden Lake, August 28 to 30, and on Artillery Lake, near the tree limit, on September 8.　It was also noted a number of times on Great Slave Lake, between Fort Reliance and The Narrows, September 14 to 19.

Gavia pacifica (Lawrence).　Pacific Loon.

The Pacific loon was first noted on Great Slave Lake to the eastward of Mountain Portage on July 24.　It was also seen near the west end of Clinton-Colden Lake on August 12, and on the eastern part of Aylmer Lake on August 13.

Gavia stellata (Pontoppidan).　Red-throated Loon.

This species was first observed among the islands of Great Slave Lake, to the west of Stony Island, on July 18, and during our journeying along the northern shore between there and the eastern extremity of the lake was observed almost daily up to July 27.　We also saw it among the lakes on the portage from Great Slave Lake to Artillery on July 27, 28, 29, and 31.　We saw one near the head of Artillery Lake on August 7, and another on Clinton-Colden Lake, August 12.　The species was common on Aylmer Lake, where it was observed nearly every day, August 12 to 26.　We noted it once or twice on Clinton-Colden and Casba Lakes in late August, and last saw it near Fort Reliance on September 15 and 18.

Stercorarius pomarinus (Temminck).　Pomarine Jaeger.

This jaeger was positively identified but once.　We observed four in the delta of the Athabaska on June 4.

Stercorarius parasiticus (Linn.).   Parasitic Jaeger.

This is the common jaeger of the region.   It was first observed near the eastern end of Great Slave Lake, where it was fairly common, July 25, 26, and 27.   It was next seen on Casba Lake, August 8, and near the southern end of Clinton-Colden Lake on the following day.   On this lake we found it rather common, August 10 to 12, and it was also observed on Aylmer Lake, August 17, 21, and 23.   Last seen on Casba Lake on August 31.

Larus argentatus Pontoppidan.   Herring-Gull.

The herring-gull is quite generally distributed over the region wherever there are lakes or good sized rivers.   It was noted on the lower Athabaska on May 29, 30, and 31; near Fort Chipewyan, June 5, and near Fort Smith on June 22, when it was apparently breeding.   We noted a few pairs about the meadows bordering the Nyarling, a branch of Little Buffalo River, on July 8 and 9.   The numerous rocky islands, which are scattered over the eastern half of Great Slave Lake, are favourite nesting places, and we observed it in greater or less numbers nearly every day, July 13 to 25, between Fort Resolution and the eastern extremity of the lake.   It was common also on Artillery Lake, where we saw it daily, August 1 to 6; on Clinton-Colden Lake, August 10 to 13, and on Aylmer Lake, August 14 to 26.   While on our return trip we noted it on Clinton-Colden Lake, August 28 and 29, and on Casba Lake, August 30 and 31, when young were observed on the wing.   It was still common and was observed daily on Artillery Lake, near the tree limit, September 3 to 8, on which last date birds of the year were observed with their parents.   During our return voyage along the northern shore of Great Slave Lake we saw it in small numbers, September 12 to 25.

Larus californicus Lawrence.   California Gull.

This gull was noted at a number of points among the islands scattered along the north shore of Great Slave Lake on July 19, 21, 24, 26, and 27.   We failed to observe it while voyaging along the lake on our return trip.

Larus brachyrhynchus Richardson.   Short-billed Gull.

This gull was first observed among the Slave River rapids, near Fort Smith, on June 22, where it was apparently breeding. We noted it also on Slave River, below Fort Smith, on July 4. About the spruce-bordered meadows along the upper Nyarling River we saw a number of breeding colonies on July 9 and 11, and we also noted it on Little Buffalo River on July 12.   It is a fairly common breeder among the islands which stud the eastern part of Great Slave Lake, and we noted it on the north side of Kah-d'nouay Island on July 19, near The Narrows on July 22, and near Red Stone Bay, where it was common, July 25.

Larus franklini Richardson.   Franklin's Gull.

This inhabitant of the northern plains was observed only on one occasion, between Edmonton and Vermilion Creek, on July 11, when we saw a pair flying back and forth over a ploughed field.

Larus philadelphia (Ord.).   Bonaparte's Gull.

The Bonaparte gull was noted on the Athabaska, near Fort McKay, on May 30, and between there and Poplar Point on June 1.

Sterna caspia Pallas.   Caspian Tern.

This tern was observed but once—in the delta of the Athabaska, June 4.   This point seems to be one of its breeding stations.

Sterna hirundo Linn.   Common Tern.

The common tern was observed on only a few occasions.   We noted it in the delta of the Athabaska, June 4; between Fort Chipewyan and Peace River, June 5, and on Great Slave Lake at the following points: north shore, near Mountain Portage, July 24, and near the eastern extremity, July 25.

Sterna paradisœa Brünnich.   Arctic Tern.

The Arctic tern was abundant and was noted daily on the lower Athabaska, between Fort McKay and Fort Chipewyan, May 31 to June 4.   We next found it common near the eastern extremity of Great Slave Lake, where we observed it July 25 and 26.   In the elevated lake country to the north-eastward we noted it as follows: Artillery Lake, at the tree limit, August 7; Clinton-Colden Lake, August 10 to 14.   It was last observed near the outlet of Aylmer Lake on August 24.

Hydrochelidon nigra surinamensis (Gmelin).   Black Tern.

The black tern was observed in small numbers along the Athabaska, below Fort McMurray, May 29, was very common near Fort McKay, May 30, and was noted in the delta of the Athabaska on June 4, and between Fort Chipewyan and Peace River on July 5.   We also saw a number on the portage between Slave River and Little Buffalo River on July 6.

Pelecanus erythrorhynchos Gmelin.   White Pelican.

Stray pelicans from the colony which nests among the Smith rapids were noted daily at Fort Smith, June 13 to 21.   On June 22 we visited the main colony, which occupied a small island at the head of the rough rapids below Mountain Portage.   The nests, which were built on the ground beneath the spruces, many of which had been killed as the result of the long continued occupancy of the island, contained from one to four eggs, most of which were on the point of hatching.   We counted seventy-seven nests within an area of a few square rods.   Other birds were seen near Fort Smith on July 2 and 4.   After we left the vicinity of this colony we observed no more pelicans until our return on October 4, when we saw a belated one, very likely a crippled bird, swimming about in the river near Fort Smith.   A specimen taken at Fort Smith on June 17 weighed thirteen pounds; the horn on its beak was only moderately developed.   It contained twelve eggs, varying in size from that of a bantam's egg to a marble. Its pouch was lined with worms firmly attached; the stomach also contained some of the same.

Mergus americanus Cassin.   Merganser.

This merganser was first observed on Lily Lake, fifty miles north of Edmonton, on May 12. We next noted it on the lower Athabaska on June 4. We saw no more of the species until our return to the Athabaska delta on October 11, when we observed four individuals.

Mergus serrator Linn.   Red-breasted Merganser.

The red-breasted merganser was noted on the Athabaska River, between Athabaska Landing and Pelican Portage, on May 18 and 19. We next noted it while voyaging among the islands scattered along the northern shore of Great Slave Lake, where we noted it between Stone Island and the Mountain Portage almost daily, July 18 to 24. We saw it also among the small lakes on Pike's Portage, July 29 and 30; on Artillery Lake, August 7; and on Casba Lake, August 8. We next noted it on our return trip across Great Slave Lake, observing it as follows: near Fort Reliance, September 18; north shore Kah-d'nouay Island, September 23 and 24. Later, while ascending the Athabaska, we saw it above Fort McKay on October 14, and above Brulé Rapid, October 23.

Anas platyrhynchos Linn.   Mallard.

This widely distributed duck was observed near Edmonton on May 10 and 11, and during our voyage down the Athabaska we noted it at various points during the latter part of May. We noted it also near Fort Chipewyan on June 4 and 5, and between Peace River and Smith Landing, June 6 and 7. It was rather common, the females now accompanied by their young, on the upper Nyarling on June 10 and 11. We did not observe it on the eastern part of Great Slave Lake nor in the lake region to the north-eastward. On our return trip, however, we observed it on lower Slave River, September 28, 29 and 30, and between

Smith Landing and Fort Chipewyan, October 7 and 8. It was one of the common ducks in the storehouses at Fort Chipewyan, and it was still common on the lower Athabaska on October 10, the last date recorded.

Mareca americana (Gmelin). Baldpate.

The baldpate was observed on the Athabaska below Pelican Portage on May 20, and in the delta of the Athabaska on June 4. It was common also on Slave River between the mouth of the Peace River and Smith Landing on June 6 and 7. While making the portage from Grand Detour on Slave River to the upper part of Little Buffalo River on June 6, we observed a number, and we saw it about the head of the Nyarling on July 11, the last date recorded.

Nettion carolinense (Gmelin). Green-winged Teal.

The green-winged teal was observed at a number of points along the Athabaska between Athabaska Landing and the mouth of the river, May 18 to June 4; and was seen also near Fort Chipewyan, June 5; and near Smith Landing, June 10. We observed it next on the Buffalo River Portage on July 6. We observed it daily, July 8 to 11, along the Nyarling, where it was a common breeder and was accompanied by young. We noted it also in the delta of the Slave River on July 17, but did not again observe it until our return to the same place on September 25. A few were noted also on the lower Slave River on September 29. The number seen in the store-houses at Fort Chipewyan in early October showed that it had been one of the common ducks during the hunting season. It was last observed on the Athabaska, near Fort McKay, on October 16.

Spatula clypeata (Linn.). Shoveller.

The shoveller, or, as it was usually called in the north, spoon-bill, was noted on only one occasion. We saw several pairs on the Athabaska between Boiler Rapid and Cascade Rapid on May 27.

Dafila acuta (Linn.). Pintail.

The pintail was observed commonly in the marshes bordering Rocher River on June 5, and on Slave River, between Fort Chipewyan and Smith Landing, on June 6 and 7.

Marila valisineria (Wilson). Canvas-back.

We did not observe the canvas-back in life, but during our return trip saw a number among the ducks which were being salted for winter use at Fort Chipewyan. The marshes about the delta of the Athabaska constitute one of its breeding stations.

Marila marila (Linn.). Scaup Duck.

These ducks were several times noted along the Athabaska, between Boiler Rapid and Fort McMurray, May 27 and 29, and were seen on the lower Athabaska on June 3 and 4. We next noted it on the Nyarling on July 9. It was next observed while we were ascending Slave River on October 1, when we noted one near Point Brulé. We also observed a flock of about twenty near Smith Landing on October 6, and noted the species on the following day. It was a common duck in the store-houses at Fort Chipewyan.

Marila affinis (Eyton). Lesser Scaup Duck.

The lesser scaup was observed in some grassy ponds on the north shore of Aylmer Lake on August 17. It was conspicuous among the ducks preserved in the store-houses at Fort Chipewyan in early October.

Clangula clangula americana Bonaparte. Golden-eye.

This fine species was observed nearly every day while we were descending the Athabaska River, May 17 to June 4. It was common also along Rocher and Slave rivers, between Fort Chipewyan and the mouth of the Peace River, June 5 and 6. We saw it also near Salt River on June 27, and near Fort Smith on June 28 and July 4. It was seen on Little Buffalo River on July 9 and 11, and near Fort Resolution on July 16. This species was next observed on our return to the Slave delta, September 25, and was seen also on lower Slave River, September 28, and near the mouth of Salt River on October 3. While ascending the Athabaska we observed several flocks on Slave River, October 11, 12 and 13.

Charitonetta albeola (Linn.). Buffle-head.

The buffle-head was observed on the Athabaska, near Fort McKay, on May 30, near the head of the Nyarling on July 11, and on Little Buffalo River on July 12. It was also a common species in the store-houses at Fort Chipewyan in early October.

Harelda hyemalis (Linn.). Old-squaw.

Migrating flocks of old-squaws were common and rather noisy on the Athabaska River, near Athabaska Landing, on May 15 and 17. This species was next observed on its breeding grounds on Artillery Lake, north of the tree limit, on August 7, on Casba Lake on August 8, and on the southern part of Clinton-Colden Lake on August 9. We found a number of birds accompanied by unfledged young on the small lakes, near the head of Back River, on August 21; and also observed the species along the south shore of Clinton-Colden Lake on August 28, and on Artillery Lake, at the tree limit, September 4. On September 10, while traversing Pike's Portage between Artillery and Great Slave Lakes, we saw flocks of this species flying southward; and we found the species common on Great Slave Lake, between its eastern extremity and Caribou Island, September 17 to 20. These were the last seen in life, but the species was common among the ducks preserved for winter use at Fort Chipewyan.

Oidemia deglandi Bonaparte. White-winged Scoter.

This species was first observed on the lower Athabaska on June 4. We next noted it on Artillery Lake, near the tree limit, on September 8, noting four; and saw it last on Great Slave Lake, near Caribou Island, on September 21.

Oidemia perspicillata (Linn.).   Surf Scoter.

The surf scoter was observed almost daily along the Atha-
baska, between Athabaska Landing and the mouth of the river,
May 15 to June 4, and a few were noted near the mouth of Peace
River on June 5.   It was observed also on Slave River, below
Fort Smith, on July 4, and on the Buffalo River Portage on
July 6.   During our voyage along the northern shore of Great
Slave Lake it was observed in numbers nearly every day, July
18 to 25.   It was not observed in the lake country to the north-
eastward, and was next noted near Fort Reliance on September
16 on the return trip.   During the next few days, while we were
paddling westward along the northern shore of Great Slave Lake,
we saw it in numbers almost daily.   We noted it also near the
mouth of Peace River on October 8, and on the lower Athabaska
on October 10.

Chen hyperboreus nivalis (Forster).   Greater Snow Goose.

The snow goose is a common migrant through the Athabaska
Lake region in spring, but had already passed northward at the
time of our northward journey.   We did not note this species,
therefore, until we reached the delta of the Slave, near Fort
Resolution, on September 25, when we noted a number.   It was
next observed on the lower Athabaska on October 10, 11, and 13.
After leaving the Athabaska delta, which is a favourite gathering
place for the species, we saw none for several days, but during
the forenoon of October 16 we saw upward of 300 flocks passing
southward, high in the air.   This marked the final exodus of
the flocks, which had lingered in the Athabaska delta until
warned of the approach of winter by a severe northern storm.
During the night we heard the migrating bands on several occasions.   A few late stragglers were seen on the Athabaska, near
Fort McMurray, on October 17, and a single one, probably a
crippled bird, near Mountain Rapid on October 18.

In the store-houses at Fort Chipewyan, which we visited on
October 9, we saw large numbers of geese, which had been shot
during the fall migration and had been salted for winter use.

Most of these were snow geese. It was estimated that upward
of 12,000 would be preserved in this settlement during the season.
The geese were reported more plentiful than had been the case
for several years, the number during an average season having
diminished very much compared with the abundance of long ago.

Chen caerulescens (Linn.). Blue Goose.

A fine specimen of this beautiful species was obtained on
October 9 at Fort Chipewyan, where it had been secured. It
had been shot in the vicinity within a week or two. It was reported to be the first one ever taken in the neighbourhood within
the experience of any of the hunters.

Chen rossi (Cassin). Ross's Goose.

This small goose, which is the latest of the snow geese to leave
the Athabaska region for the north, was observed on the Athabaska, between Fort McKay and Poplar Point, on June 1, when
we saw eight or ten flocks. Several flocks were observed in the
Athabaska delta on June 4. We did not again observe the
species until we returned to Fort Chipewyan, where on October
9 we saw large numbers preserved in the store-houses. They
had been shot in the vicinity. While ascending the Athabaska
between Mountain and Stony Rapids on October 18 a single
bird was observed and taken. It showed no wound, but was
most likely a bird which had been crippled during the fall hunt
and had been prevented from migrating with its fellows. The
following data were taken from the fresh specimen, a female:
Length, 21½ inches; alar extent, 46; wing, 14. Weight 2½
pounds. Color, pure white; primaries, all jet black; primary
coverts, gray with black ribs; head, tinged with rusty; feet, deep
carmine red; viscera, healthy; gizzard, very large and crammed
with grass.

Anser albifrons gambeli Hartlaub. White-fronted Goose.

The white-fronted goose was first noted at the western end of
Aylmer Lake, August 15, when three were seen. Others were
observed on August 16 and 17 in the vicinity of some reedy lakes

on the north shore, a few miles to the eastward. They were undoubtedly on their breeding grounds. We next saw the species in the store-houses at Fort Chipewyan on our return trip. Here several thousand are salted each year for winter use. Hunters met on the lower Athabaska on October 11 had freshly killed specimens, and the species was conspicuous among the migrating flocks which passed overhead during the forenoon of October 16, when we were ascending the Athabaska, a few miles above Fort McKay.

Branta canadensis canadensis (Linn.).   Canada Goose.

This fine species was observed on the Athabaska below Poplar Point on June 3 on its breeding grounds. We noted it also near the head of the Nyarling on July 11. We next saw the species on Great Slave Lake near Kah-d'nouay in mid-July, when a pair of birds, accompanied by their young, were seen. On our return trip we noted a flock of twenty on lower Slave River on September 28, and we saw flocks on Rocher River on October 8 and 9. It is one of the favourite food birds and was seen in large numbers in the store-houses at Fort Chipewyan, where several thousand are salted each year for winter use. We last observed it during the forenoon of October 16, when over a hundred flocks, averaging at least thirty birds each, were seen flying southward.

Branta canadensis hutchinsi (Richardson).   Hutchins's Goose.

We first noted this northern form on Artillery Lake, near the tree limit, on September 2, and, while we were making the portage from Artillery Lake to the eastern extremity of Great Slave Lake on September 9 and 10, we observed flocks flying southward. The species was next noted at Fort Chipewyan on October 9, when numbers were seen among the geese preserved for food. We noted a flock on the lower Athabaska on October 11, and saw many flocks among migrating water-fowl on October 16 when we were ascending the Athabaska above Fort McKay.

Olor columbianus (Ord). Whistling Swan.

This beautiful species, now so much diminished in numbers, was first observed on Great Slave Lake while we were paddling westward along the north side of Kah-d'nouay Island on September 23 on our return trip. Here a flock, composed of two adults and four birds of the year, probably a family party, flew overhead to the westward. A similar flock of seven was seen a few miles west of the same point on the following day. On September 25, while we were traversing the delta of Slave River, we started about eighty individuals, scattered in small flocks from the marsh bordered channels. On the evening of October 3, while encamped on Slave River, near the mouth of Salt River, we heard the soft notes of this species and we noted a few individuals in the delta of the Athabaska on October 10.

Botaurus lentiginosus (Montagu). Bittern.

The bittern was noted in the marshes bordering Little Buffalo River above Bear Creek, July 7, and in the delta of the Slave, near Fort Resolution, on July 16.

Grus americana (Linn.). Whooping Crane.

We first noted this rapidly disappearing species on the lower Athabaska on October 11, hearing its loud trumpet call in the early morning and later being favoured by a fleeting glimpse of a pair of the birds themselves. We also observed five below Fort McMurray on October 16.

Grus canadensis (Linn.). Little Brown Crane.

The brown crane is fairly common in suitable places throughout the region. We first noted the species on May 26, near Brulé Rapid, Athabaska River. On little Buffalo River and its tributary, the Nyarling, we saw a few on July 7 and 8, and on July 10, near the head of the latter stream, we observed a pair with their two young ones not yet able to fly. We noted this species also on the marsh bordering Great Slave Lake, near the mouth of Little Buffalo River, on July 12. On September 17, while at Fort Reliance, we saw the last ones of the season, noting a flock of six flying eastward.

Porzana carolina (Linn.). Sora.

The complaining notes of this marsh-loving species were heard in the swamps bordering Salt River, north-west of Fort Smith, on June 24 and 25. While making the portage from Grand Détour on Slave River to the Little Buffalo we several times heard its voice and once saw one of the little fellows running along the edge of a slough. Its familiar notes were also heard near the head of the Nyarling, July 11, and near Fort Resolution on July 16 and 17.

Coturnicops noveboracensis (Gmelin). Yellow Rail.

We did not actually see this secretive species but heard its unmistakable notes in the extensive marsh bordering Salt River, a few miles above its mouth on the evening of June 24.

Lobipes lobatus (Linn.). Northern Phalarope.

The northern phalarope was observed but once—on Aylmer Lake, near Sandhill Bay, August 20, when we saw a single bird swimming about in its customary nervous manner.

Gallinago delicata (Ord). Wilson's Snipe.

The snipe was first observed near Edmonton on May 10. While we were descending the Athabaska we heard the peculiar flight sound of the species on several occasions between Poplar Point and Fort Chipewyan on June 3 and 4. We noted it also near Smith Landing, June 10 and 11, and near Fort Smith on June 16. In the marshes bordering Little Buffalo River and its tributary, the Nyarling, we saw or heard the bird daily, July 7 to 11. We noted the last in the delta of the Slave, near Fort Resolution, on July 16 and 17, on which date it was still calling.

Pisobia maculata (Vieillot). Pectoral Sandpiper.

The pectoral sandpiper was noted only on one occasion while we were ascending the Slave River on September 29, when a small flock flew past us within a few yards.

Pisobia fuscicollis (Vieillot). White-rumped Sandpiper.

A single individual was observed on Slave River, below Point Brulé, on October 1.

Pisobia bairdi (Coues). Baird's Sandpiper.

Small restless flocks of this pretty sandpiper were seen on Casba River on August 8, and near the eastern extremity of Aylmer Lake on August 13.

Ereunetes pusillus (Linn.). Semipalmated Sandpiper.

We first observed this small sandpiper near Fort Resolution on July 17. We also noted a few on Artillery Lake, near our camp at the tree limit, on August 5, and while voyaging up the lake on August 7. We saw a few more between Casba River and the eastern end of Clinton-Colden Lake during the next three days, and again noted the species near the western end of Clinton-Colden on August 12. On Aylmer Lake we observed it at the eastern extremity on August 13, and at its western end on August 15.

Totanus melanoleucus (Gmelin). Greater Yellow-legs.

We noted the large yellow-legs but once—on Rocher River, near Fort Chipewyan, on October 9.

Totanus flavipes (Gmelin). Yellow-legs.

First observed at Edmonton on May 10, and between there and Vermilion Creek on the following day. The species was next seen at Athabaska Landing on May 17, and was also noted a few miles below that point on May 18. Next seen on the Athabaska, below Fort McKay, May 30. Birds apparently breeding were noted on the Nyarling on July 10 and 11. The species was last noted on Casba River on August 8.

Helodromas solitarius solitarius (Wilson).   Solitary Sandpiper.

The solitary sandpiper was first seen a few miles north of Edmonton on May 11.   A specimen was taken at Athabaska Landing, May 17, and the species was noted on the Athabaska, a few miles below that point, on May 18.   Next observed near Poplar Point, on the lower Athabaska, June 1, and noted for the last time near Smith Landing on June 10.

Actitis macularius (Linn.)   Spotted Sandpiper.

We first observed the spotted sandpiper at Athabaska Landing on May 18, and frequently observed it while we were descending the Athabaska.   It was common also on Rocher River, June 5, and on Slave River, between that point and Smith Landing, June 6 and 7.   Observed daily at Smith Landing, June 8 to 11, and at Fort Smith, June 13 to 15.   A nest containing four eggs was found at Mountain Portage, near Fort Smith, June 22; on Slave River, below Fort Smith, July 4 and 5; on Little Buffalo, July 7; and on the Nyarling, July 8 to 11.   A nest found there on July 9 contained eggs nearly ready to hatch.   A pair with their downy young was observed on Great Slave Lake, near Fort Resolution, on July 16.   A young one, which we surrounded and photographed, was very active, and had the characteristic habit of dipping its tail well developed.   A nest found on the shore of Great Slave Lake, near The Narrows, on July 22, contained the usual four eggs, but well-grown young were observed a few miles east of the same place on July 24.   We saw a single bird near the southern end of Clinton-Colden Lake, well north of the tree limit, on August 29.   On our return trip we noted one at Fort Resolution on September 16, and two, one of which had been wounded, on Slave River, below Point Brulé, on October 1.

Charadrius dominicus dominicus (Müller).   Golden Plover.

This plover was not observed during the spring migration, but during our return trip a flock of four was seen on lower Slave River on September 29, and a few in the delta of the Athabaska on October 10.

Aegialitis semipalmata (Bonaparte). Semipalmated Plover.

This plover was first seen in its breeding grounds on Artillery Lake, near the tree limit, on August 2, and others were observed at the same place on August 4. We observed it also near the eastern end of Aylmer Lake on August 13, and at its western extremity on August 15.

Canachites canadensis canadensis (Linn.). Hudsonian Spruce Partridge.

Although the spruce grouse occurs over the entire wooded region north of Edmonton, we failed to observe it during our passage down the rivers, and saw but few during the entire season. We noted two on the lower Nyarling on July 8. The species was next seen on lower Slave River on September 29. We noted a few near Grand Détour on October 2 and 3 while tracking along the eastern bank of the Slave between Salt River and Fort Smith, we noted eight individuals in twos or threes. Several were seen while we were driving across the portage between Fort Smith and Smith Landing on October 5. The species was last seen on the Athabaska, below Calling River, on the morning of October 1, when a single bird flew into our camp just as we were leaving it.

Bonasa umbellus umbelloides (Douglas). Gray Ruffed Grouse.

The presence of ruffed grouse, usually evidenced by the drumming, was noted on the Athabaska, below Athabaska Landing, May 18; near Brulé Rapid, May 26; near Fort McKay, May 31 and June 1, and near Poplar Point on June 2 and 3. We also heard the species drumming near Smith Landing on June 9, and noted it on Little Buffalo River on June 26. It was last noted on our northward trip in the Slave delta, near Fort Resolution, on July 16. During our return trip we saw a few while making the portage across the Grand Détour on October 2, and we saw one near Fort Smith on October 5. While ascending the Athabaska the species was noted above Poplar Point, October 13, and we heard two drumming at intervals during most of the night at our camp, near Brulé Rapid, October 22. The drumming of others was heard above Pelican Portage on October 27 and 28; and during the night of October 31, while we were encamped about fifteen miles below Athabaska Landing, we were again serenaded by one of these drummers.

Lagopus lagopus lagopus (Linn.). Willow Ptarmigan.

We first met with this Barren-Ground species on the northern shore of Clinton-Colden Lake on August 11, when we encountered an old bird which was accompanied by her brood of ten young ones. A fine male specimen was taken at our camp on the northern shore of Aylmer Lake on August 17, and another one at the same place on the following day. Although we were on favourable ground for this species for nearly three weeks the bird was seen but on one other occasion, on August 28, when we observed several on the southern shore of Clinton-Colden Lake.

Circus hudsonius (Linn.). Marsh Hawk.

The marsh hawk was seen near Edmonton on May 10 and 11, and between Vermilion and Sandy Creeks, on the Athabaska Landing road, on May 12. Another, the last one observed during the season, was noted on the lower Athabaska on June 4.

Accipiter velox (Wilson). Sharp-shinned Hawk.

This little falcon was observed near Smith Landing on June 10 and 12, single birds being observed. The species was next seen on Slave River, near Grand Détour, on October 2 during our return trip.

Accipiter cooperi (Bonaparte). Cooper's Hawk.

This hawk, which as far as known inhabits only the extreme southern part of the region visited during our trip, was noted at Edmonton on May 10.

Astur atricapillus atricapillus (Wilson). Goshawk.

Goshawks were noted on Slave River, near Grand Détour, on October 2, and on the lower Athabaska on October 11 and 12.

Buteo borealis calurus Cassin.   Western Red-tail.

A melanistic individual of this species was seen at Edmonton on May 11, and one in the normal plumage on May 12.   Another dark bird was noted near Athabaska Landing on May 13.   While we were descending the Athabaska red-tails were seen below Athabaska Landing on May 18, and below Pelican Portage on May 20.   Observed near Smith Landing, June 8; at Fort Smith, June 18 and 21; and on Little Buffalo River, July 7. In the country drained by the Buffalo and its tributary, the Nyarling, the species seemed rather common.   Several, some of which had nests, were seen on the Nyarling on July 8, 10, and 11; and while we were descending Little Buffalo River on July 12 we passed two nests of the species.   It was last observed on the Athabaska, a few miles below Athabaska Landing, on October 31.

Archibuteo lagopus sancti-johannis (Gmelin).   Rough-legged Hawk.

A bird of this species was seen a few miles north of Edmonton on May 11.   The species was next observed near Salt River, north-west of Fort Smith, on June 25.   About the large lakes to the north-eastward of Great Slave Lake the bird was fairly common.   We noted individuals near the southern end of Clinton-Colden Lake on August 9, on its northern shore on August 11, on the northern shore of Aylmer Lake on August 17, and near the outlet of Clinton-Colden on August 30.   Others were seen near the head of Artillery Lake on September 1, and at our camp, near the tree limit, on September 7 and 8.   During our return trip we observed the species in the Slave River delta, September 25; near Fort Smith, October 4; and near Fort Chipewyan, October 9 and 10.   While ascending the Athabaska we noted a few near Fort McMurray, October 16 and 17; and above Boiler Rapid, October 22.

Aquila chrysaëtos (Linn.).   Golden Eagle.

While we were descending the Athabaska on May 26 we noted a pair of these fine birds below Brulé Rapid.   The species was next seen on the Barren Grounds, near Muskox Lake, on August 21; others were seen near the outlet of Clinton-Colden Lake on August 30, and near the eastern extremity of Great Slave Lake on September 10.

Haliæetus leucocephalus alascanus Townsend.   Northern Bald Eagle.

The first bald eagle was seen while we were paddling westward along the northern shore of Kah-d'nouay Island on September 23 during our return trip.   Here we saw a bird in immature plumage, probably a young one of the year, make three attempts to capture a fish without success.   We observed the species also on the Athabaska, near the site of the old post, Pierre au Calumet. Another was seen a few miles north of Edmonton on November 3.

Falco peregrinus anatum Bonaparte.   Duck Hawk.

The duck hawk was observed in the delta of the Athabaska on June 4.   We next noted the species near the western end of Clinton-Colden Lake on August 12, noting two; and we saw one near our camp on Sandhill Bay, Aylmer Lake, August 20. During our southward voyage down Artillery Lake we saw three about the rocky mound known as the Beaver Lodge.   They were very noisy and were swooping about high in the air playing with each other.   A nest on the face of the cliff overhanging the water had probably been the home of these birds.   One of them was melanistic.

Falco columbarius columbarius Linn.   Pigeon Hawk.

Examples of this species were seen on the Athabaska, near Fort McKay, on May 30, near Poplar Point on June 1, and on Slave River, near Smith Landing, on June 7.   The species was next noted on Great Slave Lake, near The Narrows, July 22. During our return trip we saw two at Fort Reliance on September 14, one of which was collected on September 21 while we were encamped on Caribou Island, Great Slave Lake.   We saw one of these falcons pursue, but fail to capture, a Hudsonian chickadee.

Single birds were observed near Fort Resolution, September 27; on Slave River, near Grand Détour, October 3; and on the Athabaska, near Fort McKay, October 15.

Falco columbarius richardsoni Ridgway. Richardson's Pigeon Hawk.

This form of the pigeon hawk was noted but once—a few miles north of Edmonton on May 11, when an individual, which was perched on a telegraph pole, was passed at close range and positively identified.

Falco sparverius sparverius Linn. Sparrow Hawk.

The sparrow hawk is fairly common over the southern part of the territory covered during our trip. It was observed near Edmonton on May 11, near Sandy Creek on May 12, and near Athabaska Landing on May 15, 17, and 18. We saw one near Boiler Rapid on May 27. The country about Fort Smith is particularly favourable as a habitat, and the species was noted there several times between June 12 and 23.

Pandion haliaetus carolinensis (Gmelin). Osprey.

Individuals of this species were observed on the Athabaska, below Athabaska Landing, May 18, and at Grand Rapid, May 21. Another bird, which had a good-sized fish in its talons, was seen in the Athabaska delta on June 4. During our return trip we saw one at The Narrows of Great Slave Lake on September 20.

Asio flammeus (Pontoppidan). Short-eared Owl.

This species was observed but once—near the eastern extremity of Aylmer Lake on August 13, when we started a single bird from the shrubby tundra.

Scotiaptex nebulosa nebulosa (Forster). Great Gray Owl.

During the night of June 4, as we were crossing Athabaska Lake from the mouth of the river to Fort Chipewyan, a large owl, which could be referred to no other species, circled once about our boat. Although the time was not far from midnight the subarctic twilight, which prevails at this season, allowed a good view of the bird. The species was observed on but one other occasion—while we were descending the Nyarling on July 11, when a fine individual was seen perched on a low stub near the river.

Cryptoglaux funerea richardsoni (Bonaparte). Richardson's Owl.

The soft musical notes of this owl were heard for some time during the evening of May 29 near our camp on the Athabaska, about twenty miles below Fort McMurray.

Bubo virginianus subarcticus Hoy. Arctic Horned Owl.

The great horned owl was first noted on the Athabaska, about twenty miles below Fort McMurray, May 29. It was next observed near Poplar Point on the lower Athabaska on June 2. Judging by the numbers seen the species was abundant along the Little Buffalo River, for we saw no less than ten individuals during our voyage down that stream on July 7. The species was also noted near the head of the Nyarling on July 11. We saw the last one during our northward journey, perched on the granite cliffs of Stony Island, east of Fort Resolution, on July 17.

The species was next observed in the delta of the Slave River on the afternoon of September 25. While we were ascending the Athabaska we heard one, during the night of October 12, utter a long wail resembling the note of the barred owl. Later we saw single birds near Fort McKay on October 15, and above Mountain Rapid on October 18. Another individual seen below Brulé Rapid on October 22 was being vigorously assailed by a pair of Canada Jays, and one seen near La Biche River on October 31 had a good-sized fish in its talons when it was started from the margin of the river. This species was last observed on Athabaska Landing on November 1.

Nyctea nyctea (Linn.). Snowy Owl.

This Arctic species was first observed on the northern shore of Clinton-Colden Lake on August 11. The species was observed on but one other occasion—near the outlet of Aylmer Lake on the evening of August 25, when one flew by our tent in the gathering darkness. Large pellets, without doubt the rejects of this species, which we picked up on hillocks on the northern shore of Aylmer Lake, near Sandy Hill Bay, contained the bones of an Arctic weasel and several lemmings.

Surnia ulula caparoch (Müller). Hawk Owl.

This interesting owl was observed on only one occasion. This was at our camp on the eastern shore of Aylmer Lake, at the tree limit, on September 3, when we secured a fine specimen.

Ceryle alcyon (Linn.). Belted Kingfisher.

This little fisherman is quite generally distributed through the region covered by our journey north to Great Slave Lake. The species was observed on the Athabaska, near Cascade Rapid, May 27; near Fort McKay, May 30 and June 1, and on the lower river on June 3 and 4. We also noted one near the mouth of Peace River on June 7, and others on June 25 and July 7. The species was noted also on Little Buffalo River on July 7, and lastly near the head of the Nyarling on July 11.

Dryobates villosus leucomelas (Bodd.). Northern Hairy Woodpecker.

This woodpecker was observed during our northward journey on only a few occasions, as follows: Near Brulé Rapid, May 26; on the lower Athabaska, June 4; and near Fort Smith on July 2, when a specimen was collected. During our homeward journey, while ascending the Athabaska, we saw the bird near Boiler Rapid, October 22; near Grand Rapid, October 24; and daily between Pelican Portage and Athabaska Landing, October 28 to November 1. On October 30, near Calling River, several were noted.

Dryobates pubescens nelsoni Oberholser. Nelson's Downy Woodpecker.

The downy woodpecker is less common in the north than its larger relative, and was noted on only four occasions, as follows: Near Athabaska Landing on May 18; near Fort McMurray, May 28; near House River, October 25; and near La Biche River, October 31. Thus we saw it only along the Athabaska.

Picoides arcticus (Swainson). Arctic Three-toed Woodpecker.

This rather uncommon bird was observed at Smith Landing on June 10, when a specimen was taken; on Little Buffalo River on July 7; and on the Athabaska, near Pelican Portage, on October 27.

Picoides americanus fasciatus Baird. Alaska Three-toed Woodpecker.

The common three-toed woodpecker was observed near the mouth of Peace River on June 7, and on Little Buffalo River on July 7. It was next seen near Smith Landing on October 6 during our homeward journey, when several were noted, and one was taken among heavy spruce woods bordering Slave River. Others were seen on the Athabaska, near Calling, on October 29, and near La Biche River on October 31.

Sphyrapicus varius varius (Linn.). Yellow-bellied Sapsucker.

This sapsucker was first observed on the Athabaska, near Grand Rapid, on May 25, when several were seen. It was common during the next three days between that point and Fort McMurray, and here specimens were taken on May 28. The species was also observed daily along the Athabaska, between Fort McKay and the mouth of the river, May 30 to June 4; and on Slave River, between the mouth of the Peace and Smith Landing, on June 5, 6, and 7. It was common also in the country to the north-westward of Fort Smith on June 25 and 26. While on our Buffalo River trip we noted it on Little Buffalo River, July 7 and on the Nyarling on July 8 and 11. It was last noted on the lower part of Little Buffalo on July 12.

Phlœotomus pileatus abieticola (Bangs). Northern Pileated Woodpecker.

This lordly woodpecker was heard on the Athabaska, near La Biche River on May 19, and below Fort McKay on May 31. The species was next found above Pelican Portage on October 28, and on October 31, near La Biche, we were favoured with a fine view at close range of this notable species.

Colaptes auratus luteus Bangs. Northern Flicker.

The flicker was first observed near Athabaska Landing on May 16. We next saw it at Grand Rapid on May 24, and during our journey down the rivers between that point and Fort Smith, May 25 to June 18, observed it in greater or less numbers nearly every day. A tenanted nest in an aspen poplar was found to the west of Salt River on June 25, and the bird was seen in the same region during the two following days. Others of the species were seen at Fort Smith on July 1 and 2, and we noted the bird on the Buffalo River Portage, July 6; on Little Buffalo River, July 7; and on the Nyarling, July 8 and 11. In the sparsely wooded country about the Estern End of Great Slave Lake the species was fairly common, being observed near Fort Reliance, July 25 to 27; and on Pike's Portage, between that point and Artillery Lake, on July 28 and 29. The bird was next observed, and for the last time that season, near Fort Reliance on September 11.

Chordeiles virginianus virginianus (Gmelin). Nighthawk.

The nighthawk was observed as follows: Athabaska River, near Poplar Point, June 3; Smith Landing, June 10 and 11; Fort Smith, June 15 and 19; near Salt River, June 25; and near the head of the Nyarling, the westerly branch of the Little Buffalo, on July 11.

Tyrannus tyrannus (Linn.). Kingbird.

We observed the kingbird for the first time at Fort McKay on the morning of May 31. It was observed on but one other occasion—near the head of the Nyarling on July 11, when two individuals were seen.

Sayornis phœbe (Latham). Phœbe.

The phoebe nests commonly along the cut banks and rocky cliffs throughout the Athabaska region. We observed it on the Athabaska, near Pelican Portage, on May 19; at Grand Rapid on May 22 and 25; near Poplar Point, June 1 and 3; and daily at Smith Landing, June 8 to 12. At the latter point a pair had their nest on the face of a granite ledge nearly finished on June 8; ten days later the bird was observed sitting on four eggs. While descending Little Buffalo River we observed the species near Bear Creek on July 7, and near the mouth of the river on July 12. While voyaging along the northern shore of Great Slave Lake toward its eastern extremity we noted the species on the north shore of Kah-d'nouay Island on July 19, and observed several near The Narrows on July 22. These were the last seen.

Nutallornis borealis (Swainson). Olive-sided Flycatcher.

This fine flycatcher was observed at Smith Landing on June 10 and 11, and a specimen was taken at Fort Smith on June 13. Others were observed to the west of Salt River on June 25, and near the upper part of Little Buffalo River on June 26. The species was last noted near the head of the Nyarling, July 11.

Myiochanes richardsoni richardsoni (Swainson). Western Wood Pewee.

First noted on the large island at Fort McMurray on May 28, when several were observed. The species was next seen a few miles below the same point on the forenoon of May 31, when several birds were seen flycatching about a small meadow near the river. The unusually cold weather had driven the insects to seek shelter among the rank marsh grass, and the birds were usually observed within a foot or two of the ground, in striking contrast to their usual habit. The species was last observed on June 15, when a specimen was collected at Fort Smith.

Empidonax trailli alnorum Brewster. Alder Flycatcher.

This little flycatcher, whose presence is generally detected from its sprightly notes, is rather common among the willow and alder thickets bordering the water-ways of the Athabaska region. It was noted near the mouth of Peace River on June 6, and at Fort Smith on June 15, 16, 21, 26, and 28. The alder swamps of the Buffalo and its tortuous tributary, the Nyarling, are favourite haunts, and numbers of the birds were seen on July 11 and 12. These were the last observed during the season.

Empidonax minimus (Baird). Least Flycatcher.

The least flycatcher was first observed at Fort McMurray on May 28; others were seen on the lower Athabaska on June 4 and at Smith Landing on June 10. At Fort Smith the species was noted on June 15, and on June 22 the first nest, a compact structure in the forks of a poplar close beside the road, was seen.

Otocoris alpestris hoyti Bishop. Hoyt's Horned Lark.

Migrating birds of this species were seen a few miles north of Edmonton on May 11. The bird was not again observed until we reached its breeding grounds at the tree limit on Artillery Lake. Here numbers were seen, August 2 to 6, and several specimens, including newly fledged young, were taken. The bird was also observed at the western end of Clinton-Colden Lake on August 12, and was again observed commonly at our camp on Artillery Lake at the tree limit on September 5 and 6. We failed to observe the species later during our southward journey.

Cyanocitta cristata cristata (Linn.). Blue Jay.

The blue jay is a fairly common species along the Athabaska. During our northward trip we saw it near Pelican Portage on May 20; near Brulé Rapid on May 26, and near Poplar Point, on the lower Athabaska, June 3. We did not again observe the species until we were ascending the Athabaska during our return trip, when we noted it below Iron Point on October 28. It was also noted near La Biche River on October 30, and on October 31 above that point the species was common and noisy, apparently migrating.

Perisoreus canadensis canadensis (Linn.).   Wiskajon or Canada Jay.

The Canada jay is one of the commonest and most widely distributed birds throughout the region covered by our journey north to the tree limit, and was observed almost every day during the entire season, excepting the period when we were on the Barren Grounds.   It is one of the most familiar of the feathered inhabitants and its thieving propensities make it at times a nuisance, yet on account of its trusting ways it is seldom molested by the traveller.   It is usually seen in pairs.

Corvus corax principalis Ridgway.   Northern Raven.

The raven, though much less abundant than its smaller relative, the Canada jay, is even more widely distributed.   It was frequently seen as we descended the Athabaska and Slave Rivers, and was noted also on Little Buffalo River.   The precipitous rocky islands, which abound in the eastern part of Great Slave Lake, furnish favourite nesting sites, and the bird was noted almost daily during our voyage there, July 17 to 26.   It was also observed on Pike's Portage, between Great Slave Lake and Artillery Lake, and was abundant about the latter body of water. Wherever game is killed, numbers of the birds soon collect, and on August 5, near our camp on Artillery Lake, we observed twenty-eight of the birds at once.   They had been attracted by the bodies of several caribou which we had taken for specimens. The bird was rather common also on Aylmer Lake, along the northern shore, and at Sandhill Bay, where it was noted August 18 and 20.   During our return trip through the chain of lakes to Great Slave Lake, and westward among the islands of that great sheet of water, during late August and September, the bird was observed almost daily.   It was abundant also while we were ascending the Slave River and the Athabaska during October and was observed practically every day.

Corvus brachyrhynchos brachyrhynchos Brehm. Crow.

The crow, except in certain favourite localities, is less abundant than its larger relative. It was noted between Edmonton and Athabaska Landing on May 11, 12, and 13, but after that was not seen again until we reached the delta of the Athabaska on June 4, when we saw several. Others were seen on Slave River, near the mouth of the Peace, on June 6, and on June 9 a nest containing four eggs was found at Smith Landing. The species was fairly common about Fort Smith, where it was noted on June 13, 14, and 15. It was observed also on Little Buffalo River on July 7. The delta of the Slave, near Fort Resolution, is frequented by numbers, and we noted the species there on July 14 and 15. After this it was not again observed until we returned to the same point on September 25, when we saw a number of individuals, and we noted the species for the last time on Slave River, a few miles above its mouth, on September 29.

Molothrus ater ater (Bodd.). Cowbird.

This parasite was observed on the Athabaska at Athabaska Landing on May 17; near Grand Rapid, May 20, 24, and 25; at Fort McMurray on May 28 and 29, and near Fort McKay on May 30 and June 1. The species was next noted, and for the last time during the season, at Fort Resolution on July 16.

Xanthocephalus xanthocephalus (Bonap.). Yellow-headed
  Blackbird.

This notable blackbird was observed on but one occasion. This was near Poplar Point on the lower Athabaska on June 3, when a small company, numbering about five individuals, one of which was collected, was seen.

Agelaius phœniceus arctolegus Oberholser. Northern Red-
winged Blackbird.

This red-wing inhabits suitable places, of which there is an
abundance throughout the region north to Great Slave Lake.
We noted it at Edmonton on May 10, and while on the Athabaska observed it on a number of occasions between Athabaska
Landing and the mouth of the river, May 17 to June 4. The
species was common along Slave River, and was observed near
the mouth of the Peace River on June 7, and at Smith Landing
on June 10. During our trip through the Little Buffalo River
country red-wings were noted on the Buffalo River Portage,
July 6; on Little Buffalo River, July 7; daily on the Nyarling,
July 8 to 11, and on the lower part of the Little Buffalo on July
12. It was last observed in the delta of the Slave, near Fort
Resolution, on July 17.

Euphagus carolinus (Müller). Rusty Blackbird.

The rusty blackbird is quite generally distributed through the
swamps of the Athabaska region north to the tree limit. It was
nesting in the country west of Salt River on July 27, and was an
abundant species about the Nyarling and along the lower part
of Little Buffalo River, July 8 to 12. It was next observed near
the eastern extremity of Great Slave Lake on July 25, and was
noted on Pike's Portage on July 29 and 31, and old birds accompanied by newly fledged young were observed on the following
day. It was next noted near the same point on our return trip
on September 10, and a specimen was taken at Fort Reliance
on September 16. Others were seen among the islands between
Fort Reliance and Fort Resolution on September 23, 24, and 25,
and while ascending the Slave River we observed numbers on
lower Slave River on September 29; near Point Brulé, October 1,
and near Grand Détour, October 2 and 3. Others were seen
near Fort Smith on October 4, and while crossing Smith Portage
between that point and Smith Landing on October 5 we observed
one being pursued by a Northern Shrike. During the remainder
of the month, while we were ascending the Slave and Athabaska

Rivers, we frequently observed migrating companies, and we noted the bird for the last time that season near Athabaska Landing on November 1.

Euphagus cyanocephalus (Wagler).   Brewer's Blackbird.

This blackbird is found but a short distance north of Athabaska Landing.   We found it common at Edmonton on May 10, and observed large numbers between that point and Athabaska Landing, May 11 to 13.   It was common also at the latter point, May 13 to 18, and was last noted on the Athabaska below La Biche River on May 19.

Quiscalus quiscula æneus Ridgway.   Bronzed Grackle.

The bronzed grackle was seen on the Athabaska Landing road, near Sandy Creek, on May 12, and was rather common on the Athabaska below Athabaska Landing on May 18.   It was next observed on the lower Athabaska on June 4, and on Rocher River, near the mouth of the Peace, on June 5.   It was common at Smith Landing, June 10.   During our trip to the Little Buffalo River region we observed it on the Buffalo River Portage on July 6, and found it rather common about the head of the Nyarling on July 11.

Pinicola enucleator leucura (Müller).   Pine Grosbeak.

We did not observe the pine grosbeak during our northward journey, but while on our homeward trip saw a few on Caribou Island in the eastern part of Great Slave Lake on September 21. The species was next seen while we were ascending the Athabaska, near Pelican Portage, on October 27, when we saw three individuals which were the forerunners of the migrating flocks which were seen daily between Calling River and Athabaska Landing, October 29 to November 1.   The species was observed also between Athabaska Landing and Edmonton on November 2 and 3.

Carpodacus purpureus purpureus (Gmelin).   Purple Finch.

This is a rather common bird along the Athabaska.   Numbers were observed near Grand Rapid on May 21, 22, and 24, and

the species was noted near Cascade Rapid on May 27.   It was
common at Fort McMurray on May 28, the last date observed.

Loxia curvirostra minor (Brehm).   Crossbill.

The red crossbill was observed on but one occasion, while we
were ascending Slave River, a short distance above its mouth,
on September 28, when a specimen was collected.

Loxia leucoptera Gmelin.   White-winged Crossbill.

This beautiful bird was noted but once.   A small flock lingered
for a few minutes among the spruces on the island which bore
the nesting colony of white pelicans in the Slave River Rapids
on June 22.

Acanthis linaria linaria (Linn.).   Redpoll.

The redpoll was first noted near The Narrows of Great Slave
Lake on July 22, and next near the eastern extremity of Great
Slave Lake, July 25, 29, and 30.   At our camp on Artillery Lake,
near the tree limit, it was observed daily, August 2 to 7.   While
on the Barren Grounds to the northward, we observed a few near
the eastern end of Aylmer Lake on August 13, and near Sandhill Bay, August 21 and 24.   It was again observed in numbers
on Artillery Lake on September 2, 5, and 6.   While voyaging
along the northern shore of Great Slave Lake toward Fort Resolution, we observed it on Caribou Island on September 20 and
21.   These were the last dates recorded.

Spinus pinus (Wilson).   Pine Siskin.

The little siskin was first noted on the Athabaska during our
return trip.   We observed it below Iron Point on October 28,
near Calling River on October 30, and found it abundant near
La Biche River on October 31 and November 1.

Piectrophenax nivalis nivalis (Linn.).   Snow Bunting.

During the spring migration the snow bunting was observed
but once—on May 12, between Vermilion and Sandy Creeks on

the road between Edmonton and Athabaska Landing. The species was next observed on or near its breeding grounds on the north shore of Clinton-Colden Lake, where three individuals were seen on August 11. A few others were observed on the north shore of Aylmer Lake on August 14, and a bird of the year was taken near the same place on August 19. Others were seen near the south end of Clinton-Colden Lake, August 29.

During our homeward journey we saw the first southward migrants on the Slave River, near Point Ennuyeux, on September 30. During the month of October, between Point Brulé on lower Slave River and Athabaska Landing, we saw large flocks of the birds practically every day. On October 2 and 3 we noted that some of the flocks, on being disturbed, would alight in trees after one or two circuitous flights. Near Athabaska Landing, and between that point and Edmonton, November 1 to 3, we saw large numbers daily.

Calcarius lapponicus lapponicus (Linn.). Lapland Longspur.

This species was observed between Edmonton and Vermilion Creek on May 11, and between Sandy Creek and Athabaska Landing on May 13. During the spring migration it was seen on but one other occasion, near Fort McMurray on May 29. On reaching the Barren Grounds, near the southern end of Artillery Lake, on August 1, we at once began to observe the bird now on its breeding grounds, and it was seen in large numbers on Artillery Lake, Casba Lake, Clinton-Colden Lake, and Aylmer Lake every day during our trip north of the trees until we again entered the wooded country on September 8; then we left the bird for a period. We next observed it migrating to the southward at Fort Resolution on September 27. During our ascent of the rivers on our way south we noted it near Point Brulé on Slave River on October 2; on the Athabaska, near Pierre au Calumet, on October 14; near Fort McMurray, October 16 and 17, and between Mountain Rapid and Stony Rapid on October 18.

Calcarius pictus (Swainson).   Painted Longspur.

This beautiful species was seen on only one occasion—on August 13—when we observed a single individual near the eastern end of Aylmer Lake.

Passerculus sandwichensis alaudinus Bonaparte.   Western Savannah Sparrow.

This little sparrow is a common breeder throughout the region visited by us, even within the Barren Grounds. We first saw it near Edmonton on May 11. During our descent of the Athabaska we noted it near Fort McKay on May 30 and 31, and on the lower Athabaska on June 2 and 3. Other localities and dates follow: Forth Smith, June 16; mouth of Salt River, June 25 and 27; Little Buffalo River Portage, July 6; Nyarling River, July 9 to 11, and Fort Resolution, July 15. It was common on Artillery Lake, near the tree limit, where specimens were taken, August 3 and 5. We also saw it on Casba River, August 8; on Clinton-Colden Lake, August 10 and 11, and at various points on Aylmer Lake, August 14 to 27. During our homeward trip we took specimens at Fort Reliance, near the eastern extremity of Great Slave Lake on September 14 and 15, and noted the species for the last time that season on September 16.

Zonotrichia querula (Nuttall).   Harris's Sparrow.

This interesting sparrow was first noted on the Athabaska, near Fort McKay, on May 30, when we saw a small flock of migrants. Several others were seen and one was collected below Poplar Point on June 3.

We next saw the species on its breeding grounds on the semi-barren islands in the eastern part of Great Slave Lake. The first pair was seen on a small island in the channel bordering Kah-d'nouay Island on July 20. Other birds, usually in pairs, and betraying by their excited actions that they had eggs or young near by, were seen near The Narrows, July 22, and near the eastern end of the lake on July 25 and 26. We noted the species also under similar conditions while crossing Pike's Portage between Great Slave Lake and Artillery Lake on July 29, 30, and 31. Near our camp at the tree limit on Artillery Lake the species was common. It was common, August 1 to 7. The first nest, containing young a week or ten days old, was found by Seton at this place on August 6. It was a well built, compact nest, placed on the ground at the base of a clump of dwarf birch (*Betula nana*). One or two other nests in similar situations, but deserted, were subsequently found near the same place, and it is likely that this is a favourite nesting place. A few specimens, including young ones, were preserved. North of this point the species was not observed, but upon our return to the same place in early September it was still common there and the song was heard by Seton on September 3. He noted that it resembled that of the white-throated sparrow in tone, but was less of a whistle, and the low notes were slightly trilled. The bird was still common when we left there on September 8. During our homeward trip through the chain of lakes leading to Artillery Lake, the species was common on September 9 to 11, and we saw many adults and young of the year, now in the complete autumnal plumage, about Fort Reliance, September 12 to 17. The species was last seen at Fort Resolution on September 26 and 27.

Zonotrichia leucophrys gambeli (Nuttall). Gambel's Sparrow.

Migrating birds of this species were seen at Athabaska Landing on May 17, below Poplar Point on June 3, and near Chipewyan on June 5. The species was next seen on its breeding grounds at Fort Resolution, where it was common, July 13 to 16. It was noted also on the north shore of Kah-d'nouay Island, July 20, and among the islands to the eastward between that point and The Narrows on July 21 and 22. Young birds just from the nest were seen on the north shore of Great Slave Lake, near the Mountain Portage on July 24, and the species was observed also near the eastern end of Great Slave Lake on July 25. During our return trip through the bird's haunts, the species was not observed, evidently having migrated to the southward.

Zonotrichia albicollis (Gmelin). White-throated Sparrow.

The white-throated sparrow is a common breeder throughout the region covered on our trip north to Great Slave Lake. Some localities with dates of observation follow: Grand Rapid, Athabaska River, May 24; Fort McMurray, May 28 and 29; Fort Chipewyan, June 5; Smith Landing, June 11; Fort Smith, June 24; Little Buffalo River, July 7, and Nyarling River, July 9 to 11.

During our southward trip we observed the species on lower Slave River on September 25 and 29.

Spizella monticola monticola (Gmelin). Tree Sparrow.

Migrating tree sparrows were seen during our northward trip, near Edmonton, May 11; at Athabaska Landing, May 13 to 18, and on the Athabaska River, near Pelican Portage, on May 19.

The bird, now on its breeding grounds, was next observed on Pike's Portage between Great Slave Lake and Artillery Lake on July 28. From this point onward it was abundant and was observed in numbers practically every day during August on our trip through the great lakes between this point and the head of Black River, and during our return trip through the same bodies of water. It was common also, and was observed almost daily, usually in numbers, during our voyage westward among the wooded islands of Great Slave Lake during the latter part of September. We noted it also on the lower Slave on October 1; near Grand Détour, October 3; near Fort Smith, October 4 and 5; above Smith Landing, October 7; near Fort Chipewyan, October 8; near Fort McKay, October 15, and below Fort McMurray, for the last time during the season, on October 16.

Spizella passerina arizonæ Coues. Western Chipping Sparrow.

The chipping sparrow was not seen during our descent of the Athabaska, and was first observed near Fort Chipewyan on June 5. Others were seen at Smith Landing on June 8 and 9, and at Fort Smith daily, June 13 to 20. A nest was found near the mouth of Salt River on June 27, and the species was observed after our return to Fort Smith on June 29 and 30. We failed to record it at any point north of this place.

Junco hyemalis hyemalis (Linn.).   Slate-colored Junco.

This familiar little species was common along the road between Edmonton and Athabaska Landing, May 10 to 12, and at the latter place, May 17 to 19. During our descent of the Athabaska we found it common at Grand Rapid, May 22 to 25; at Fort McMurray, May 28 and 29. The species was common at Smith Landing, June 8 to 11, and a nest nearly ready for the eggs was seen on June 10; this nest held two eggs on June 17. It was common also at Fort Smith during the latter part of June and the early days of July. We saw many on the Buffalo River Portage on July 6, on the Nyarling on July 10, and on the lower part of Little Buffalo River on July 12. While voyaging eastward among the islands of Great Slave Lake we saw the species near the western end of Kah-d'nouay on July 18, on Caribou Island on July 20, and on the northern shore of Great Slave Lake, near Mountain Portage, July 23. Beyond this point it was not seen during our northward journey, but on our return trip the bird was observed near the eastern extremity of Great Slave Lake on September 11, and near Fort Reliance on September 14, 15, and 16. While voyaging westward among the islands of Great Slave Lake, we observed the junco on Caribou Island on September 20. During our ascent of the rivers on our southward journey, the species was noted as follows: Lower Slave River, September 29; near Point Ennuyeux, September 30 and October 1; near Grand Détour, October 2 and 3; near Fort Smith, October 4 and 5; on the Athabaska, near Fort McKay, October 15, and near Calling River on October 29, the last date recorded.

Melospiza melodia melodia (Wilson).   Song Sparrow.

We noted song sparrows near Edmonton on May 11, and at Athabaska Landing, May 16, 17, and 18. While descending the Athabaska we observed the species near Pelican Portage on

May 19, and at Grand Rapid, May 22, 23, and 25. The bird was next seen at Fort Chipewyan on June 5, and was noted for the last time that season near Fort Smith on June 22.

Melospiza lincolni lincolni (Audubon). Lincoln's Sparrow.

Over most of the territory covered, this sparrow replaces wholly, or in part, the more familiar song sparrow. We saw it at Athabaska Landing on May 17, and near Fort McKay on May 30 and 31. Other birds were observed at Poplar Point on the Athabaska, June 1, and at Fort Smith, June 28 and 30. The swamps bordering the Nyarling seemed a favourite habitat, and we saw numbers there, July 8 to 11, and on the lower part of Little Buffalo River on July 12. Others were seen at Fort Resolution, July 13 and 17.

Melospiza georgiana (Latham). Swamp Sparrow.

The swamp sparrow is quite generally distributed, though seldom abundant north to the region of Great Slave Lake. We noted it at Fort Smith on June 24, and in the delta of Slave River on July 17.

Passerella iliaca iliaca (Merrem). Fox Sparrow.

This beautiful sparrow was noted at Athabaska Landing on May 17, and on the Athabaska, below that point, on May 18. We also noted the species and took a specimen at Grand Rapid, May 22. It was next observed on the Little Buffalo River on July 6 and 7. We noted a few near Fort Resolution on July 16 and 17, but did not again observe the species until August 5, when one was seen in the alders bordering a small stream on the eastern shore of Artillery Lake at the tree limit. The bird was last seen on September 11, near the eastern end of Great Slave Lake, during our homeward trip.

Passer domesticus (Linn.). House Sparrow.

The so-called English sparrow has apparently established itself at Athabaska Landing, where a few pairs were noted on May 16.

Zamelodia ludoviciana (Linn.).   Rose-breasted Grosbeak.

This beautiful bird was first observed on the Athabaska at Fort McMurray on May 28 and 29, being then fairly common and represented by both sexes. Other localities and dates of observation follow: Fort McKay, May 30; near Poplar Point, June 1 and 2; below Poplar Point, June 3; Athabaska delta, June 4; near Smith Landing, June 7 and 10, and near Fort Smith, June 28. Its rich, clear song was often heard in the willow and poplar thickets bordering the lower Athabaska.

Piranga ludoviciana (Wilson).   Western Tanager.

This tanager was first seen on the Athabaska, above Pelican Portage, on May 19. The next ones were seen between Boiler Rapid and Cascade Rapid on May 27, when the species was noted as common. It was rather common at Fort McMurray, May 28 and 29. Noted on the lower Athabaska, June 4; near Fort Chipewyan, June 5, and near the mouth of Peace River, June 6. We observed it also on the Smith Portage, June 12, and at Fort Smith, June 13, 14, and 17. It was noted near the mouth of Salt River on June 27. The country drained by the Nyarling seems to be a favourite habitat, and numbers were observed there on July 8, 9, and 10. It was last noted on the lower part of Buffalo River on June 12.

Petrochelidon lunifrons lunifrons (Say).   Cliff Swallow.

The cliff swallow was first observed on the Athabaska, near Fort McKay, on May 30, and others were seen near Fort Smith on June 28. We next observed the species about some precipitous islands, near the north shore of Great Slave Lake, near the Mountain Portage, where it was nesting abundantly on the cliffs of a small island which we recognised as one figured by Captain Back in the geological appendix to his narrative. This island forms one of a group called by the Chipewyans Tha-sess San-d'ouay, the name meaning in their language "Swallow Islands." Other nesting colonies were observed on the cliffs to the eastward of the Mountain Portage on July 24, and in Big

Stone Bay, where upwards of 100 pairs had nested, on July 25. On the precipitous face of a high rocky point, which is washed by the waters of Artillery Lake, called the Beaver Lodge, a considerable colony was noted on August 1, and a male bird, probably belonging to this colony, was collected at our camp at the tree limit on August 3. This was the last date recorded. During our ascent of the Athabaska in October, we saw many nests, now deserted and in ruins, on the limestone cliffs near Fort McKay.

Hirundo erythrogastra Boddaert.   Barn Swallow.

A few barn swallows were seen at Fort Smith on June 16. Our only record otherwise was of a small colony, undoubtedly nesting on the cliffs, near the eastern extremity of Caribou Island in the eastern part of Great Slave Lake, July 21.

Iridoprocne bicolor (Vieillot).   Tree Swallow.

The white-bellied swallow was noted at Athabaska Landing on May 15, was common on May 16, and during our descent of the river was seen near La Biche River, May 18 and 19; above Brulé Rapid on May 25, and near Fort McKay on May 30, when it was very common. We found it nesting in the country west of the mouth of Salt River, June 25 to 27. It was noted also at Fort Smith on June 28, and was seen on Little Buffalo River on July 7, and on the Nyarling on July 10. The northernmost point recorded was Fort Resolution, where we observed it, July 14 and 16.

Riparia riparia (Linn.).   Bank Swallow.

This widely distributed swallow was noted on the Athabaska, below Grand Rapid, on May 25, and near Fort McKay on May 30. Observed also at Fort Smith on June 16 and 22, and daily, June 28 to July 3. A nesting colony was seen at this point on June 22. While we were descending the Slave, between Salt River and Grand Détour, on July 5, we noted many of the birds, and many nesting colonies, now of course deserted, were seen on the lower part of Slave River in late September during our southward trip.

Bombycilla garrula (Linn.). Bohemian Waxwing.

This interesting species was first observed near the mouth of Salt River on June 27, when a nest containing six eggs was collected. The nest resembled closely that of the cedar waxwing, but was larger and more compact. It was settled on the horizontal limb of a Banksian Pine (*Pinus divaricata*). The eggs were in varying stages from fresh to advanced incubation. While descending Little Buffalo River on July 12, we saw a small company of these birds leisurely flycatching. The species was next seen on October 18, while we were ascending the Athabaska, a small flock being observed. Others were seen above Boiler Rapid on October 22. We last noted the bird on November 2, a few miles south of Athabaska Landing, a flock containing thirty or forty individuals.

Lanius borealis Vieillot. Northern Shrike.

This bloodthirsty species was first noted at Fort Reliance on September 15, when one in brownish plumage, evidently a bird of the year, was seen in close pursuit of a tree sparrow. The shrike was collected. The species was elsewhere observed as follows: Slave River, near Point Ennuyeux, September 30; Smith Landing, October 5 (when we saw one in pursuit of a rusty grackle); Athabaska River, near Fort McKay, October 14; below Iron Point, October 28; near Calling River, October 29, and on the road south of Edmonton on November 3, when two were observed.

Vireosylva olivacea (Linn.). Red-eyed Vireo.

The red-eyed vireo was common at Fort Smith, where it was observed at various times, June 13 to 24, and again, June 28 to July 4. Other points and dates of observation were as follows: Mouth of Salt River, June 25; west of the same point, June 24 and 27, and Nyarling River, July 8. The species was last seen at Fort Resolution on July 16, when it was still in full song.

Vireosylva gilva swainsoni (Baird). Western Warbling Vireo.

The warbling vireo was first noted at Grand Rapid on the Athabaska on May 22, and was noted at the same place on the two following days. It was observed also at Smith Landing on June 10, and at Fort Smith on June 15, 17, and July 3. We last saw it on the lower part of Little Buffalo River on July 12.

Lanivireo solitarius solitarius (Wilson). Blue-headed Vireo.

This rather uncommon species was noted but once—near Fort Smith, where a specimen was taken on June 18.

Mniotilta varia (Linn.). Black and White Warbler.

Noted but once—on the Athabaska, below Fort McKay, on May 31.

Vermivora celata celata (Say). Orange-crowned Warbler.

A specimen of this warbler was taken at Smith Landing on June 10. This was our only observation of the species.

Vermivora peregrina (Wilson). Tennessee Warbler.

This little warbler was collected at Fort Smith on June 15, where it seemed to be much less common than during previous summers. The species was next seen, and for the last time, on Pike's Portage, near the eastern extremity of Great Slave Lake, on July 28.

Dendroica æstiva æstiva (Gmelin). Yellow Warbler.

The yellow warbler was first observed on the Athabaska River, near Fort McKay, on May 30. It was seen also at Fort Smith, July 3, and on the lower part of Little Buffalo River on July 12. While voyaging eastward among the islands of Great Slave Lake, we saw the species near The Narrows on July 22, and near Mountain Portage on July 24. Our last observation of the bird, and the north-easternmost point of its occurrence, was near the eastern extremity of Great Slave Lake, where we saw one on July 25.

Dendroica coronata (Linn.). Myrtle Warbler.

The yellow-rumped warbler was first noted on the Athabaska, near Fort McMurray, on May 28, when one was collected. Others were observed at Fort Smith on June 13, and near the head of the Nyarling on July 11. During our trip to the eastward of Fort Resolution we noted the species near the western end of Caribou Island on July 20, and on Pike's Portage, near the eastern end of Great Slave Lake, on July 28. At our camp on Artillery Lake at the tree limit a specimen was collected on September 3. A deserted nest seen in a small spruce shows that this point is a breeding station. During our homeward trip, two individuals, the last observed that season, were seen at Fort Reliance on September 16.

Dendroica striata (Forster). Black-poll Warbler.

Although this species occurs in the Slave River region, we did not observe it there, but saw the first one on Pike's Portage on July 30. Already birds attending young, which had just left the nest, were seen near our camp at the tree limit on Artillery Lake on August 5, the last date recorded.

Seiurus aurocapillus (Linn.). Oven-bird.

The familiar song of the oven-bird was heard on the lower Athabaska on June 4. We noted the species on but one other occasion, near the upper part of Little Buffalo River on June 26.

Seiurus noveboracensis notabilis Ridgway. Grinnell's Water-Thrush.

The water-thrush was first noted near Fort McKay on May 31, and was again seen on the lower Athabaska on June 4. Observed also at Fort Chipewyan, June 5; near the mouth of Peace River, June 6, and near Smith Landing, June 7 and 10. Other points and dates of observation follow: Fort Smith, June 14 to 22; Buffalo River Portage, July 6; Little Buffalo River, July 7;

Nyarling River, July 9 and 10, and lower Little Buffalo River, July 12. It was last noted near Fort Resolution on July 16, being then in full song.

Wilsonia pusilla pusilla (Wilson). Wilson's Warbler.

Wilson's black cap was noted but once—at our camp on Artillery Lake at the tree limit. Here a specimen was taken in an alder thicket on September 5.

Anthus rubescens (Tunstall). Pipit.

This species was observed in migration at Edmonton on May 10. It was next seen, apparently on its breeding grounds, on the north shore of Great Slave Lake, east of Mountain Portage, on July 24. On reaching Artillery Lake it was evident that we had found the true home of the bird, for it was common there, August 3 to 5. It was noted also at a number of points on Aylmer Lake, August 13 to 26, and on Clinton-Colden Lake, August 28 to 30. During our return trip we again found it common on Artillery Lake during the early days of September, and we observed it also at Fort Reliance on September 16 and 17, and near The Narrows, Great Slave Lake, on September 19.

Sitta canadensis Linn. Red-breasted Nuthatch.

The Canada nuthatch was observed only during our southward trip in the autumn, when individuals were observed as follows: Poplar Point, Athabaska River, October 13; near Brulé Rapid, October 23, and below Pelican Rapid, October 26.

Penthestes atricapillus septentrionalis (Harris). Long-tailed Chickadee.

This chickadee was first observed at Edmonton on May 10, and was not again seen until June 10, when it was noted at Smith Landing. A few were seen on the Buffalo River Portage on July 6, and on Little Buffalo River on July 7. We saw no more until we reached lower Slave River during our return trip, when we noted the species on September 28 and 29. Others were seen near Point Brulé, October 1 and 2, and near Fort

Smith, October 4. While ascending the Athabaska, we observed the bird as follows: Near Grand Rapid, October 24; above House River, October 25; near Pelican Rapid, October 26 and 27, and below Iron Point, October 28. It was noted also between Athabaska Landing and Edmonton on November 2 and 3.

Penthestes hudsonicus hudsonicus (Forster). Hudsonian Chickadee.

We did not note this chickadee during our northward journey, but while on our return trip found it common on several occasions. A number were seen on Caribou Island on September 21, and others near Stone Island, east of Fort Resolution, on September 25. A band of about a dozen were observed on the Point Ennuyeux Portage on September 30. In response to Seton's low whistling they came very close and responded with a low lisping note but would not whistle in response. We noted the bird later as follows: Slave River, below Point Brulé, October 1; near Salt River, October 3 and 4, and Athabaska River, near Poplar Point, October 13.

Hylocichla aliciæ aliciæ (Baird). Gray-cheeked Thrush.

The gray-cheeked thrush was observed in migration on the Athabaska at Grand Rapid, May 24. We next observed the bird on its breeding grounds among the islands in the eastern part of Great Slave Lake, noting it as follows: Caribou Island, July 20; near The Narrows, July 22, and near Mountain Portage, July 23. We noted the bird also on Pike's Portage between the eastern end of Great Slave Lake and Artillery Lake on July 28, 29, 30, and 31. We next observed the species near the same point on September 11, and we saw one, the last recorded for the season, at Fort Reliance on September 14.

Hylocichla ustulata swainsoni (Tschudi). Olive-backed Thrush.

This is the commonest thrush in the Athabaska region. We first noted it already in full song on the Athabaska, near Fort McMurray, on May 28, and we next saw it below Fort McKay

on May 31 and June 1.   It was seen also on the lower Athabaska
on June 3; near Fort Chipewyan, June 5; near the mouth of
Peace River, June 6, and near Smith Landing, June 7 to 12.
It was abundant at Fort Smith, and was noted on many occasions
during the latter part of June and the first few days of July.
We noted it also near Salt River, July 4 and 5; on the Buffalo
River Portage, July 6; on Little Buffalo River, July 7; on the
Nyarling, July 9 and 10, and on the lower part of Little Buffalo
River on July 12.   Our last observation of the species was at
Fort Resolution on July 16.

Hylocichla guttata pallasi (Cabanis).   Hermit Thrush.

The song of the hermit thrush was first heard on the Athabaska, near Boiler Rapid, on May 26 and 27, and the bird was
noted also near Poplar Point on June 3.   It was rather common
at Smith Landing, June 10 and 11, and near Fort Smith during
the latter half of June.   We noted it also on the Buffalo River
Portage on July 6, on the Nyarling on July 9 and 10, and on the
lower part of Little Buffalo River on July 12.   We last observed
the species among the islands in Great Slave Lake, noting it
on the shores of Kah-d'nouay Island on July 18 and 19.

Planesticus migratorius migratorius (Linn.).   Robin.

The robin is abundant throughout the region covered by our
canoe trip north to the tree limit.   It was common and in song
at Edmonton on May 10, and during our northward journey
down the Athabaska was noted almost daily.   The first nest
with eggs was seen on the lower Athabaska on June 4.   It was
especially common at Smith Landing and Fort Smith, a nest
containing three eggs being found at the latter place on June 15.
The country drained by the Buffalo and its tributary, the Nyarling, seemed to be a favourite habitat, as the bird was observed
on a number of occasions in early July.   It was also common
at Fort Resolution about the middle of the month.   It was fairly
abundant among the islands in the eastern part of Great Slave
Lake, and was noted on Kah-d'nouay Island on July 19.   A

nest found on a small island near this point on July 20 contained one egg. The bird was observed also at Caribou Island on July 20; on other islands to the eastward on July 21 and 22; near the Mountain Portage, where it was nesting, on July 24, and near the eastern end of Great Slave Lake on July 25 and 26. The bird was not common on Pike's Portage between Great Slave Lake and Artillery Lake; but a deserted nest was seen near Toura Lake, near the summit of the divide, where nearly typical Barren-Ground conditions prevail. There being no trees suitable for nesting, the bird had placed its home in a cranny on the face of a low cliff, where it was well protected from the elements. At our camp on Artillery Lake at the tree limit, a few individuals were seen on August 3, and one or two deserted nests in the stunted spruces showed that the bird had bred there. On the occasion of our second stay on this lake during our return trip, September 2 to 7, the bird was observed in greater or less numbers nearly every day, several flocks being noted on September 6. It was observed also at Fort Reliance, September 11 to 17, and was especially abundant on September 14, when migrating flocks aggregating several hundreds were seen. The bird was also observed on several occasions, September 21 to 24, among the islands of Great Slave Lake during our westward voyage. We noted it next on Slave River on September 29 and 30, and while ascending the Athabaska, saw it near Brulé Rapid on October 22 and 23, above House River on October 25, and near Calling River on October 30.

Sialia currucoides (Bechstein). Mountain Bluebird.

This species, not improperly styled the Arctic bluebird, was noted along the road between Sandy Creek and Athabaska Landing on May 13, when three individuals were observed.

INDEX

INDEX

This does not include the Appendices (as follows):

A. The new North-west, treating of its soil, climate, and suitability for settlement
B. The Buffalo summary; giving a full report on the wild Buffalo of the region.
C. The Yak—The Range Beast for the North-west.
D. Insects collected by the Seton expedition of 1907.
E. Plants collected by the Seton expedition, 1907.
F. Mammals noted on the Seton expedition, 1907.
G. Birds noted on the Seton expedition, 1907.

INDEX

413

HARPER NATURE LIBRARY
New Paperback Editions of Outstanding Nature Classics

☐ CN 846   THE ARCTURUS ADVENTURE *by William Beebe. Illustrated.* An account of the New York Zoological Society's first oceanographic expedition. $5.95

☐ CN 840   SIGNS AND SEASONS *by John Burroughs. New illustrations by Ann Zwinger.* An enduring classic from one of the most popular nature writers of the nineteenth century. $5.95

☐ CN 839   THE WORLD OF NIGHT *by Lorus J. and Margery J. Milne. Illustrated by T. M. Shortt.* The fascinating drama of nature that is enacted between dusk and dawn. $5.95

☐ CN 841   THE ARCTIC PRAIRIES *by Ernest Thompson Seton. Illustrated by the author.* A canoe-journey of 2,000 miles in search of the caribou, being the account of a voyage to the region north of Aylmer Lake. $5.95

☐ CN 806   THE INSECT WORLD OF J. HENRI FABRE *by J. Henri Fabre. Selected, with interpretative comments, by Edwin Way Teale.* The best writing of J. Henri Fabre, the great French entomologist. $5.95

☐ CN 842   BEYOND THE ASPEN GROVE *by Ann Zwinger. Illustrated by the author.* Zwinger has written "a collector's item that even nonbotanists will enjoy ... a book of charm and distinction." *Library Journal* $5.95

Buy them at your local bookstore or use this handy coupon for ordering:

HARPER & ROW, Mail Order Dept. #28CN, 10 East 53rd St., New York, N.Y. 10022.

Please send me the books I have checked above. I am enclosing $_____ which includes a postage and handling charge of $1.00 for the first book and 25¢ for each additional book. Send check or money order—no cash or C.O.D.'s please.

Name _____

Address _____

City _____ State _____ Zip _____

Please allow 4 weeks for delivery. USA and Canada only. This offer expires 4/1/82. Please add any applicable sales tax.